Zachariah Pearson: Man of Hull

A tale of philanthropy, boom and bust

Marian Shaw

The Grimsay Press

Published by:

The Grimsay Press
An imprint of Zeticula Ltd
Unit 13
196 Rose Street
Edinburgh
EH2 4AT
Scotland
http://www.thegrimsaypress.co.uk

First published in 2016.
Reprinted 2016

Front cover illustration. The portrait of Zachariah which
hangs in the Guildhall, Hull.
Back cover illustration. The ceremonial arch designed as
the gateway to Pearson Park, Hull.

ISBN 978-1-84530-156-9 Paperback
ISBN 978-1-84530-161-3 Hardback

Zachariah Pearson, Man of Hull

Dedicated to
Finn, Jasmine, Georgia and Barnaby Pearson

The author lending scale to one of her great-great-grandfather's Enfield rifles. It was research on the stocks of rifles such as this that has led to a scientific breakthrough in the conservation treatment of wooden structures that have been submerged for decades. The time capsule that was the Modern Greece *(page 172) has revealed more than 11,000 artefacts over the years, and much of the cache is still being uncovered and catalogued.*

Acknowledgements

I wonder how many people there are who, on first stumbling across something interesting enough to explore further, know for certain that they will eventually write about it? I certainly did not set out to document the life of Zachariah Pearson when I first visited Hull opportunistically twelve years ago, and if it had not been for the prompting and encouragement – sometimes verging on the nagging – of key people along the way the book would not (and could not) have been written at all. These are folk who have unconsciously played a central role in ensuring that I remained on track, drawing me back to the life of Zachariah time and again. I owe them a huge debt of thanks.

In the beginning, there was Martin Taylor. He now leads the magnificent Hull History Centre, but way back in 2004 he was the Director of the Hull City Archives. What he thought about a dishevelled cyclist turning up in his office with no appointment, and patently no historical background, I don't know, but he was kind enough to spend sufficient time with me to light the spark of further enquiry. Since then, he has been the central pivot of so much over the years – always enthusiastic, full of practical knowledge, and with the patience to point me in the right direction. Living as I do in the south, Martin's insider knowledge of how Hull works has been invaluable, and he has linked me with a number of people who have been wonderfully helpful.

One of these was the late Elizabeth Scott-Whipkey, an American Civil War historian specialising in locating the graves of Englishmen who had in some way supported the

Confederates. Her enquiries about Zachariah Pearson's grave came initially to Martin, who linked us together. It was Elizabeth's in-depth knowledge, introducing me to the digitised naval records of the 'War of the Rebellion', that led me to what Zachariah called his 'American Adventures' – one of the turning points that converted a gentle family tale into something more profound. Elizabeth has walked with me over the years until her recent death, and I cannot express how valuable her contribution has been; she was always interested in the next stage and not afraid to chivvy when my 'radio silence' went on for too long.

Another Hull figure who has been most helpful is Counsellor John Fareham, Chairman of the Pearson Park Trust. Not only has he supported my research with access to archived council documents, but he was also instrumental in planning the Pearson Park celebrations of 2010 when we held a Pearson clan gathering to commemorate the 150th anniversary of the date when Zachariah handed over the deeds to the people of Hull. In a city where even today Zachariah Pearson's name can still be controversial, Counsellor Fareham has always been a champion for this 'Marmite' figure. As ever, one contact leads to another, and he handed me to Richard Barry, who was kind enough to entertain me with his lively descriptions and recollections of Zachariah stories. I'm also grateful to Gavin Render, one of the earliest people to whet my appetite for research by sending me a tantalising account of Zachariah from the archives.

Dr Barry Hovell who has written widely on the Masonic history of Hull has been central to this book, and I am eternally grateful to him for his patient encouragement over the years. Unlike my sloppy stop-start approach to writing, he is meticulous and systematic. Wherever the name of Zachariah Pearson emerged from his own research, he kindly sent me snippets and links. His eclectic support ran to checking out those sorts of facts that only a physical presence in the archives can lead to, such as addresses from directories, or photos of relevant places – things I had neglected to follow up whenever I had been in Hull. Barry's fascinating guided walks through Hull brought Zachariah's past alive. And on those occasions when 'life' took over, and my research/writing project stalled, Barry has gently nudged me back to the keyboard, determined that the accumulated information would eventually emerge as a book. He also cast his eye over a few sections for me, tactfully steering my phraseology in more appropriate directions; a background in science had not prepared me for the niceties of historical writing.

Gillian Mawrey, Editor of Historic Gardens Review and author, was the inadvertent catalyst for my starting the book. As she stood in my kitchen reading the poster for the Colossal Fete of Pearson Park in 1860, she asked about the park and its history. So skilful and persuasive was she that before she departed she had extracted a promise that I'd write her an article. She it was, then, who pushed me off the diving board of hesitation – and I'm eternally grateful to her for making me take my first plunge. Arthur Credland, as Curator of the Hull Maritime Museum, was one of the Hull figures from whom I learned much. Not only did he answer my naïve questions about Hull's shipping business, pointing me in new directions, but he was the second editor to make me write something – in this case for the East Yorkshire Historian. Another nudge off that diving board...

I am also beholden to the late Chris Ketchell, local historian and Pearson Park enthusiast, who helped me with some of the background research. His lively emails were full of scurrilous information which shone shafts of light into unexpected corners. The Hull Trinity House was kind enough to provide details of Zachariah's deep involvement with their organisation throughout his life. Local historian Prof. David Neave kindly help me to trace the source of a particularly elusive drawing, and the Hull Library Services have been most helpful in providing both permissions and top quality photographs. The Hull History Centre, already mentioned as pivotal, has also been wonderfully supportive in releasing permissions and directing me to new areas to search for what I needed. Most of the other Hull-based news has been extracted from the extensive contemporaneous press via the National Newspaper Archive.

On an illuminating visit to the Confederate ports with my husband in 2005 the museum staff at the Fort Fisher State Historic Site in North Carolina, and the branch of underwater naval archaeology based there, were all incredibly helpful. We were also grateful to all the volunteer American Civil War aficionados who imparted their enthusiasm and knowledge as they walked us through New Orleans, Mobile, Charleston, Savannah and Wilmington and brought alive the whole blockade-running issue.

I'm afraid I have leant heavily and shamelessly on friends and relations in preparing this text. Richard Mawrey, QC, realising how naïve I was about Victorian law, was kind enough to advise me on the legal implications of bankruptcy in the nineteenth century, and I am indebted to him for helping me interpret the case notes. My sister, Pam Stafford, was subjected to some of my more difficult passages, as I relied on her brutal honesty to comment on their readability (or not!). After spending years in the merchant navy, the insider knowledge of my brother, Dick Stafford, also proved invaluable in correcting my terminology and helping me get to grips with the various parts of ships and maritime hierarchies. He it was who set up the family website, where distant relatives from far-flung parts of the globe have 'discovered' us in their efforts to find out more about their mythological and hazy ancestor. Thus John Pearson from Melbourne got in touch and, being descended from Zachariah's first-born son, managed to provide some unique photos. Then Frank Brunngräber, having been cut off in East Germany, found us once the Berlin Wall had toppled. Not only were our own lives enriched by our delightful 'new' German cousins, but suddenly the book was enhanced by the discovery of a hitherto anonymous son of Zachariah.

The first rule about uncovering family history is to pester some of the older relatives, so after returning from my first visit to Hull, fired up and fascinated, I chatted with my Aunt Phyllis Hodkin, and her brother, Uncle Arthur Pearson. They could both recollect their grandmother, Zachariah's daughter, and it was tracing their leads via Google and eBay that translated their snippets of family gossip into new discoveries about the life of this remarkable ancestor; they even generated an entire Garibaldi chapter. Additionally, Arthur, a one-time boat builder and enthusiast, especially knowledgeable about the design and use of sailing ships, has helped me side-step several potential traps of ignorance. Our conversations are always lively and highly valued; it is he, in fact, who has been uppermost in my mind as I pieced together the bits of jigsaw to build a picture of Zachariah. Second cousins Paul Woodhead and Ralph McCleod also opened up new vistas to explore, and innumerable other first, second and third cousins have added to the tapestry.

Once it was clear that 'the book' was actually happening, Mike Spencer was a star. He read the script twice, once to help me shape it, and then again a year later to proofread – and to point out my most annoying literary habits. Diane Pearson (no, not a relative) also proofread – and identified some quite different annoying literary habits. I owe each of them a huge debt for their hours of reading and patient English tutorials; I am not the easiest writer to mentor, and they were both endlessly encouraging. They have my deepest thanks.

Trying to sew up the loose ends of Hull illustrations whilst living in Oxfordshire has not been easy, but in addition to the substantial support I have received from those already mentioned, my neighbour, Brian Roantree, introduced me to Hull-based Brian Rylance, who was good-naturedly prevailed upon to take some last-minute photos for me. I am grateful to my talented artist friend, David Pelling, who has helped me to see things through a different lens. Chrys Bavey has diligently kept me in touch with the workings of The Friends of Pearson Park, and provided me with the occasional platform to write short articles for the FoPP Newsletter. Hull City Council and the Mayor's parlour have been helpful with mayoral insignia.

Of course, the closest and most constant support has been provided within the close family. Derek, my long-suffering husband, has tirelessly striven – in the face of considerable sense-of-humour failure on my behalf – to trace and locate relevant descendants to harass, or to make my recalcitrant computer do as I commanded. He has the patience of a saint, and deserves my deepest thanks for being the means of enabling this book to appear. Credit is also due to offspring Chris and Penny Shaw, and to Jack Pearson, who all, despite enthusiasm-followed-by-scepticism, maintained faith long enough to be amazed when the book did finally materialise.

My colossal thanks to everyone who has, knowingly or not, played a role in this book.

Foreword

by the Lord Mayor of Hull

It gives me great pleasure to be asked to write the Foreword for this book about Zachariah Pearson, a local legend whose name is familiar to many, but whose story has so far only been told in soundbites and rumour. This is the first time his biography is told in full.

As a child I played in Pearson Park, never really wondering about who founded the place I loved – or why he did it. This book tells the story of Zachariah, a local boy made good, who ran away to sea, fell in love with life on a ship, built up a shipping business from humble beginnings and who, once he was rich, became a generous benefactor to the poor in Hull. He wanted the factory workers to have somewhere to relax and breathe fresh air away from the pollution of the Industrial Revolution, and Pearson Park, his lasting legacy, was the result.

Zachariah's meteoric rise, though, came to an abrupt end when, at the peak of business success, and as Mayor of Hull, he suffered a catastrophic business collapse. This book relates in grisly detail how he was laid low by poor judgement and bad luck arising from a war thousands of miles away. This venture into the American Civil War was his nemesis – Abraham Lincoln's forces sent him into the bankruptcy court.

As the Lord Mayor following in Zachariah's footsteps more than a hundred and fifty years later, I can empathise with his world of local politics and tricky decisions. No doubt development and enterprise played as major a part of the Victorian world as it does today. Decisions are made for complex reasons, and Zachariah's motives were a combination of philanthropy and profit. But while his concern for the poor was appreciated by the masses, he was ostracised by many of his previous friends and colleagues after his dramatic financial crash: Victorian bankruptcy was a serious disgrace, and he spent many years gradually rebuilding his reputation.

Zachariah's story was certainly one of boom and bust but, with his rise to pre-eminence, from cabin boy to shipowner, and from nobody to twice-Mayor, he was undoubtedly one of Hull's significant figures. This book, carefully researched and narrated by his great-great-granddaughter, is a most welcome addition to our city's history.

Rumours may still circulate about Zachariah, but I urge you to read the full story in these pages, then you can judge the man for yourself.

Sean Chaytor
Lord Mayor of Hull
September 2016

Contents

Illustrations

Preamble

It was one of my earliest childhood recollections - the white statuette on my grandparents' mantelpiece in Kent. "That," they said, with pride, "is your great-great-grandfather". He was dressed in ankle-length flowing robes and a peculiar hat, and he was leaning on a large ship's rudder at his side. The grandparents supplied a few more scanty details: his name was Zachariah, he had been Mayor of Hull (yes, the hat was a tricorne), and there was a park 'up there' named after him – which was where the proper statue was. This little one on the mantelpiece was, we were told, the model the sculptor had made before he carved the large one. There were also some blurry, *sotto voce* mutterings about Zachariah losing the family fortune, and an aunt who vaguely felt that Garibaldi came into the picture somewhere. An elderly uncle, much closer to the tales handed down first hand, later experienced unnerving *déjà vu* when he watched BBC TV's 1970s series 'The Onedin Line' for the first time; the story lines were *very* familiar – he'd heard them first-hand from Zachariah's grandson.

That summarised the family folklore. But how was curiosity to be satisfied? In the 1970s a couple of Zachariah's great-grandchildren, my uncles, made the long trek north to Hull and visited Pearson Park but they found no statue, only a tasteful bas-relief plaque on an ironstone pillar. When an opportunity arose for me to visit Hull in 2004, I set out to track down what had actually happened to the mythical statue of Zachariah Charles Pearson. Everyone was delightfully helpful with information about Zachariah:

the City Archive office, the Council, the Guildhall, the Pearson Park Hotel – but every trail led into a cul-de-sac. There was no statue. There never had been. The sculptor had apparently never made it. Why not? Where had the plan been de-railed between the maquette and the statue?

The trail through Hull was fascinating and it had sown far more seeds of curiosity than merely hunting down an elusive statue. Everyone knew about Zachariah but no-one was neutral to him. People saw him through different lenses, and parted with different snippets of his story to illustrate their view. There was clearly far more to this controversial ancestor than I could possibly have imagined. With a young grandson of my own now bearing Zachariah's name, I decided to unravel the story of this remarkable man and set it down, not only for future generations of Pearsons but also for the people of Hull, as his tale has never been told before in its entirety – and he was, above all, a 'man of Hull'.

This is Zachariah's story. His life was a full one, packed with hard work, success and triumph, surprise and disaster, followed by a low-key life lived out in the corner of the park he gave to the people of Hull. The book traces Zachariah as he built up his business from very humble beginnings and rose to fame, fortune, and philanthropy. It shows how he capitalised on events to turn them to his and to Hull's advantage, but also how world events, bad luck and poor judgement brought him disaster. His was an eventful life. Some of the events were central and had a forceful impact on his story, while others were relatively tangential. All have been included though, as they add colour to his story and help us to understand him better in his own context.

Resources for the research have been eclectic. They include the handed-down folklore, a Masonic scrap of white leather found in a box of effects, some forgotten and hitherto unidentified photos discovered in an Australian attic, a Confederacy historian in Kentucky, and family contacts coming forward from genealogy research undertaken by my husband and put 'out there' in the public domain by my brother on a family website. Meeting local people in Hull, listening to folklore, talking with councillors and historians - all have all been most illuminating in helping to follow new leads. The evidence stored in the Hull City Archives, now the wonderful purpose-built Hull History Centre, has been both plentiful and tantalising – each little gem leading the search in new directions. There are contemporaneous accounts by journalists and historians, newspaper articles and advertisements from around the world, Register Office records, Bankruptcy Court proceedings, and National Archive records.

Zachariah's businesses were global enough to supply world-wide sources. One of the most illuminating episodes – the Garibaldi incident – was drawn almost entirely from Hansard and the Parliamentary papers accompanying the House of Commons debate. On our field trip to America, my husband and I visited each of the ex-Confederate ports and their museums, from New Orleans in Louisiana to Wilmington in North Carolina, gathering more background to the American Civil War so that we could better understand Zachariah's 'American adventures', as he himself called them. North Carolina's Maritime Museum at Fort Fisher, and the back rooms of the U.S. Naval Archeological Department, were particularly instructive, as half the artefacts on display are there courtesy of Zachariah – all recovered from the *Modern Greece,* his blockade-running steamer which sank in 1862, thanks to President Abraham Lincoln.

Another terrific resource has been the world of continuously-expanding digitised data. Fully searchable without having to travel, these collections include, among others, the British Newspaper Archive, the Census records, Ancestry.co.uk, and the 'Official Records' from the American Civil War. The internet also obliged with some unexpected surprises, like a bolt of ammunition from one of Zachariah's ships' cannons for sale on eBay, and a shipwreck site now used for recreational diving but which led to a gripping account of how survivors from one of Zachariah's vessels escaped being massacred in the Maori Wars. Before long, any historian will be able to do most of the research from the computer desk, although nothing can substitute for conversations with real people to bring colour and perspective to hard evidence.

These sources have provided thousands of pieces of jigsaw to spread out on the table, and together they make up a picture of Zachariah's life. But there are inevitably some pieces missing. It would, for example, have been good to know more about him as a family man, although sound parenting does not make it into the newspaper headlines and we have discovered no handy cache of personal letters in a loft. It would have been fascinating to know why Zachariah took certain critical decisions. We can only conjecture. Some parts of the picture have had to be pieced together by deduction and evidence-based speculation, but it is always made clear where this is the case. If anyone is able to contribute new bits of the jigsaw puzzle, they would be most welcome to do so via email.

Zachariah was a contentious figure who left a controversial legacy. Some saw him as a swindler, others a victim, some even a racist, though most as a philanthropist. Actions and motives can be in interpreted in many different ways. This book aims to unpack them.

The story would not be authentic without identifying source material, and a bibliography can be found at the end. References are built into the text in a general way in order to make the story more readable, avoiding the narrative being interrupted with frequent multiple individual references, footnotes and superscripts. This is not an academic treatise, but more of a life-story that anyone interested in the ups and downs of a Victorian philanthropist might like to read. It is nevertheless a historically accurate account, not a novel, and I hope it makes a useful contribution to the history of Hull.

Finally, because Zachariah was 'a man of his time', his story has to be interpreted in the context of the mid-nineteenth century, so where direct passages are thought to lend character and veracity to a section of the story, they have been quoted liberally. Seeing and 'hearing' the words used at the time, either by him or about him, brings the characters alive. This has nevertheless been a difficult transition for me – as an academic I would have hammered my students for being so free with raw data, and being so negligent in precise referencing.

But this is a story, not a thesis...

Marian Shaw
marian.shaw@meadow-croft.org.uk
Spring 2016

This is a correct Register of the time of Birth of myself, Wife and Children

I was born on the 24th April 1788. at evening 9½ Oclock. called Saint Marks

Zachariah Pearson

Laus Deo.

My Wife Elizabeth was born on the 30th April 1788 and died 24 November 1825 Thursday ½ past 2 Oclock

1 *Our Daughter Mary was born the 20th March 1808 and died on the 23rd of same only being three days*

The first part of the decorative entry in the family Bible where Zachariah Pearson (the elder) recorded the births of himself, his wife and his ten children – and the deaths of four of the children and his wife.

1

Beginnings

Laus Deo, "thanks be to God", was the epithet which heralded the earliest personal reference to the subject of this book, Zachariah Charles Pearson. It was the entry in the family Bible, inscribed in beautiful copperplate writing by his father, Zachariah Pearson the Elder – here referred to as 'Mr Pearson'. Kingston-upon-Hull, a thriving port in Yorkshire, and ideally placed on the North Sea for trading around the world, is where Mr Pearson was born in 1788, just ten years after the first dock in Hull opened. When he married Elizabeth Harker in 1810, he had the foresight to start a record of his family in the customary manner, inscribing his name and those of his wife and descendants into his family Bible. This *Laus Deo,* the decorative embellishment with which he started his record, is a sentiment echoed by his numerous descendants – although not necessarily on every occasion.

Hull had initially made its money by exporting wool, a product so symbolic of Britain's wealth in medieval times that even today in the House of Lords 'The Woolsack' is the Speaker's seat. Later, Hull's wealth was based on the whaling industry until fishing took over with the arrival of the 'trawl', a more efficient way of catching fish. By the early nineteenth century, small businesses were booming, and Mr Pearson was one of numerous traders who, having started life as mariners, now capitalised on any entrepreneurial activity that would support a family.

The Pearsons lived in the Sutton region of Kingston-upon-Hull, on the east side of the town by the River Hull, the main artery of the town. The area had once been used for pasture, but was now becoming more commercial. Shipping businesses and factories were springing up and, to accommodate the many workers who were moving into the district, numerous small houses were built. It was in one such terraced house, in Sutton Row, that the burgeoning Pearson family lived.

'Burgeoning' meant producing ten children – by no means unusual at the time. Traditionally, large families were an insurance policy; children were a cheap source of labour and gave parents plenty of help on the land, growing crops and tending animals. But the relentless march of the Industrial Revolution was changing the shape of traditional society; large portions of the population were shifting from their agrarian way of life to a town-dwelling one where they could earn wages in the new sorts of jobs that were opening up. There were opportunities for the entrepreneurial with goods to trade; new markets appeared in order to sell the goods, and services like finance and insurance expanded to service the developing commerce. Society now needed more teachers, lawyers and civil servants and, for the less well-qualified, there were plenty of jobs as machinery operators in factories or as servants to the expanding number of middle class households. With workers now using their wages to buy food instead of growing it themselves, large families were no longer quite so necessary. Extra mouths to feed could even be more of a liability than a support...

This was the rapidly-changing environment which the Pearson family inhabited in a developing part of Hull, and bearing ten children between 1810 and 1825 must have turned Elizabeth into a breeding machine. They rolled off the production line at the rate of one every 18 months – but such huge families came at a human cost. There were multiple hazards associated with birth: statistically, 25 per cent of the babies born at that time failed to reach 12

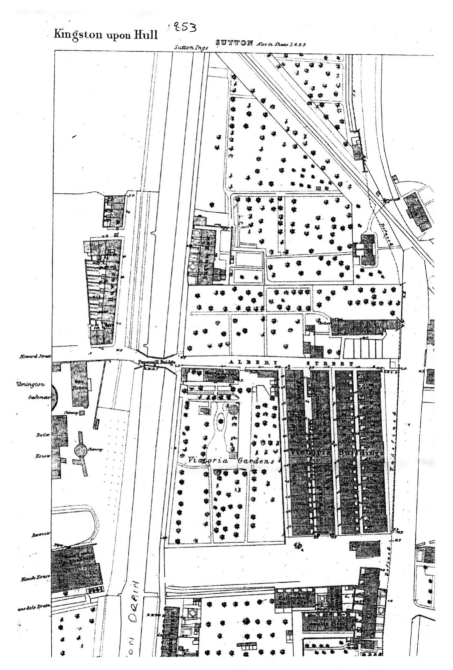

1853 map of the Sutton area of east Hull where Zachariah and Elizabeth Pearson lived – in one of the cottages at the NE of this map. The region was rapidly-developing, offering many opportunities for a hard-working family man.

months old. Only six of these Pearson children survived, giving Mr and Mrs Pearson a tragic failure rate of 40 per cent, well above the average. The Pearson tally was: Mary (died), John (lived), unnamed daughter (died), Isaiah (died), Robert (lived), Elizabeth (lived), Mary (lived), Zachariah (lived), Emily (lived), unnamed daughter (died).

Fitting a family of this size into a small dwelling cannot have been easy, and for Mr Pearson as the sole provider this would have been a substantial financial strain, though his wife would no doubt have been creative in bringing up the family. A map of the east part of Hull in 1817 shows that while considerable green space remained between Sutton Row and the River Hull, which flowed into the Humber, there were also shipyards, docks, timber yards and brickyards. The new Reckitt and Colman factory was to be built here a few years later. Clearly, there was not only a good deal of outdoor space for a family to grow up in, but also plenty of work to be had for a resourceful breadwinner.

And we know that Mr Pearson *was* resourceful. From the local newspapers it is possible to trace his rise from clerk to shipowner and shipping merchant. He bought a vessel called the *Midas* in 1812; she was described as a *'prize ship'*, probably one of the spoils of war that the government was selling off to private shipowners. *Midas* was a 41 ton two-masted vessel, with which he traded.

We also know that in 1822 Mr Pearson was a bit of a local hero when he saved the life of a neighbour's child. The Sutton area of Hull, very low-lying and marshy, was drained by a series of waterways, known as drains. While today the word 'drain' might summon up images of a small unsavoury ditch, photos of the Sutton Drain, flowing right past the row of houses where the Pearsons lived, show it to be more akin to a large canal. It was into this that a little girl, daughter of one of their neighbours, fell whilst playing – despite being ostensibly under the supervision of her nurse. The account in the *Hull Advertiser* describes the Sutton Drain as in a *'swoln state [...] from the high tide and the previous heavy falls of rain'*. None of the horrified on-lookers was able to rescue the girl, but the mother, *'hearing of its* [sic] *dreadful situation shrieked, and her cries of agony alarmed Mr Zachariah Pearson, merchant, neighbour, who ran to the place with utmost speed and plunging into the water, caught the child by the foot just as it was sinking to rise no more'*.

Apparently he was no swimmer, and as he was wearing his coat, hat, and boots (not even having had time to remove his watch from his pocket), he began to sink, and onlookers thought that both were lost. Luckily, his efforts prevailed, the child survived, and Mr Pearson was widely praised for his bravery. The local paper, in true Aesop-fable style of moralising, used the opportunity to make a salutary lesson about nurses needing to take more care of their charges...

It was in this terrace of small dwellings where Zachariah Charles was born in 1821, and into this canal, or drain, that Zachariah's father – not a swimmer himself – heroically leapt, boots and all, to rescue a drowning girl the following year.

Mr Pearson was a working-class man like many others, taking full opportunistic advantage of every opportunity that offered itself. He was feeding his wife and his six surviving children by trading as and where he could, as a *'Merchant, Dealer and Chapman'* – the latter being a person who earned his living by travelling, perhaps, in his case, referring to his shipping ventures, or other trading. The Trade Directory of 1826 lists him as *'merchant, general agent and spirit importer merchant'* under three different addresses.

This was wise; as a merchant, it was useful to have several income opportunities. Business generally was not doing very well anywhere during the 1820s, and people had to scratch a living wherever it was possible. Hull was probably slightly better off than some other places; being a thriving seaport in an entrepreneurial age, with ships unloading cargoes on his doorstep, Mr Pearson was clearly taking full advantage of the opportunities offered and he earned his living by buying and selling commodities.

Elizabeth, the homemaker, must have been exhausted. By 1825, having lost three children at birth, she had six living children to care for. Zachariah Charles, the fifth of these, had made his entry into the world on 28th August 1821, and he was only four years old when his mother went into labour with her tenth pregnancy. Sadly, her run of giving birth to sickly babies continued, but this time with a truly tragic consequence: the baby died after 45 minutes, and Elizabeth succumbed four days later to what was most likely to have been puerperal fever. This lethal bacterial infection accounted for most of the maternal deaths at childbirth at this time, and there was no defence against it in a pre-antibiotic era.

Elizabeth's death was a severe blow to the family. She had been the pivot around which the whole family moved, and her death left a devastating crater. Her widower was now left to provide as best he could for his surviving six children; this was just at a time when there was an economic downturn, causing difficulties for shipping and trading, leaving the father of the house exposed and vulnerable.

It became clear to Mr Pearson that looking after six children on his own was not an option: changes had to be made. The two oldest boys, John, aged 15, and Robert, aged 10, were deemed old enough to be looked after in their father's household, but the other four children, Zachariah, aged four, and his three sisters, Elizabeth, Mary and Emily, were sent to live with their uncle's family. Before an era where a social service safety net rescued families in difficulties, the extended family stepped into the breach where possible. The workhouse was the only alternative for abandoned children, or for those whose parents were unable to look after them. Life in the workhouse, though, was so awful that many escaped and took their chances on the streets.

It is unclear who the uncle was, as he is not named in any accounts, but he was described later by the *Illustrated London News* as *'a gentleman of independent means'*. Given that he already had children of his own, these 'independent means' must have come in quite handy. The sudden influx of an extra four children must have made new demands on his crowded household, but doubtless there was sufficient income to meet the challenge with servants and nursemaids. Whoever he was, it was his household that provided the new environment for the early development of young Zachariah Charles, who now found himself living, alongside his sisters and cousins, with his uncle and aunt. There is no way of knowing the degree to which he remained in contact with his father and older brothers, but as none of them are evident at all later in Zachariah's life, one wonders whether his childhood was not especially conducive to keeping the family bond alive.

Meanwhile, back at the household of widower Pearson, all was not well. The national depression was now taking its toll on traders small and large alike. Was it the national economy that caused him now to have financial difficulties? Or did his recent bereavement spur him to take greater risks or make ill-judged decisions? Whatever the circumstances, in less than two years after the loss of his wife the London

Gazette of 27th February 1827 announced that he was summoned to appear on a bankruptcy charge at the Dog and Duck Tavern in Scale Lane. This was a pub in the heart of Hull, just across the river from where he lived. Pubs, being the only buildings with large enough rooms, were often used for judicial hearings, such as bankruptcies and inquests, and Mr Pearson, *'Merchant, Dealer and Chapman'* was *'hereby required to surrender himself to the Commissioners'* as he was required to *'make a full discovery and disclosure of his estate and effects'*, when *'the Creditors are to come prepared to prove their debts'*.

The outcome of his bankruptcy case is shrouded in the mists of time but we do know that Mr Pearson eventually picked himself up and re-built his businesses. Hull soon started to emerge from the depression and shipping, with its associated trades, was vibrant again. Mr Pearson was now able to leave the house in Sutton and move to the more salubrious area of Portland Place – to one of the addresses from which he had been doing business. Later on, he became a wine merchant, based in the High Street. Having several strings to one's bow certainly seemed to be paying dividends.

Hull's businesses were enhanced by the arrival of the railway in 1840, which could convey goods across England to and from the docks. The port was thriving, and the possibilities must have fascinated the young Zachariah as he was growing up. A world out there was waiting to be discovered, no doubt brought alive by story books. While we don't know how much of a reader Zachariah was, we do know that he attended Hull Grammar School, a small, endowed school, struggling at that time to compete with the new private schools which had been founded to attract the sons of the new middle-class parents. Hull Grammar School was more geared to providing boys with practical and engineering skills than preparing them for university. Nevertheless, it ensured that Zachariah was both literate and grammatical, his later letters and speeches bearing witness to the fact that he had been well-educated.

Perhaps his school had introduced him to Daniel Defoe's story, published 100 years earlier? Robinson Crusoe went to sea against his parents' wishes, became shipwrecked, and had many exciting exploits along the way. Further adventure stories, like *The Swiss Family Robinson*, followed in the wake of the amazing literary success of Defoe's novel. Was it these books which gave an imaginative young man a yearning for an adventurous life? Whatever his motivation, when he was about twelve years old the young Zachariah, together with another like-minded adventurous youth, stowed away aboard a ship that was setting forth from Hull. Was it purely coincidence that it was actually from the Queen's Dock in the centre of Hull that Defoe's hero had also embarked on his adventures?

Unlike the story book, though, the boys did not succeed in their quest: they were discovered and summarily returned to Hull. The account of one of the local reporters, Whiting, writing about Zachariah some 25 years later, paints us a vivid picture of this episode:

Not many years ago, two little fellows secreted themselves as stowaways on board a seagoing vessel. Nestling among the cargo like a couple of young rats, these adventurous gentlemen had nearly got safely out to sea, when one of the ship's crew thought he heard something in the hold, so the hatches were taken off, the hold searched, and the enterprising lads bundled out and sent back to Hull in the pilot boat, as returned parcels.

After this little escapade, Zachariah continued his education at Hull Grammar School, until he was eventually allowed to join a merchant ship as a legitimate apprentice to Jenkins and Tonge. A likely lad could make good progress if he learnt fast and showed enthusiasm although life would not always have been easy. As Whiting went on to say, *'the romantic boy discovered how little of romance abides within the smell of bilge water, and that the airs of heaven are about as uncomfortable as the airs of the captain'.* Nevertheless, Zachariah seemed to take to sea naturally, as he was made Second Officer by the time he was 17, and First Officer, or Mate, the following year. His meteoric progress continued: by the age of 21, he was captain, and as the Illustrated London News was to report later, *'he commanded the finest ship then sailing out of Hull'.*

A typical barque in full sail. As he built his business, this was the type of vessel that Zachariah used for his trading around the world. It was the 'fore and aft' sail at the stern which enabled the barque to be more versatile than the square rigger which it replaced.

Pausing for a moment to consider what a tremendous responsibility it was to be in supreme charge of a sailing ship, it is clear that Zachariah must have proved himself in all the complex aspects of being the commander. A captain needed enough knowledge of the winds and currents to get to his destination economically, together with enough technical knowledge about how the vessel worked to be practical. He would also need a sound business head to handle the cargo and, possibly the most challenging aspect of captaincy, have enough personality, leadership and strength of character to bind together the crew – who, in Zachariah's case, were probably older than he was. A shipowner looking to appoint a captain to safeguard both his vessel and his cargo must have been very confident indeed in Zachariah's ability to take him on at the extremely young age of 21.

Now that he had an established career, Zachariah's next move was to get married, which he did at the age of 23. Mary Ann, born in 1824, was the oldest of another huge family, the Colemans. Edward and Mary Ann Coleman lived in London, but some time between 1838 and 1842, before the last of the children was born, the Coleman family moved to Kingston Street in Hull, and it must have been soon after this that their daughter Mary Ann met Zachariah. We must assume that she saw good husband-potential in Zachariah, as they were married in Hull on 10th April, 1844. Although he did not know it yet, Mary Ann's dowry was her father and a substantial supply of siblings who were to furnish Zachariah with several partners-in-waiting for his future enterprises.

It was an exciting time for Zachariah. Within a couple of years of getting married, and by time he was 25, he was master of his own vessel, and 'was noted for making the quickest voyages across the Atlantic'. We know nothing about how he financed the first of his many subsequent vessels, but one of my elderly uncles, after watching 'The Onedin Line' in the 1970s, found the plot lines of this television serial so familiar that there was no doubt in his mind where the authors had found their inspiration. In the beginning, the young Onedin struggled to raise enough money to get his own vessel, then traded judiciously, sometimes in the teeth of competition from the big shipowners, and paid back what he borrowed with the profit he made in trading goods with this vessel. It does sound like the plausible sort of scenario that Zachariah might have written – and was it entirely a programme-naming coincidence that Zachariah owned a sailing vessel called the *Odin*?

It was probably not uncommon for young ambitious men to create this sort of plot-line for themselves, but Zachariah's own story was endorsed later in *The Illustrated London News*. Just as he was embarking on his career in local governance in the 1850s, this journal gave its readers Zachariah's potted CV: '*whilst in command of his own vessel, he acted also as a merchant, always buying his own cargoes and chartering other vessels, and he subsequently established a line of packets*'.

Zachariah was making a success of life, and in keeping with the spirit of the age, he took to international trading like a duck to water. Despite his prolonged absences at sea, though, Zachariah managed to spend enough time in Hull between trips to perform his husbandly duties, embarking on the family-making business with gusto. Mary Ann proved to be almost as fecund as their own mothers, who had each borne ten children, but she achieved a considerably greater success rate than Zachariah's mother. Mary Ann bore eight children, seven of whom survived into adulthood. Charles Edward arrived in 1846, and Mary Elizabeth early in 1849. James Harker appeared at the end of 1849, though he was to die two years later from 'slow fever', a type of typhoid fever caused by Salmonella – the same disease from which Prince Albert was thought at the time to have to died ten years later (although he had been ill for some time, so this diagnosis was later disputed). Alfred Coleman was born just before James died, and Arthur Henry in 1854. Three more daughters eventually completed their family: Emma Jane (my great-grandmother) in 1858, Beatrice Maude in 1860, and Eveline Rose in 1862.

Zachariah was working hard and playing hard. As well as establishing his family in Hull, he passed his Master's Certificate in 1849, a qualification introduced on a voluntary basis in 1845 but which was to become mandatory in 1850. No doubt he felt this certificate would help him succeed in business. So now, with proliferating family ashore, qualifications afloat, and an adventurous approach to life, he was set fair for a promising career. It was this eye for the main chance in trade, and the resources and experience to handle it, that enabled him to develop, to 'grow his business' – and the next chapter traces his rise from captain to merchant and shipowner.

2

Building the business in an entrepreneurial age

As his career took off, Zachariah now became increasingly involved with expanding his trading routes and establishing his businesses around the world. In the fast-changing young nineteenth century, new opportunities were continually opening up. It was a good time to be an entrepreneur – at least whilst one's star was in the ascendant.

With his instinct for good business, Zachariah developed trading routes wherever he could see a profit. As he expanded around the world, he built up eclectic business interests, developing a good instinct for the best deals. At the same time, he was becoming increasingly involved in local matters such as the development of the port of Hull, and concerning himself with the welfare of seafarers and their families. During the decade of the 1850s, his life altered substantially; he progressed from captain to shipowner, from sail to steam, and from an average income to a healthy one. All this time, his family was increasing and by the end of the decade his offspring tally was six, with two to follow in the early 1860s.

In tracing Zachariah's meteoric rise, a substantial amount can be pieced together from the advertisements he placed, initially in the local papers and later on, as he expanded more widely, in *The Times* as well. In addition to the plethora of adverts, the newspapers also carried miscellaneous reports of meetings, activities and events, particularly as he took on increasingly public roles in Hull.

The first indication that Zachariah was coming up in the world is an advert in the shipping column of *The Hull Packet and East Riding Times*, the local paper that traders might use if they had goods to export. This entry, placed in April 1850, read in full:

```
For Elsinore and St Petersburg. The regular
traders Helen, Capt. Z. C. Pearson, and Royal
William, Capt. G. H. Broadhead, are loading,
and will be dispatched with the first ships.
```

Here were two captains sharing an advert, and demonstrating with their 'first ships' comment that they understood this northern route. Around the end of October, rivers and passageways froze, cutting off access to the Russian ports until the thaw around April, but canny shipowners were able to maximise the Baltic trade by utilising the latest and earliest dates when the passages were 'open', advertising that they would be leaving as soon as the ice had melted and the passage was clear to get through.

Before long Zachariah was advertising on his own for the same route, but was also now starting to act as an agent for others. As well as commanding his own vessel *Helen*, he was advertising cargo space on other vessels too; any merchant who wished to export goods to Russia could find the right ship easily, as the docks were in the centre of the town. Zachariah was now embarking on his career as both a shipowner and a service-provider, and learning to become more proactive and media-savvy in the process.

His preferred type of vessel at this time was the barque. Described as the 'workhorse of the Golden Age of Sail', the barque was versatile, swift, and economical compared with more traditional vessels such as the square-rigger. The latter had a great many sails, and was consequently very labour-intensive to operate. But because the sails were at right angles to the direction of travel, they caught all the wind, and in full sail this vessel could zip along. However, when the wind was not in the right direction she was stuck. The barque, on the other hand, could sail into the wind, as the mast at the stern had sails aligned 'fore-and-aft' (in the direction of the vessel) so she could tack like a modern yacht. And because the sail pattern was less complicated, the barque could be operated with a smaller crew. While it could not beat a full square-rigger in a following wind, its combination of sails made it more versatile, and so ultimately it was more economical – which, of course, appealed to Zachariah.

Over the next three years, Zachariah's business became more successful. By 1853 he was advertising:

```
For Elsinore and St Petersburg. Now loading,
the first class barque, Vivide, 387 tons, being
the last ship for St Petersburg this season,
will sail about 28th October. For freight &c,
apply to Z. C. Pearson, High-street.
```

Operating from one's own premises in the High Street was a significant step up the career ladder. Advertisements were no longer naming him 'captain', but indicating his broader business interests. His judicious trading had paid off, and now, seventeen years after embarking on his life at sea, he had completed the transition from commander to businessman.

New horizons were opening up. In addition to the Russian trips, he embarked on Australian and American routes, and this global commerce meant acquiring more barques. Not only was he sending his own vessels but he was also chartering others to deliver his cargoes, though it is not always easy to see from the adverts which ships were owned and which were chartered. He had been making his money by buying and selling his own cargoes but now he could augment his income by providing a carrier service for other merchants who wished to trade overseas.

Before long, he acquired another string to his bow when an exciting and newly-emerging income stream presented itself: passengers. Until now, vessels had been used for cargo transport but if people happened to want to go where he was sending ships, Zachariah was keen to oblige. Passenger requirements naturally meant that appropriate accommodation was needed, but once the adaptations to his freight barques had been made, Zachariah could now add a travel agent service to his portfolio. He was climbing the ladder even faster now, and income from any source was grist to his mill – and to his bank balance.

Once Zachariah had brought his brother-in-law into the business, this was the flag that flew at the masthead of all their vessels. The letters, representing Pearson, Coleman and Co., were written on a white band sandwiched between two red bands.

But success presented its own challenges: he was by now struggling to do it all single-handedly, and he needed reinforcements. Fortuitously, having married into the Coleman family, there was a ready-made team of willing workers prepared to support his enterprises, and he now turned his business into a family affair by taking on James Coleman as his business partner. James was one of Mary Ann's brothers, and at twenty-two years old was eleven years younger than his brother-in-law, but Zachariah clearly valued him enough to enter into a formal arrangement. The public announcement in the *Hull Packet* of January 1854 proudly launched the name of their new company:

```
Z. C. Pearson, ship broker, shipping agent
&c, has this day taken into partnership Mr
Jas. Coleman, and that the business in future
will be carried on under the firm of Z. C.
Pearson, Coleman and Co.
```

Hull High Street today. Russia Chambers, the business premise of Pearson, Coleman and Co. was situated here – the ideal location for a shipping company between the River Hull to the east and the docks to the west.

The new firm of Z. C. Pearson, Coleman and Co. at once sought larger premises to handle the increased business, moving into Russia Chambers, prestigious quarters in the High Street. These buildings backed on to the River Hull, quite close to where this river opened into the Humber, and the Queen's Dock lay very close to the west of them, so an office here between the two was a very convenient headquarters for a busy shipping agent.

Over the following six years Z. C. Pearson, Coleman and Co. became one of the more prominent shipbrokers in Hull, and they started to develop their trade with Australia, by now heavily colonised by the British. Early explorers had 'discovered' it, but from the late eighteenth century onwards, a different sort of emigrant had unwillingly experienced life there: criminals deported from England. The Industrial Revolution in Britain had generated such displacement of people that there was a corresponding rise in petty thefts. Lawlessness needed to be stamped out, but the gaols became overcrowded, so shunting them all to the other side of the world was a practical alternative. Many of those sentenced to transportation had been convicted of nothing more than stealing food for survival, and they found life out there very tough. These 'criminals' were made to build roads as well as their own prisons; they were, in fact, the first sizeable labour force in Australia.

But as the continent's potential for development was recognised, populations of voluntary settlers built up, keen to experience life in a less crowded place than industrial England. Land was cleared for cultivation, often wrecking the habitats of the indigenous population in the process. Mineral deposits were discovered and exploited, and before long settlers were calling for more manpower to work the land and run the businesses. They were keen to import more folk from England so that they could populate and exploit the 'The Colonies', as Australia and New Zealand were collectively known. These lands were treated as far-flung bits of Britain and eligible people such as agricultural workers, masons, blacksmiths, and of course, women, were given assisted passages in order to establish successful colonies and increase the population out there.

Zachariah, naturally, wanted to secure a slice of this action, but the competition was fierce. If they wanted to stay ahead of the game while the world was opening up in the mid-1800s, Pearson and Coleman had to entice merchants and passengers to travel with them rather than with other shipowners, so their advertisements now started to extol the safety, speed and comfort of their sailing ships. Their barques were frequently described as 'A1' – surely a vessel with the highest possible rating in Lloyds' insurance list could be trusted with one's goods and family? Some of their ships were *'coppered and copper-fastened'*; not only did this help the ship to go faster by reducing growths on the bottom of the hull, but copper bolts would not corrode like iron, so the wooden planks forming the hull would be secure: passengers could be reassured of a safe voyage in a copper-fastened vessel. Even today, a copper-bottomed guarantee is the best available.

Zachariah was clearly proud of the good speed his vessels could make, and in one advert the incentive for passengers heading for Melbourne was that the clipper was *'expected to make the passage in 70 days'*– an excellent time. Passengers might also be enticed by the greater comfort of a head-space of eight feet between the decks, a luxury compared to the normal cramped conditions and low ceilings suffered by passengers. As a final inducement, Zachariah threw in a banking service as well: *'money orders on Australia granted free of charge'* – perhaps a well-valued bonus if one was paying out 16 guineas (£16 and 16 shillings) for a one-way emigration voyage to Australia. The Pearson-Coleman travel agency was pulling out all stops to attract customers.

With the extra business to Australia involving passengers as well as cargoes, Zachariah needed a reliable agent over there, someone to sort out the practical arrangements for travel and commerce. People needed to be looked after, goods needed to be sold and money needed to be collected. Around the same time that Zachariah formally joined forces with James, the Coleman family came up trumps with a suitable agent. James' father, and Zachariah's father-in-law, Edward Coleman, emigrated to The Colonies and became a distant agent for Pearson, Coleman and Co. Did he volunteer to go to Australia, or was he persuaded for the sake of the family business? Was it living in such fluid and adventurous times that caused a man in his late middle-age to uproot so dramatically? We shall never know, but it seems that his wife and family followed him, for Mary Ann's next two sisters, Louisa and Emma, were both married in Bathurst, New South Wales, in 1856 and 1859 respectively.

Whatever the circumstances of his arrival in Sydney, Edward's job was to acquire building supplies from England to help make Australia. There were plenty of raw materials, but the country was still very basic and rugged. Manufactured products were desperately needed, but there were as yet no factories. Edward's advert displayed in the local paper on 4th November 1853 helpfully identified those construction materials he knew would be most needed 'down-under', and at the same time he was promoting sales-opportunities to his friends in England:

```
Mr Ewd. Coleman, Sen., late of Hull and now of
Sydney, will be glad to receive consignments
of goods per the Orwell Lass, now loading
here, and would strongly recommend to his
friends their sending building materials,
consisting of deals, slates, paints, oils,
etc. which are in great consumptive demand.
```

Business was thriving but now getting increasingly complex. To attempt to get inside the juggling act of running a shipping service, we can use the movements, all drawn from local and national newspapers, of a few of Zachariah's vessels to gain an insight into how hectic life was at the organisational end. By February 1854, Zachariah had a large number of barques on the go, and on 10th February he placed four advertisements selling freight and passenger spaces. These were positioned for maximum impact in highly visible, consecutive slots in the *first* column on the *first* page of the Hull Packet: to Boston on the *Ulverstone,* to New York on the *Stentor,* to St John (New Brunswick, Canada) on the

Everthorpe, and to Melbourne in an unnamed barque. How would one fill up and sell space on all these vessels at the same time, let alone find crew for them?

Zachariah certainly believed in letting people know what was on offer, but it can't have been easy to plan voyages with precision when there were so many unknowns, not least the winds and the rate at which merchants were loading their goods. The *Stentor,* bound for New York, gave a good example of time slippage: on 20th January he had introduced her, and then each week for the next *nine* weeks he put another advert in the local paper. Most took the form of reminding merchants that this barque was in dock, *'now loading',* but eventually the adverts announced that there was some freight and passenger space left, and she finally sailed for New York on 25th March. How did shipowners make plans or recruit crew when the departure date was so variable? But flexibility was part of the condition of travelling by sea.

At least *Stentor* was a specific, named ship, but the voyage to Melbourne in the same list must have been rather an organisational nightmare. Initially, Zachariah had advertised freight space in an unnamed vessel, but it seems Zachariah had a specific barque in mind, as she was described as an A1 ship of 240 tons. Perhaps he was in negotiation for her and could not specify her by name? Whatever the reason, he continued to place weekly advertisements for loading over the next four weeks, and then abruptly the deal must have fallen through in early February, because he was now obliged to place an 'URGENTLY WANTED' advertisement:

```
To load for Melbourne, Wanted immediately, a
vessel of light draught of water. Will meet
with a good freight and quick despatch.
```

He had already sold the freight space for a ship he suddenly didn't have, and was now desperate for a vessel to replace her. The same urgent call for a ship was placed in the following two weeks' editions – and then all went quiet until October. Presumably he got a suitable ship for his Melbourne cargo, for no more was heard after this.

A postcard from the archive shows how busy the Queen's Dock was in the 19th century. This inland dock was used until 1930 when it was filled in, as more accessible docks opened in the Humber. Today it is known as the Queen's Gardens.

Managing the simultaneous loading of cargoes, stocking up with provisions for a long voyage, and hiring competent crews demanded considerable organisational skills. It is hard to imagine running a high-powered business life without today's communication systems, but topography was on their side. Positioned as the firm was, in their very central location between Queen's Dock and the River Hull, co-ordination could be achieved in person. The tiny lanes and close proximity of businesses to each other enabled easy face-to-face communication when negotiating cargoes, ship charters, and crews. All the same, the challenges became more complex as the business grew...

Judging from a single huge advertisement he placed, not in the local paper, but nationally in *The Times* in June 1855, things were now operating more smoothly, and they would appear to have sorted out their ship-flow problems.

```
Pearson, Coleman and Co. are now loading the
following vessels, which will be dispatched
```

immediately:
Maria to Constantinople (from London)
Neptuna to Quebec (from London)
Leo (neutral flag) to Stockholm (from London)
Margarita to Constantinople or Scutari and
    Balaklava (from London)
Cato to Hamburg (from Hull)
British Queen to Hamburg (from Hull)
Aphrodite to Konigsburg (from Hull)
Howden to Bombay (from Grimsby)

Here were eight sailing vessels, all being loaded simultaneously and about to be dispatched to many different destinations. Zachariah had clearly spread his wings, and he was now loading in London as well as Hull and Grimsby, which meant advertising at a national level. Quite apart from the sheer number of shipping movements, this was a tremendous amount of business to handle at the same time. Well-trusted employees were essential to buy and manage all these cargoes and reliable agents were needed in foreign ports, not only to dispose of these cargoes at their destinations but to load up with new cargoes for the return trip. His 'address book' must have been extensive.

At this stage the Baltic timber trade was the bread-and-butter of Pearson and Coleman, and very lucrative this seemed to be for shipowners generally. England could not get wood fast enough to supply the massive house-building programme and the rapid expansion of the railway system. The country was hungry for timber, and the vast forests in Russia were a ready source of wood. To supply a keen commercial outlet in the west, huge platforms of timber from the boreal forests in Russia were floated down-river to St. Petersburg and Riga, where they were loaded onto ships and brought back to England. The port of Hull was ideally placed and particularly well-connected since the railway had arrived, so the consignments of timber could be readily distributed throughout England. The Hull wood trade, in fact, was so vigorous during the 1840s and 1850s, with so many ships unloading, and so much timber stacking up on the docks, that there was considerable congestion, a key factor in initiating the dock-expansion programme with which Zachariah would become active a few years later.

International trade on this route, however, was precipitously interrupted when the Crimean War broke out in 1854. Russia invaded Turkey; France and England subsequently declared war on her, so the Russian ports were now out-of-bounds for merchant vessels. Trade was suspended and Zachariah's wood import business was naturally in the firing line. But on such a lucrative route as this, it was important to keep a foot in the Russian door, poised to pick up trade as soon as the war drew to a close. For the duration of the war then, Zachariah still ventured as far as the Prussian ports of Pillau and Konigsburg on routes he had already established, but he had to stop short of St. Petersburg, which was now firmly in enemy territory. All the same, with a keen eye on the political situation, to allay fears and attract passengers he was careful to state in his advertisements that his ships flew a neutral flag. In this way he shrewdly contrived to keep open these routes as far as was practicable, because there was a ready market for his cargo. Perhaps more importantly, by doing so he was making very sure that he would be well-placed to pick up the trade when hostilities eventually ceased.

In addition to protecting his own trade routes, Zachariah played his part for the defence of the realm during the Crimean War. England needed to prepare to defend itself, if necessary, against Russia (*'the great autocrat of the north'*), and the government called on seamen of experience to help check that the *'belts and passages in the North Sea'* were in good order. So Zachariah and nine other Brethren of Trinity House, the organisation for the well-being of sailors and the safety of shipping, were selected by the Ministry to form part of this North Sea inspection party. The *Hull Packet* newspaper had *'no doubt that the Hull pilots and seamen [would] do their duty in the coming struggle'* because the sailors of Hull were *'the foremost in England in knowledge of the navigation of the Baltic and North Seas'*.

This Trinity House party accordingly set out to do their duty for Queen and Country, but all was not plain sailing; they met with some unexpected and demeaning conditions aboard *HMS Hecla,* the Royal Naval vessel chosen for this survey. They found themselves accommodated in hammocks slung *'before the mast'*, the place where Ordinary Seamen were quartered. Commissioned officers were usually quartered aft, a more favourable position in the ship, so it was hardly surprising that they felt insulted; they were senior in many ways to the sailors of the *Hecla.* So incensed were they that Zachariah and his nine colleagues wrote an impassioned letter to the House of Lords:

> *18th Feb 1854*
> *My Lords,*
> *We the younger brethren of the Trinity-house at this place, selected to form part of the expedition in HM steamer Hecla, appointed to survey the passages, harbours, &c &c, in the North Sea and the Baltic, beg most respectfully to complain to your lordships of the want of berthing accommodation on board that vessel.*
> *Some among us are shipowners, and retired from the sea, and the remainder are masters in the merchant service, and we are all accustomed to the comforts of a respectable home or cabin while afloat. Before we accepted the appointment in the Hecla, which included great sacrifices or pecuniary losses on the part of several of our number, we were assured that our position would be respected, and proper berths in the after cabins allotted for our use, your lordships may, therefore, imagine our astonishment and disgust when we were informed that hammocks were slung in the cockpit for our reception. [...]*
> *We cannot for a moment suppose that the degradations thus imposed upon us (and desire to acknowledge with*

thanks your lordships' order that we are to mess with the officers) neither do we attach any blame to those gentlemen, from whom we have received the greatest kindness, and have no better berths to offer us, but we humbly submit that the Hecla is unsuitable for the purposes intended, [...] and we entertain no doubt that if a steam ship of a more superior class had been dispatched, we could have persuaded a large number of seamen from this port to accompany us as volunteers for H. M. navy.

In conclusion, we beg to state that nothing but a solemn sense of the duty we owe to our country at the present crisis, to which at all times British sailors will cheerfully respond, if properly treated, would have induced us to embark upon the Hecla. We are aware that this appeal will come too late to admit of a remedy being provided on the present occasion, but we would respectfully urge your lordships' attention, should our services be required hereafter, that orders be issued to provide suitable berths for us among the commissioned officers on board HM ships, and that the indignity of huddling us in the cockpit with the men before the mast, be not again practised upon the younger brethren of the Trinity House of this port.

We have the honour to be

Your Lordships's very Obedient Humble Servants.

History does not tell us whether Zachariah sacrificed himself to further patriotic duties after this humiliating debacle, or whether their Lordships responded, but we get a flavour here of how the Russian War (only later known as the Crimean War) impacted on the lives of seamen in the merchant navy as well as those in the Royal Navy.

Ever the opportunist, the war provided Zachariah with the opportunity to diversify his businesses, and intriguing little adverts leave us wanting more detail about his money-making activities. In 1855 he decided to rent out the cellars under his new office in the High Street to anyone wishing for a location *'suitable for storing wine or oil, £12.'* And in another advert, he sought a buyer for 350 bales of *'cotton wool, slightly damaged by salt water. Saved from the wreck of the* Robert, *stranded at Hunsdon, near Lynn.'* He was selling this consignment by auction on behalf of Oates, Son and Capes, for the underwriters. Was this one of his own cargoes? Or had he managed to acquire a consignment of shipwrecked goods at a knock-down price in order to sell it on? In either case, it was yet another way to bring in money.

Trading was not all smooth, however: *'Wanted immediately, the holders of the Bill of Lading for abt. 840 qrs. of linseed ex* SWESDA *from St Petersburg, and which, if not shortly claimed, will be landed and warehoused'*. The importer of this consignment had not, for whatever reason, come to collect their cargo once it had arrived in Hull. It is unclear here whether the *Swesda* was one of Zachariah's vessels, or whether his firm was acting as an agent to dispose of the linseed for a third party.

This next advert could also have been the consequence of an unclaimed cargo: *'On sale, 50 bags fine Russian Manna Croup'*. The hard bits of wheat kernels that had escaped being powdered by the millstones was known as manna croup, and it was popular as the basis for puddings like semolina. Perhaps a merchant who had imported it from Russia had been unable to pay his transport fees? Or maybe a dodgy consignment had come his way? Whatever the story, one must assume that Zachariah made a profit of some sort on it.

Again, a barbed little one-liner inserted into the shipping column in April 1856 raises all sorts of questions: *'We hereby give notice that we have DISMISSED Mr GEORGE. C. WEAR from our employ'*. Why? Had Mr Wear been notorious? There was nothing further in the press to indicate why he'd been sacked. Elsewhere, however, there is media evidence to indicate that Mr Wear was a Master Mariner – a merchant captain. Under the circumstances, it is not unreasonable to infer that, until March 1856, George Wear had been commanding one of Zachariah's vessels. But what could he possibly have done to incur such public disgrace as an announcement on the front page of the town's local paper? He had either committed a cardinal sin, or Zachariah was keen to demonstrate that he would not stand for any nonsense from his employees.

As well as exposing scandal and failures, the local press also celebrated success, and this short congratulatory piece appeared in the Hull Packet in June 1855:

```
Extraordinary passage.
We [the editors] are happy to observe that
the barque Empress, Capt. Soulsby, belonging
to Messrs Z. C. Pearson, Coleman and Co., of
this port, arrived at Constantinople laden
with government stores, after a remarkable
passage [...] of only 27 days. We believe
this is one of the quickest passages for a
sailing vessel on record. The same vessel
on her voyage out rescued the crew of the
Schooner Lively, of Stockton, which was
seized by pirates in the Mediterranean.
```

While the speed of the *Empress* appears to have been more newsworthy than the pirates in the Mediterranean, publicity like this did Zachariah's firm no harm at all; not only did Z. C. Pearson, Coleman and Co. deploy the fastest ships in the business, but these speedy vessels were also seen to be commanded by caring, socially-minded captains.

Zachariah was now an established shipowner with a fleet of barques trading around the world. But this world was changing, and steam technology was being channelled into transport. Zachariah's disposition did not allow him to stand back if there were potential advantages to be gained from steam. Now a whole new chapter of his life began.

3

Zachariah embraces steam

It was during the eighteenth century that steam power had come into its own, with advances in coal mining and iron-production fuelling the relentless march of the Industrial Revolution. By the nineteenth century, the textile industry in the north had already been completely revamped by steam, producing the 'dark, satanic mills' of William Blake together with massive profits for the mill-owners. It was a natural progression for these industrial technologies to revolutionise travel, and with the arrival of steam locomotives the railway network expanded to make rail transport efficient and attractive. The same engineering principles could also be applied to mechanise travel on water. This was a game-changer for Zachariah.

The early steam vessels were paddle-steamers, ships propelled by using the engines to turn a pair of side-paddles. These worked well for calm waters, where the vessel lay evenly in the water, but they were less suited to the open seas where a stormy ocean could toss the ship about, bringing one or other of the paddles completely out of the water, thus playing havoc with the steering. But technology and design were constantly moving forward, and by the 1840s a new generation of ships evolved that could deal with heavy seas on the open ocean. These used their steam engines to turn a screw propeller at the stern, and because this was constantly under water – unlike side-paddles – it was more reliable, even in the roughest weather. All the same, hedging their bets, many ship designers initially provided both propeller and paddles.

The other step-change in ship design was the material from which the hull was constructed. Now that the production of iron had been streamlined, timber hulls could be replaced by stronger iron hulls and vessels no longer needed the bulky internal cross-bracing that stabilised traditional wooden ships. In addition to being a stronger vessel, there was also more room in the hold for cargo, notwithstanding the storage space needed for fuel. Coal bunkers had to be sizeable, as the ship had to be able to reach the next point on land where it could take on fuel, but when access to coal was uncertain, small coal tender vessels accompanied the transport steamers to top them up as needed.

Zachariah was intrigued: steam clearly offered tremendous advantages over sail, one of which was predictability – shipowners and merchants were no longer victims of the wind direction, but could now plan voyages more effectively, regardless of wind or current. It was inevitable that a man of such global shipping experience as Zachariah would investigate steam. All the same, steam-powered vessels did not arrive with an unblemished record; Zachariah and James must have seriously weighed up the pros and cons of investing in these expensive new vessels with all their machinery and engineering. There was no single 'best'. While shorter journey times knocked down transport costs, this had to be weighed against the expense of buying fuel – and there were still some merchants who preferred free wind to pricey coal to get their cargoes to the other end of the world. Still others wanted to keep their options open, and they chose vessels with paddle, screw *and* sail – although, given the size and weight of steamships, sail was really only useful as a back-up rather than a main method of propulsion.

Zachariah had plenty of choice when it came to buying steamers. Shipyards were rolling them out at a prodigious rate, and the Shipping Register shows that vessels changed owners quite frequently. Z. C. Pearson, Coleman and Co., always at the cutting edge of their trade, now augmented their fleet with steamships which ran in parallel with their sailing ships. This meant that they now had a real choice of what to send where. The world was their oyster. Possibly their first steamship ever was the *Spurn*, as this advert in *The Times* of 27th March 1856 shows:

> Steam to Copenhagen and Riga (subject to the declaration of peace). The fine A1 screw steamer Spurn, 600 tons, is intended to leave Grimsby for the above ports about the 15th April. For freight from London and all parts apply to Z. C. Pearson, Coleman & Co, Hull, Grimsby, and 34 Great St Helen's, London

This '*subject to the declaration of peace*' demonstrated that Zachariah was ahead of the game. Having diversified while the Baltic was being a bit tricky in the Crimean War, at the same time keeping the northern door open for business when the crisis was over, he was poised to pounce as soon as peace was on the horizon. So poised was he, in fact, that he placed this advertisement three days before the signing of the Peace Treaty.

His perseverance in maintaining the Baltic route, and his newly-acquired office in London, seemed to mark the point at which Zachariah's trade took off with gusto, and he soon acquired a fleet of steamships including *S.S. Gertrude, S.S. William France* and *S.S. Emmeline* to complement the *S.S. Spurn*. His routes were already established, and now that he could offer a more regular timetable, all he had to do was to attract passengers aboard. He launched his new services with seductive advertising: '*These fine steamers are all new, and built expressly for the requirements of the trade; their cabins are most elegantly and conveniently fitted up for the accommodation of first-class passengers*'.

It sounds here as though he had commissioned these steamers to be built for him, but we don't know for sure. What we do know is that he was now setting out to woo passengers. The predictability of steamers made travelling far easier to plan, and the passenger trade was in transition. People could be more deliberative: rather than hang about and wait for the moment ships had finished loading their cargo and were ready to depart, passengers were now given priority, and timetables were published. The transport lists of 'Packet Boats and Steamers in the Humber' show that every fourteen days the *S.S. Gertrude* left Hull for Riga to collect consignments of timber, but that she also offered passage to paying customers who paid a single fare of either £6 or £4, according to the quality of the accommodation they could afford.

Z. C. Pearson, Coleman and Co. were now in a period of huge expansion, which was arguably due to being so quick off the mark at the end of the Crimean War. The new fleet of steamers brought in a profitable passenger income alongside the timber import trade and with it new prominence. Success bred success; Zachariah was now firmly established in the ship-owning world.

It was around this time that he started to have ships built especially for him, the *Hull Packet* announcing the launch of one of these in May 1857: '

```
A new screw steamer, built for Messrs.
Pearson, Coleman and Co., was launched on
the new plan, namely, sideways, at Messrs
Samuelson's iron ship-building yard in the
groves. She is the sister ship to the Lord
Ashley (recently launched for the same firm)
and was christened the Lord Worsley.
```

Perhaps it was this strategic investment in new steamers that put the firm in pole position for an innovative and significant business venture, for in 1858 they landed a plum contract to provide the first regular mail service for Australia and New Zealand. This was a real coup: a lucrative ten year contract, with twelve months' notice on either side. The New Zealand government had been trying for over a year to get a provider for this service, and this Hull firm with its new steamers looked ideal to step into the breach. From Zachariah's own perspective, an added incentive must have been a ready-to-go agent: father-in-law. It would be a relatively short hop for Edward Coleman, who was already in Australia on company business, to transfer to New Zealand and handle the distant end of the new enterprise. Thus the 'Intercolonial Royal Mail Steam Packet Company Ltd.' was born.

THE

Inter-Colonial 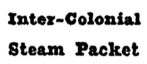 **Royal Mail**

Steam Packet **Company.**

(Limited.)

CAPITAL—£125,000, IN 12,500 SHARES OF £10 EACH.

2000 Shares reserved for the Colonies.

Colonel the Honorable **Robert Fulke Greville,**
Castle Hall, Milford, South Wales, *Chairman*
Rear-Admiral the Right Honorable **Lord George Paulet,** C.B., *Vice-Chairman.*
Z. C. Pearson, Esq., Hull and London, *Managing Director.*
Edward Coleman, Esq., New Zealand, *Manager in the Colonies.*

This was the press launch of the Intercontinental Royal Mail Steam Packet Co. Ltd, with the aim of raising the £125,000 needed to capitalise the new company.

They needed to raise capital from investors to finance the proposed service, and Zachariah used his now-impressive address book to assemble an enviable board of directors, headed up by the Hon. Robert Greville. Rear-Admiral Lord George Paulet and eight others completed the Board, which included James Coleman and Managing Director Zachariah Pearson. They launched their new company in *The Times* in September 1858, initially proposing to raise capital of £125,000 by selling shares worth £10 each. The advertisement took the form of a prospectus, spelling out the aims of the Company:

This co. has been formed to acquire and work out the valuable contract entered into by Messrs Pearson, Coleman and Co, with the Lords of the Admiralty, for an exclusive monthly mail service between Sydney and the principal ports of the colony of NZ, for a term of 10 years, and for the further object of meeting the requirements of the increasing trade between Australia, New Zealand and this country.

The prospectus pressed all the right buttons: Admiralty involvement, exclusivity, and increasing trade. They pointed out that it would be a '*highly remunerative prospect to the contractors*' as four efficient steam vessels were being furnished, '*to be inspected and approved by the Admiralty before leaving England*'. To run this service the government had granted a subsidy of £24,000 a year for the first four years of the contract, and a further £22,000 a year for the remaining six years of the term, plus an additional 11 shillings per mile for all extra distances. Lucrative indeed.

They could boast that the steamers were '*at liberty to carry passengers and cargo in addition to the mails*', and needed to prove reliability, so to guard against malfunction, they were at pains to point out that the steamers had all been fitted with '*duplicate machinery*' – a spare engine in case the main engine broke down. Perhaps it was this that enabled them to have an extra clause inserted into the contract, letting them off the hook if the steamers were late. Unfair fining for lack of punctuality had apparently been *'detrimental to some subsidized companies'*, and Zachariah, wearing his business hat, succeeded in having this contract worded so that they would not be fined *'except in cases of wilful neglect'*. Investors were impressed, and accordingly bought into the scheme: the company was soon a going concern.

It is hard to over-emphasise the value of a regular coastal service to the inhabitants of The Colonies. At this stage, the infrastructure of Australia and New Zealand was ruggedly rudimentary, with neither a road nor rail network, so coastal ships were their life-line. In adhering to the published timetable for his key vessels, the *Prince Alfred, Lord Worsley, Lord Ashley* and *Airedale,* Zachariah dared not leave anything to chance, and he organised a range of coal tenders to supply the fleet with fuel where local coal on the coast was not available.

Before they could start in earnest, the company had to get their steamers out there, which enabled them to capitalise on another source of income: the emigration traffic. As the Company was not contracted to carry the mail from England to Sydney, it made sense to off-set costs by attracting passengers – and there was now no shortage of people wishing to start life afresh in The Colonies. Similarly, there was no lack of shipping firms offering deals, so Zachariah set out to entice them aboard his own vessels: he advertised nationally, he offered 'superior accommodation', and he gave his customers a choice of embarking at either London or Milford Haven.

In getting the business off the ground in The Colonies, the new services were advertised in the local newspapers: the *Bay Courier,* the *Otago Witness,* the *Nelson Examiner and New Zealand Witness* and the *Taranaki Herald.* They would be taking a monthly route from Sydney to six ports in New Zealand: Wellington, New Plymouth, Auckland, Canterbury, Nelson, and Otago, and by publishing the schedule in advance they aimed to build up a regular passenger clientele. They assured potential travellers and traders that they were *'establishing houses at each station, and [...] sending out clerks for the whole of them'*, and these agencies were in place at each port by January 1859. New Zealand had been looking forward to this service for a long time, as the previous deal they had struck with the Australian contractor had fallen through. So they were delighted when Zachariah stepped into the breach, and it was with relief that the NZ newspapers now heralded the new mail service.

Royal Mail **Line of**

Company's **Steam-ships.**

T HE "*PRINCE ALFRED*," 1200 tons,
400 horse-power.

The *Lord Ashley*...... 550 tons ...180 h.p.
„ *Lord Worsley* ... 550 „ ...180 „
„ *Airdale*............ 350 „ ...100 „

Until further notice, one of the Company's splendid Steamers will leave Otago on or about the 25th of every month, taking Passengers and Goods for Port Lyttelton, Wellington, Nelson, and Sydney.
For Freight or Passage, apply to
JONES, CARGILL, & Co.

One of the adverts placed in the New Zealand press to publicise the monthly route of the 'splendid steamers' around the coast.

The Intercolonial Royal Mail Steam Packet Company Ltd. went into service on schedule, and operated so successfully that soon they were looking to buy a fifth vessel to expand their operation. In the advertisement in *The Times* of March 1860, aiming to raise money with a second tranche of shares, their exemplary track record was extolled: *'the service commenced on the 1st Nov 1858, and has continued uninterruptedly to the present times, giving entire satisfaction to the general and local governments of New Zealand and the colonists generally.'*

To attract shareholders, they were keen to point out that all their ships had *'invariably performed their voyages under the stipulated times'* and they reassured investors that they had obtained a considerable reduction in both insurance premiums and the cost of coal. An intriguing insight into the sort of challenge the new arrivals had faced can be gleaned from this sentence in the advertisement: *'although the business and connexions of the company had to be created, and <u>the opposition of established and competing interests subdued</u>,* [my emphasis] *the progress of the trade, and the results of the working to the present time, have been highly satisfactory'.*

Clearly, Edward Coleman had driven a hard bargain with everyone: suppliers, colonial government, and even with the local competition. His correspondence to Zachariah indicated his difficulty in breaking into the locally-favoured practices, but he was nevertheless optimistic. *'There is no doubt we have entered on the contract at an excellent time',* the other contract having fallen through, and he quoted the pay-rates for able-seamen, firemen etc. before saying *'there is a prospect of getting the work done at a more advantageous rate. It is my firm opinion that the enterprise will pay well. You may rely upon my leaving no stone unturned to the effect of this most desirable object.'* Edward was just the sort of father-in-law a chap needed – 12,000 miles away *and* making money for his son-in-law.

The Intercolonial Royal Mail Steam Packet Company certainly revelled in its achievements; the Directors gave a dinner for the retiring Superintendent of Canterbury, New Zealand, and the Chairman gave a resounding speech, praising the role the English played out there, and especially the Company's part in colonial development. But despite all the good press, there were nevertheless a few grumbles.

Notwithstanding the fact that they had chosen to travel on mail steamers, some passengers were less than

*It was to these New Zealand ports that Zachariah's new shipping line, the
Intercontinental Royal Mail Steam Packet Co. Ltd., delivered mail from
Sydney. Being a scheduled, regular service, it also provided a coastal route for
passengers – much-needed as the infrastructure of roads across the country
had yet to be developed. The coast was treacherous, however, and the Lord
Worsley ran aground here on North Island – carrying a consignment of gold
for the Bank of New Zealand.*

enchanted with the standard of accommodation provided – they complained that the ships were too small, and the accommodation caused *'miserable inconvenience and discomfort'*. The selling-points of the Company had naturally emphasised the best points of the service, and glossed over any local problems, such as passenger dissatisfaction, but a pack of correspondence from 1861 throws light on some of the background challenges they had to face. The letters were between the House of Representatives of New Zealand, the New Zealand Post Office, and the Company. While the New Zealand government was happy with the mail part of the service, and could not fault its punctuality, they were unable to ignore these passenger complaints, and requested larger vessels to satisfy the paying passengers.

Zachariah felt justifiably miffed, as he had provided ships that were actually larger than those specified in the contract. In the original negotiations, as he pointed out in his letter to Lord Claud Hamilton, who was handling the matter at the UK end (and after whom Zachariah named his next vessel intended to be dispatched to New Zealand) he said he had *'asked [the NZ negotiator] to fix himself the size of the boats he would recommend'*. After hearing what size vessels the client wanted, Zachariah had then provided ships that actually exceeded this requirement, so he felt that they had no right to complain. If they were now requesting still larger ships, he could not justify this: the contract simply was not paying enough.

The issue seemed to be a political one, fanned by flames of local envy towards the runaway success of the new shipping line, and when there was a route and timetable shake-up, Zachariah and his colleagues had a very clear suspicion that other shipping lines were being given favoured routes. Was one of the contributory factors due to Edward's ruthless 'subduing of established interests' – a festering sore waiting to come to a head?

Eventually, of course, the inevitable British compromise was reached. The Company was forced to share its business with a new postal service for part of the route, which meant that the *Claud Hamilton* was not, in the end, sent out there at all. And Zachariah responded to criticism by upgrading the Company's ships, inviting reporters to view and publicise his ship *Victory,* which he had fitted out especially for the service. *A Hull Advertiser* journalist in May 1860 described the passenger accommodation in glowing terms:

> She has three saloons aft; one for general use, and two for ladies only. She can accommodate in these 46 passengers. The fittings and furnishings of the main saloon are superb. The seats are covered with rich crimson velvet, and the panels are decorated with oil paintings of no mean order. These are principally battle scenes, and represent some of the most stirring events in our national history. A hasty glance through the cabins leads us to the conclusion that nothing which can tend to the comfort of the traveller is wanting.

The story of the Intercolonial Royal Mail Steam Packet Co. Ltd would not be complete without some hair-raising observations of a ship-wrecked passenger. It contributes nothing to the life of Zachariah, except, one assumes, the bureaucracy involved in the aftermath of losing a ship, but it is a colourful little incident which illustrates the rugged experience of life in The Colonies at the time. The Taranaki Wars were the result of local Maoris rebelling against white settlers arriving from Australia and taking over their land. Emigrants had assumed, based on centuries of land ownership and transference of title deeds in Britain, that they could buy land and set up deals with local chiefs – but they had no understanding of the Maori culture of communal land, and sometimes the chiefs 'sold' land that was not, in fact, owned at all.

This had led to a number of skirmishes, and things really came to a head in 1860 in the Taranaki district on the west coast of New Zealand's North Island, when the local Maoris finally took a stand against the government. Some bitter battles took place, and many people on both sides were killed. The Company's vessels played a role in this struggle, sometimes being used to carry stores and troops to the scenes of action as they travelled round the coast. The outcome of the Maori wars at Taranaki was generally considered to be indecisive but there was residual nervous tension in the area, and the attitude of the local Maori chiefs towards white men was unpredictable.

So there was much anxiety when, on 1st September 1862, the *Lord Worsley,* one of the coastal fleet, was driven ashore by a storm and wrecked on the rocks at Opunake on her regular route up the west coast. The crew of a previous ship wrecked in enemy territory had been massacred, so *Lord Worsley*'s crew and passengers were justifiably nervous of what sort of reception they would get from the local inhabitants. The captain must have been especially anxious about perceived failure; unbeknownst to the passengers, he was carrying four cases of gold for the Bank of New Zealand.

But they lived to tell the harrowing tale, and nine months later a survivor, M. J. Briggs, related to *The Times* what happened after they came ashore at dawn:

> *We were 66 men, women and children, completely in the hands of the Maoris. There was consultation between them all night long for several nights as to whether we should be tomahawked or made slaves of or allowed to proceed to New Plymouth. At length it was agreed that the ship, which was safely beached and upright, should be given up to them with all her cargo and stores, and all firearms and ammunition. But that the passengers with their personal baggage should be allowed to proceed to New Plymouth.*

They were lucky that they had come ashore in the territory of a friendly Maori, King Matukatea, who defended them against the more warlike members of other tribes. Instead of being tomahawked or enslaved, they were put in bullock drays, and set free. They travelled over wild and devastated country, partly under water, through burnt out settler villages and wrecked crops. They went through considerable hardship in this rugged country in seeking safety, struggling through 18 rivers before they met one with a bridge. Briggs ended his first-hand account of the adventure with a (rather culture-centric!) view about the local state of law and order:

> *... no-one wishes more kindly to the Maoris than I do. I look on them as naughty, spoilt children, who have had everything they cried for, and apologists for their worst crimes; but they must be governed before they can be elevated. There can be no lasting peace till they are disarmed, till roads are made through the heart of the country, and till the English language is taught among them.*

He was also scathing about the money *'foolishly wasted in reducing the Maori to a written language, or rather to a mongrel language, invented by the missionaries.*

Considerable fuss was made about the incident by others, too. That part of the coast was notorious for shipping accidents, and the local colonial government was apparently too ineffective to have built land routes, so consequently everyone had to resort to travel via the dangerous coastline. After this shipwreck, an anonymous letter to *The Times* in May 1863 blamed the loss of the *Lord Worsley* and other vessels on negligence by the authorities. He pointed out that the reason they were so reliant on the coastal steamers to travel between provinces was because the sheep farmers resisted all attempts to make roads. He said that not only was more law and order needed, but that better manpower was vital if they were to do the work properly. He ended his rant with the memorable punch-line: *'the Romans had slaves and legions, the Normans had serfs, we have convicts'!*

To put a more cheerful spin on the sad tale of the *Lord Worsley*, her wreck is currently advertised as a desirable New Zealand dive-site, though apparently with a reduced sense of anticipation as the cargo of gold is no longer in it.

As the *Lord Worsley* illustrates, even with a successful fleet of vessels, secured routes, and thriving businesses, all was not necessarily plain sailing for Zachariah. Sea was unpredictable and coastlines were treacherous, and Zachariah was not alone among the early steamship owners to suffer some significant shipping disasters. Steam presented a new set of dangers – perils that had not afflicted sailing ships. For one thing, steam engines could be unreliable, and with boiling water under huge pressure it was not uncommon for the boilers to explode when valves got stuck, or when furnaces were too fierce. One wonders, from reading the accounts of wrecks, whether there was also an element of recklessness. Steam power had freed up captains from the tyranny of wind, and allowed them to steer more direct routes to their destinations, but did this also involve ignoring some of the environmental signals that captains had traditionally observed? Was steam seducing them into a more arrogant approach to the elements? Whatever the causes, steamship owners lost vessels in uncomfortable numbers, and *The Times* reported a great many of these, including several of Zachariah's.

His steamer *Emmeline* was '*wrecked on her passage from Riga'* in Nov 1860, and his *Wesley* was lost with all hands on the Baltic run in 1861. The *Z. C. Pearson* [whose idea was it to name one's ship with one's own name?] was a bit of a mystery at first. No-one knew for a couple of months exactly what had happened to

    ...this splendid vessel. [...] The vessel
    left Riga for Hull on 28th of last month [July
    1861], and although she should have passed the
    Elsinore Sound three days afterwards, nothing
    whatsoever has since been heard of her.

She disappeared with no trace, and there were great fears for the crew of 25 and the captain's wife and servant. Then nearly two months later, a piece of the name-board from her bow was washed up 120 miles from Riga, spelling out: 'ARSON', painted in the tell-tale Pearson livery of '*gilt letters on a blue ground*'. The article in the *Yorkshire Gazette* went on to say that

> the fact that the bow board was found would seem to confirm the statement that the loss of the vessel was attributable to collision

and that no hopes could be entertained for any of those aboard. It was bad enough to lose a ship, but to lose the whole crew, with captain, wife and servant was tragic.

Zachariah's vessels, however, were not more accident-prone than others, as *The Times* reported in August 1861:

> ... the frequency of the loss of Hull steamers, and the lamentable loss of life and property thereby, within the past year, is really fearful; and the inquiry is now beginning to be pretty general in the town as to whether the mode of construction of iron steamers may not in some measure be the cause of these painful disasters. Certain it is, that since last October no fewer than eight Hull steamers have been wrecked in the Baltic trade.

Eight steamers from Hull inside ten months was certainly a heavy toll, and concern was being voiced: was it really the design of the steamers, or was it something to do with the Baltic? The region does seem to have had special challenges, as this *Times* passage in June 1861 indicated when accounting for the loss of yet another Hull vessel near Dagoe, not far from the Gulf of Finland:

> This area is noted for its powerful magnetic attractiveness, and several Hull vessels have been wrecked in its vicinity, from no other cause but the derangement of the ship's compasses.

Whether or not the Dagoe area really had some environmental magnetic hazard is a moot point, but direction-finding in steamships presented a new challenge, as iron hulls and engines interfered with the compass and gave false information. In 1854 John Gray had patented his binnacle, a useful piece of kit that compensated for magnetic interference, but it took a while before all ships could be fitted with it.

Around this time, insurance companies were starting to take more interest in what was going on; they were, after all, the ones paying out on these shipping disasters. Before the nameplate of the *Z. C. Pearson* had surfaced, *The Times* had reported the initial disappearance of her thus:

> ... considerable alarm is felt about the safety of the steamer Z. C. Pearson, which sailed from Riga for Hull on 26th ult. Twenty guineas insurance was paid at Lloyd's yesterday, and fifty guineas was asked today. It is feared that this is another case of loss through deck-loads.

This comment about deck loads indicated a real issue. There was not yet any official limit as to how fully-laden ships could be, and ruthless shipowners were tempted to cram as much cargo as possible aboard to maximise their profits – jeopardising ship, cargo and crew in the process. It was to be another fifteen years before Samuel Plimsoll's determined efforts to resolve the problems caused by this greed resulted in legislation on how much load ships could carry. His visible 'Plimsoll Line' markings are painted on ships even today. Nevertheless, in the case of the *Z. C.*

Pearson, The Times was later proved to have been wrong in its assumption: the broken name plate had established that it was collision rather than overloading that sealed her fate.

It seems that Zachariah had an apparently endless supply of steamers to replace the ones that were lost. Only three months after the *Z. C. Pearson* went down, *The Times* reported a double loss. The

> *Beatrice* was only placed on the Rotterdam line on Sunday night, in place of the steamer *Entrantress*, which was lost last week with 16 hands at Helvoet in Holland, [...] driven during a strong gale onto the stone-pier there, rebounding from which she went onto a bank, from which she slipped into deep water. And sank in less than half an hour, her crew succeeding in saving part of the cargo and also themselves.

It is hard to determine how blame was apportioned when a ship went down. Were punishments meted out to the captain, crew or owner for losing a ship? Were there always enquiries to establish what happened? There was certainly one that hit the headlines in 1861: an unfortunate shipowner called Wilson lost three Baltic steamers in one year, and the Board of Trade, after an enquiry, cancelled the master's certificate of one of the captains. Could it have been a similar fate which had befallen George Wear, the captain mentioned earlier who had been sacked in 1856 so publicly by Zachariah on the front page of the local paper?

A particularly gruelling loss for Zachariah came at a rather significant point in time in his life. He had bought an old and historic vessel, the *Indian Empire*. She was a huge ship at 1857 tons, and needed considerable work done on her, so Zachariah had sent her for a complete repair after purchasing her. Her pedigree was impressive, and she bore the scars to prove it, so we shall divert for a moment to contextualise this amazing vessel which Zachariah chose to buy. She was built in New York as the first steamship specifically designed for ocean travel, and launched in 1848 as the *United States*. She was a wooden paddle-steamer, and on her maiden voyage she crossed the Atlantic; 46 passengers aboard her had paid $120 each to be part of history and, being the first American vessel powered solely by steam to enter the Mersey, her arrival was heralded by loud cheers from the locals.

The inauspicious paddle steamer, the Indian Empire, *which Zachariah bought and sent for a complete refit, and which was then destroyed by catching fire in the Thames. She started life as the* United States, *but is seen here in her next incarnation as the* Hansa *before she became the* Indian Empire.

This route was uneconomical, though, as she was consuming coal at the alarming rate of 48 tons a day, and making no income from carrying mail; she had to be sold. The Confederated German States bought her, renamed her *Hansa* and armed her, using her in the Battle of Heligoland in 1849. By 1852 she had reclaimed her role as a transatlantic passenger ship before being adapted by the British Government to carry troops and supplies to the Crimea; afterwards the Honourable East India Company chartered her as a transport vessel during the Indian Mutiny.

Her many reincarnations and adventures included considerable collateral damage: she had run into ice, lost an engine, run aground on a sandbank, lost one of her side-paddles, and hit rocks – but still she went on. She was sold in 1858 to become a fleet ship for the Atlantic Steam Navigation Co., and her new British owner renamed her the *Indian Empire* – but changing her name did not change her fortune. On her final voyage, carrying a cargo of cotton from New York, she had run into prolonged storms which delayed her so much that she ran out of coal, and she improvised on fuel, having to *'burn cotton from her cargo, woodwork and spars to reach Broadhaven, Ireland'*. This ship had certainly carved her place in history.

One can only guess at the reason Zachariah now bought the *Indian Empire.* He certainly got a lot of ship at presumably a bargain price after all her accidents, and he sent her for a complete repair at Deptford Dock on the Thames in 1862. With her huge hold, and the American Civil War now in full swing, it's quite likely that he was preparing her to play a role in trading with the Confederate States – although sadly she didn't make it. The refit was completed in July 1862, but the *Indian Empire* caught fire while she was in mid-Thames having her paddles refitted. According to *The Times* of 25th July, she burned spectacularly through the night, but despite the attentions of most of the London fire brigade, she sank and, due to a technicality with the wording of the insurance policy, Zachariah reckoned to have lost £35,000 on her. The significance of the timing of this disaster becomes apparent in the context of the rest of Zachariah's adventures in mid-1862.

Zachariah was a caring man, and concerned for the welfare of his employees, as contemporaneous accounts show, so each shipping disaster must have sliced into him. Could it have been the loss of so many of his steamers that motivated him to re-examine the potential of sail? Certainly he seemed to fall in love all over again with wind power.

Perhaps he had always harboured a nostalgic preference for sailing ships? With wind, it was you, the ship and the elements – and your own skill and experience. There were no boilers to blow up, coal to be loaded, or engines to operate – only clean sails. And wind came free.

Whatever the reason, an advertisement in *The Times* of April 1862 shows Zachariah with seven others launching a new company to

> ... establish a fleet of first class iron sailing ships, built upon the most approved and scientific plans, of the best materials and workmanship, and fitted with every modern improvement for the general passenger and cargo trades between this country, our eastern and colonial dependencies, and other suitable ports.

Alongside Zachariah, the Directors of this new 'United Kingdom Shipowning Company Ltd.' consisted of the great and the good of sea and banking, including the President of the Chamber of Commerce in Southampton, which was interesting: Hull and Southampton had always been competitors for trade, and here were Directors from both ports collaborating on a new venture...

In choosing iron over wood for its lower maintenance costs, they hoped to tempt investors, and added that as there had been a 30 per cent increase in shipping since 1845, this was a good time to invest. Extolling the virtues of sail versus steam, they pointed out that *'in sailing ships, no sacrifice of stowage room has to be made for engine space and fuel, while in steamers the cost of fuel, as well as of the staff of engineers and firemen, is very heavy.'* They were combining maximum space with lower costs and the fastest sailing ships on the sea, and they ended by exhorting people to buy into *'one of the most profitable investments that has ever been brought before the public'*.

The company set out to raise capital of £300,000 by selling shares. Their prospectus outlined plans for designing 'medium clippers', and hoped that by *'adopting carefully selected models, combining all the best qualities of the most approved specimens of naval architecture, as well as by prudent management both afloat and on shore'* they would *'produce returns amply sufficient to pay the shareholder large interest on their outlay'*.

The *Hull Packet* of 18th April applauded the scheme, noting that the new materials technology was a timely innovation. *'The adoption of iron for wood in the construction of ocean ships [...] and the superior economy of sailing vessels'* marked a much-needed breath of new life into the port of Hull, which had shown stagnation over the previous twenty years. Passengers would only take slightly longer by sail than with steam, and the minor inconvenience of this was nothing compared with the extra cost of going by steamer.

It would round off this part of the story neatly to report that the new company flourished, but the success of the venture is unclear. Zachariah's life was about to change for ever, and would exclude him from any such entrepreneurial activities. But leaving his own personal disaster aside, if the company did ultimately take off, its success was likely to have been short-lived due to the effect that the Suez Canal was to have on shipping routes. This great engineering feat was started in 1859, but not opened until 1869, seven years after the fleet of iron clippers was proposed. Once shipping was able to cut directly through the canal to India without having to circumnavigate Africa, the economics of trading with the east improved immensely – but only for steam ships. The canal was not sail-friendly as there was no space to manoeuvre and take advantage of the winds: clippers still had to go round the Cape. The opening of the Suez Canal cast a fatal blow to trade by sail.

4

Zachariah's increasing civic involvement

Amidst all the success and disaster that accompanied Zachariah's business ventures, it is easy to forget that there was more to the man than shipping, and this is an opportune moment to explore the other things that were going on in parallel with his working life. From the mid-1850s onwards, Zachariah became more visible in society. Having proved his credentials in all things maritime, he had earned a reputation as a man with sound judgement. He was proud of Hull and, having worked hard to safeguard its trade, his opinion was now widely sought to influence policy, both locally and nationally.

Even at the age of 28 he felt strongly enough about marine policy to be one of the signatories to a letter about the repeal of the historical Navigation Acts. These had originally been passed to protect Britain's trade, but they represented restrictive practices, preventing other nations from sharing the trade between Britain and its colonies – and Parliament was about to repeal them. In Hull this worried a group of merchants, bankers, shipowners and traders, and they cajoled the Mayor to hold a public meeting to discuss how to oppose the movement by *'petitioning the House of Lords, praying their Lordships not to process the said Bill'*. The Hull meeting was held – but the Acts were eventually repealed anyway, opening up free trade and the import of cheap food.

By the time he was 30, Zachariah was taking part in campaigns, and chipping in financially as well. He was one of many who subscribed £5 towards a fundraising effort to reduce port dues and other local charges at Hull. As an up-and-coming shipowner, he did not want to see Hull being priced out of the market, losing trade to other ports. He now had business premises in Hull, London and Grimsby, so no doubt he was able to choose whichever dock was most appropriate for his various purposes, but as the businessman in him evolved, so did the political animal, and Hull was very close to his heart.

Zachariah became known to the Department of Trade at Westminster, and was summoned to Parliament on a number of occasions to give evidence to Select Committees, the bodies which collect evidence from experts and report to the Lords or the Commons before policy is made. He had a considered opinion on most things maritime, and Sound Dues were one of his *bêtes noires*. This was a tax levied by the Danes on all shipping that passed through their busy strait *en route* to Russia, but the nations who used this passage were getting very tired of enriching the Danish Crown by paying it. It was certainly a tax which would have been onerous for Zachariah, substantially sapping his Baltic income, so in 1856, when he was invited as *'an experienced commander in the Baltic trade'* to answer questions to a Select Committee in Whitehall, he would have had no problem in sharing his experiences. Gratifyingly, Sound Dues were abolished the following year by the Copenhagen Convention.

One of the positions that was fundamental to Zachariah was his role as one of the 'Younger Brethren' of Trinity House. In an era where there were no social services to support those experiencing difficulties, Trinity House was a sort of sailors' guild which fulfilled charitable roles for the mariners, such as providing schools, hospitals and homes for orphans of seamen. At an operational level, the Younger Brethren were volunteers of recognised maritime experience who assisted the main business of Trinity House. Once they had become more senior, they might be elected into the small elite group of 'Elder Brethren', the body of decision-makers. Zachariah was closely involved throughout his life, from auditing the accounts in 1852 to being elected unanimously as one of the four Pilot Commissioners – the men with the responsibility of licensing pilots for the port. In later life he was to become one of the Elder Brethren.

A mariner through and through, Zachariah lost no opportunity to align himself with the marine tradition publicly, reinforcing the value of naval services to Britain whenever he could. The local paper reports that, at a dinner in 1856, when he was asked to reply to a toast on behalf of the navy, he responded by saying that *'if it had not been for the noble pluck and stout heart of the British sailor, England would not have attained the proud position which she enjoys amongst the nations of the earth'*. A further sign that Zachariah was earning trust and respect among his peers was his election in 1857 onto the Local Marine Board. These boards were relatively new, having been established as a result of the Mercantile Marine Act in 1850, and their purpose was regulatory, for *'improving the Condition of Masters, Mates, and Seamen, and maintaining Discipline in the Merchant Service'*. Each Board was to include *'six members to be elected by the owners of the foreign going vessels'* every third year – and Zachariah was one of these, freely elected as a respected local shipowner.

One can never be sure what direct influence an individual ever has on policy, but where he believed something could be improved, Zachariah stood up to be counted. Perhaps perceiving that one could have more influence in achieving change as part of a democratically-elected body than as an individual, it was around this stage in his life that he took his first steps into local governance, and in the local elections in 1856 he won the seat of Councillor to the Ward of West Sculcoates, just north of the centre of Hull. His council hat and his business hat would have frequently swapped places in his life as a public servant, for he took up and fought causes in both arenas.

Wearing both of these hats, one of the things he felt strongly about was the unfairness of shipowners' liability under the new Merchant Shipping and Passenger Act. Accidents at sea were blamed on the shipowners, who had to foot the bill regardless of whether it was their fault or not – and this had unintended consequences. Shipowners now had to consider whether or not they could offer a passenger service to the public. Early in 1857, Zachariah was picked to be one of a deputation seeking a policy change; they wanted their liability for passengers limited in law to realistic levels, and Zachariah explained to the Prime Minister, Lord Palmerston, that *'unless the government relieved the shipowner of his liabilities, he must either have his vessels registered abroad, or cease to carry any passengers whatever, and that it was unfair on the part of the British government to place the shipowners of this country in competition with the foreigner, who is totally exempt from all such responsibilities'*.

Lord Palmerston, though, pushed the responsibility firmly back onto the shipowners; they should be hiring the right captains in the first place. Shipowners, he maintained, *'were bound to see that their ships were entrusted to commanders not merely who had been passed by the Board of Trade, but men in whose judgement they could place confidence'*. *The Economist*, in February 1857, had no sympathy with shipowners either, interpreting the situation in a class context: the Bill would be an added security, *'particularly to the poorer classes of emigrants'*, and anyway, shipowners who had no such liability would be getting rich too fast. On this matter, it seems, the delegation's argument with the establishment fell on deaf ears. One might reasonably assume that the outcome sharpened Zachariah's determination to employ the best possible Masters and crew.

Another bone of contention in the shipping business was the issue of 'Primage Dues'. These were controversial tariffs payable by the recipient when freight was landed – a sort of gratuity to the captain for safely delivering the goods. The dues were unfair, as they were locally-decided, which meant that ships were charged unequally in different ports – and shipowners wanted them outlawed. The Court Circular of

The Times records how Zachariah and his business partner, James Coleman, were invited in 1858 as part of a deputation to the Board of Trade to discuss the issue. This particular visit appeared to have met with success, as three years later an Act was passed abolishing Primage Dues. He won some battles, and lost others.

Zachariah's humble beginnings must have shaped his outlook, because once he was in a position where he could influence what happened, he made the welfare of seamen one of his concerns. Seamen from all parts of the world found themselves in the town, either temporarily or longer term. Some were poor, sick or lonely, and without much English. Zachariah knew from first-hand how hard the life at sea was, and he understood how uncomfortable it could be staying in foreign ports so, with the well-being of sailors at heart, he helped in setting up a fund to provide a hostel for foreign sailors on shore leave. He was one of the secretaries for the 'Port of Hull Society for the Religious Instruction of Seamen', and the launch of their appeal sounds rather a jolly affair: after the speeches, the ladies provided tea, and then the *'orphan children sang some beautiful hymns'*.

A tried-and-tested way to raise donations at the time was to publish in the local paper a list of people who had subscribed to the cause, alongside the amount donated – *pour encourager les autres*. Zachariah started the initial list with a donation of £100, and the strategy in this instance worked, as shortly afterwards a second, much longer, list of subscribers appeared in the newspaper. With a total of £3,500 raised by public subscription, the Hull Sailor's Home on Salthouse Lane later opened in 1860. Yet another report a couple of years later has him attending a fundraising dinner on behalf of the Merchant Seamen's Orphan Asylum, this time at a national level in London.

Another of Zachariah's concerns affected the prosperity of both Hull and his own purse. There was a closed-shop practice of getting work done on ships while they were in dock: shipowners were not allowed to bring in their own workmen to speed things up, but were forced to use the labour provided on site. This slowed things down, as the docks were heavily over-used, and there were dysfunctional bottlenecks. Ships had to wait and take their turn to be loaded and unloaded, losing shipowners and the town time and money. In 1856 Zachariah made a strong case to be able to get the work done in his own way, but with factional interests at stake this was controversial, and he found himself having to argue his case publicly in the correspondence columns of the *Hull Packet.*

Whether this was the final issue that chivvied Zachariah into action with a radical solution is not known, but over the next few years he worked tirelessly to improve dock conditions. He really wanted Hull to succeed, and the matter of ship turn-around was very close to his heart. The more import-export business a port could attract via its docks, the wealthier it became, but competition between ports was fierce, and Hull had to win and maintain business by providing efficient dock facilities. The docks were not necessarily owned by the town: many were privately owned by individuals or conglomerates, and the owners could decide how much to charge for servicing the ships that passed through them. Even adjacent docks in the same port could be in competition with each other – and reducing dock handling charges was a key factor in attracting trade.

In an effort to secure a bigger slice of the dock revenue, dirty dealings were not unknown, and in 1856 we find the *London* Victoria Dock company announcing in the *Hull* local paper that it was reducing its dock charges. Knowing what Hull's docks charged, they deliberately advertised to Hull shipping how much cheaper it would be to use their own dock. By undercutting them, the London dock was aiming to attract some of the business away from Hull – exactly what Zachariah was worried about and prepared to act on.

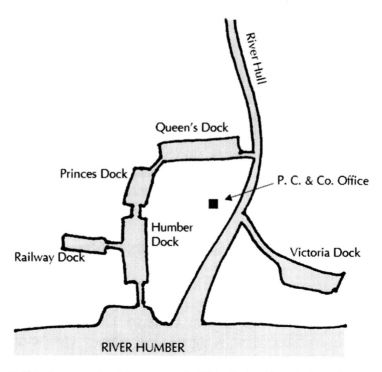

The Hull dock system in 1860 consisted of this chain of interlocking basins. Vessels had to queue for access, and as shipping increased so did congestion, wasting time and money, and prompting the scheme for a new dock to be built on the Humber.

In addition to dock charges, the other frustrations to shipowners and traders were congestion and wasted time. The existing docks, run by the Hull Dock Co., comprised a series of interlocking inland basins in the heart of the town. One can understand the issue of access by visiting the Queen's Garden, today's historical remnant of the Queen's Dock that Zachariah was using in the nineteenth century. Vessels had to queue and take their turn while others were being unloaded and loaded, but with the increasing trade in Hull through the advent of steam and rail, Zachariah among others felt that this system was now inadequate, and plans were hatched for a radical solution. In the early 1860s he was one of the delegates invited to a meeting with ministers at the Board of Trade to discuss a new potential development – the 'Hull West Dock'. This would be a purpose-built, modern dock further west up the Humber and linked to the railway.

This new dock would be safe, deep, and easy to access, allowing ships to dock at half tide instead of depending on high tide. The plan sounded logical enough to win ministerial support, and the following month Zachariah was heading a long list of 32 provisional Directors in a prospectus that launched 'The Hull West Dock Company'. The scheme had the backing of the Town Council, Trinity House, and the North Eastern Railway, and the directors promoted the all-round advantages. While the benefits to merchants and shipowners were obvious, owners of warehouses and shops would also reap extra business from the new dock, and for the labouring classes the scheme would bring new work and trading opportunities. As it would clearly bring advantages to all classes of Hull citizens, the directors suggested that a few shares might be bought by everyone. Zachariah, being passionate about this issue, had naturally already invested substantially in the new dock.

The launch, however, precipitated a big battle, as the Hull Dock Company, which had hitherto monopolised all the shipping business in Hull, was operated by the old names in Hull. They were shocked to have the monopoly of their docks challenged, but realised that they could not logically oppose the new scheme, so they put forward a rival copycat plan for a dock to the west of the town. The editors of the *Hull Packet* were incensed, and weighed in on behalf of the original proposal: *'if it be made by an independent company, we shall have competition, and competition means freedom. Let everybody understand that the context upon which we are about to enter between the existing Dock Company and the new West Dock Company is virtually a contest between monopoly and freedom.'*

The local press could see the benefits of a free market, but in the Town Council the project generated a great deal of heated debate and polarisation. By February 1862, members were either for or against the new West Dock development. No-one was neutral, as many councillors were on the boards of either one or the other company. The newspaper reported much of the debate verbatim, so we can 'hear' Zachariah speaking in quite a low-key way, stating facts and attempting to counteract the emotion being generated by others, particularly Mr Samuelson (a man who was to lead a vitriolic campaign against Zachariah a few years later). Samuelson was a shareholder in the original Hull Dock Co., and clearly on the defensive, stirring things up by emotive argument and personal attacks, until the Town Clerk eventually commented: 'his [Samuelson's] remarks are calculated to mislead the council'.

Analysis of the reportage shows Zachariah basing his arguments on fact rather than personality, returning repeatedly to the main point of the West Dock project: the current dock arrangement was haemorrhaging business to other ports where ships could be loaded and unloaded in a much shorter time, and the only reason the Hull Dock Co. had put forward their new proposal was because they were jolted into it by the threat of competition. The debate raged on, Zachariah littering his speeches with phrases such as 'solely for the best interests for the town of Hull', believing that it 'was the only chance [we have] to save her from bankruptcy', and he was supporting the West Dock scheme 'for the benefit of the town which [he] had at heart'.

The town's most powerful personalities were publicly engaged, and no-one stood on the sidelines. The argument rattled on for years, both locally and in Parliament, but in the end Zachariah's team was not successful. The 'establishment' movers and shakers of the old Hull Dock Co. managed to align more of the great and the good with their cause than the West Dock Co. could, and they won the contract. The new dock opened in 1869, achieving the original purpose of expansion – but would it ever have happened if the gauntlet had not been thrown down by Zachariah and the other directors at that time?

Alongside Zachariah's involvement in specific projects, his progress in local governance was following an upwards trajectory. Following on from his election as the West Sculcoates Councillor, he was made Sheriff in 1858, although his elevation was apparently not regarded with universal delight. He had come from nowhere, but despite being a nobody he was now achieving distinguished positions in Hull. How dare a 'self-made man' aspire to such heights – and so fast? While we have no direct evidence of where the mutterings were coming from, it is clear that they were being made. In some eyes, members of the landed aristocracy were more suitable to be office-holders, as there was a perception that there was something slightly sordid about money made by trade. Nevertheless, in the spirit of the new age, the local press was having none of this old way of thinking in announcing who the next Sheriff would be:

Mr Samuelson's successor in the Shrievelty, it is pretty well known, will be Mr Z. C. Pearson. A better appointment could not be made. Mr Pearson is an active, enterprising, liberal-minded, successful merchant and ship owner. He has done much to further the trade of the port, and he is a man against whose honour and uprightness no charge has ever been made. The only accusation we ever heard against him was that which was made a year ago, viz., that he is a self-made man. The same charge, however, may be made against nine-tenths of the men of mark in our town and to our mind it is a distinction rather than a reproach. There can be no greater absurdity in a place of commerce like Hull than this affectation of sneering at new men. If Hull were left to the aristocrats by birth who dwell in it, all talk about further dock accommodation would be superfluous and the town would soon become about as lively and as thriving as Herculaneum or ruined Carthage.

The choice of Mr Pearson for Sheriff is, we repeat, an excellent one.

(*Hull Packet*, 8th October 1858).

While it was very satisfying to be backed by the local press, the latent hostility generated by this self-made man's rise through the ranks of local government lurked darkly beneath the surface, as he was to discover to his cost only four years later when the politics of envy emerged with a vengeance.

Z. C. PEARSON, ESQ.

1860 etching of Zachariah in his Mayoral robes and chains – and sporting magnificent whiskers.

For the moment, though, he was clearly performing well, and earning the respect of his townsfolk – a respect which culminated a year later with his election as Mayor of Kingston-upon-Hull, the highest office in town. We cannot be sure how ambitious Zachariah was, but this honour would surely have been quietly gratifying. He had worked his way up the social and civic ladders to the top – and was clearly making an impression, judging by *The Illustrated London News* the following year:

Some time ago Mr. Pearson's fellow townsmen elected him a member of the Town Council; subsequently he was appointed to the office of Sheriff; and the Town Council of Hull have done honour to themselves by raising him to the Mayoralty, which dignity he at present holds. Ever since Mr. Pearson entered on his municipal duties he has devoted himself assiduously to public business, and has been throughout a steady and strenuous advocate of dock improvement and extension. Since he has occupied the civic chair, the well-known though unostentatious benevolence of Mr. Pearson has been necessarily made more manifest. The activity of his benevolence is exhibited in the warm interest he has always taken in the Port of Hull Society, in the Sailors' Home, and in many other most useful institutions. Though a Wesleyan, Mr. Pearson has amply vindicated the charity and liberality of his sentiments by taking a leading part in the restoration of Holy Trinity Church; and it was only last week that the local papers had to chronicle a further instance of his liberality by the commencement of a new Wesleyan chapel, towards which he is the chief contributor.

This '*well-known though unostentatious benevolence*' is interesting. There were expectations of men in public office that they would, if rich enough, share their wealth with society. In this pre-social-services society, Victorian philanthropy was a basic building block of society. Embracing good causes was a sign that one had made it in society, although hereditary aristocrats were less likely to set up charities than the newly emerging middle class, many of whom were driven by a conviction that, having 'made it' themselves, the disadvantaged needed their patronage. Some have argued that the purpose of charitable work was social control, and that not far beneath the surface was an underlying aim to promote moral values of self-improvement and good citizenship. Certainly, the local press reported extensively on worthy causes with their fundraising events, and the list of contributors that followed meant that all donations could be scrutinised by the public. Perhaps philanthropy needed to be seen as well as felt.

The Mayoral Chain used now by the Lord Mayor of Hull. It is the same one that Zachariah wore in office, but since his day it has been remodelled. The stones are bright blue with gold inlay of the triple crown of Hull.

For some, their philanthropy was underpinned and motivated by religious principles and this was almost certainly the case with the Wesleyan Zachariah. Was his

Methodism where his 'unostentatious benevolence' came from? Being a Methodist undoubtedly shaped both his social conscience and the way he lived, though one might debate which influenced what: was he a Methodist because of the way he felt about life, or were his actions prompted by his Methodism? John Wesley had encouraged personal morality – working hard, saving for the future, giving generously and avoiding gambling and drinking. What a Methodist *did* was as important as what he *believed*, which was why so many Methodists were involved in setting up charitable organisations. They were the non-conformist conscience of society attempting to remedy social injustice – the new 'liberals'.

Although Zachariah stayed outside party politics *per se*, in keeping with his Methodist background he leant towards liberalism. At election time, therefore, it was the Liberal candidate who tended to get his support – but only if he deserved it. In 1856, the unfortunate Liberal candidate, Edwin James, was asked by Zachariah publicly to explain his views on shipping dues and passing taxes – but the poor man apparently had no idea how to reply, and the *Hull Packet* reported how Zachariah's searching questions had embarrassingly floored him. On another occasion, three years later, just as the liberal philosopher John Stewart Mill was extolling free-thinking and personal liberty, Zachariah was still supporting the Liberal cause, and the local press reported how he used his influence – and presumably his wealth – to host a *'sumptuous breakfast'* for 300 gentlemen on behalf of the Liberal parliamentary candidate.

With his convictions and his wealth, it was only to be expected to find that Zachariah was active in supporting the Methodists both in fundraising and by chairing meetings, such as the Methodist New Connexion Missions. At a fund-raising event for a new Wesleyan chapel at Withernsea he made a rallying speech at a tea for 700 at which, in the words of the local paper, the *'large and respectable assembly sang the National Anthem in right good style'*.

Once he had sufficient funds, Zachariah's commitment to Methodism became even more visible: he instigated, and was the major donor towards, a Wesleyan Chapel in Beverley Road. He chose the Hull architect, William Botterill, to design it and the result was a flamboyant building, described by Neave (writing about lost churches of Hull) as having an *'elaborate Gothic pinnacled façade with richly traceried five-light windows'*.

The elaborate Wesleyan chapel in Beverley Road that Zachariah initiated, and towards which he contributed very generously. He laid the foundation stone in 1860, and beneath this was buried a copy of the Methodist newspaper 'Watchman'. The flamboyant Gothic building by William Botterill provided seating for a congregation of 1200.

With a silver trowel, Zachariah officially marked the start of the building in a formal ceremony on 26th August, 1860, and Sheahan, the local historian, tells of that day and the chapel itself. At the head of the procession, Zachariah laid the first stone, beneath which was buried a bottle enclosing a copy of the *Watchman* (the Methodist newspaper) and a *'parchment document containing some interesting particulars of the Wesleyan body'*.

When the building was completed, the description of it at the time was packed with superlatives. The interior was constructed of woodwork in *'red fir, stained and varnished'*, and the chapel was lit by *'ten coronae of medieval design, with eight branches to each, suspended from the intersection of the ceiling timbers'*. The organ, reckoned to be the *'largest, handsomest, and most effective in the town'*, was built by Forster and Andrews, a well-respected Hull organ manufacturer. It contained nearly 2000 pipes, had three keyboards and a pedal organ, and it was *'blown by the patent hydraulic engine'*. The latter must have been hugely welcomed, as traditionally someone would have had to hand-pump bellows to make the air flow through the pipes. The new hydraulic pump dispensed with the bellows boy as it was operated by water – of which there was no shortage in Yorkshire.

The cost of the chapel, together with the heating and lighting, was £5,900, of which £1,000 was contributed initially by Zachariah, another £100 being donated later when they ran out of money. Zachariah's donations amounted to more than ten times the value of anyone else's contribution. It was built to seat 1200, and it was opened 17 months later. It would be fascinating to know how many people attended each Sunday. Did Zachariah really expect it to be filled to capacity? Or did the design fall victim to the current wave of expansion in Methodism: during a spate of chapel-planting, were chapels trying to outdo each other on size?

Once the chapel was completed, some classrooms and a Sunday School were built to the rear, opening in May 1865, and the ongoing history of this church is a sideline to Zachariah's story. The chapel itself sustained bomb damage in 1941 when the German Luftwaffe dumped one of its left-over bombs on Hull as they headed back home after a World

War II air raid. After this, the building could not operate as a church, but the main structure was still standing, and a syndicate of Masonic Lodges, including the Kingston Lodge, bought it. They converted the school rooms into their Masonic Hall, and provided themselves with an income by renting out the church premises to a printing firm until a fire destroyed it in 1954. Today only the west end of the church remains, sealed off with a wall and doorway to form some useful rooms, which are still used by Masons.

Today this is all that remains of the Beverley Road chapel after the World war II bomb and the fire that caused the front of the church to be demolished. The rear section of the old church can be seen here, together with the old school rooms behind it, and today the building is home to a syndicate of Masonic lodges.

Had he been alive to witness the evolution of 'his' chapel in this way, Zachariah would have approved – for two reasons. He himself, having attained civic honours with his Mayoral position, was proposed as a Freemason in 1860, and he joined the Minerva Lodge in Dagger Lane. The members here were mainly doctors, merchants, lawyers and other professional men, and the Lodge eventually became so successful that it split and spawned the Kingston Lodge. What a happy co-incidence that, 83 years on – and to this day – the offspring of Zachariah's own lodge was operating out of the remnants of his own Methodist Chapel. And to round off the Masonic connection, William Botterill, the chapel architect, was later to become a member of the Kingston Lodge himself, little knowing that it would in the future be moving into the church which he himself had designed.

Zachariah's interest in churches was not limited to Wesleyan chapels, as noted in the earlier quotation from *The Illustrated London News*, and he supported the restoration of Hull's main church, Holy Trinity – the largest parish church in England. It had deteriorated to a parlous condition due, in the words of the historian Sheahan in 1866, to *'the ignorance and indolence of the remote predecessors of the present townspeople'*. Architect Gilbert Scott found that the wrong stone had been used in previous restoration efforts, and warned that restoring the church fabric would be more extensive than initially thought. Funds would need to be found. Mayor Pearson was Chairman of the Restoration Committee and, at a meeting in the Mansion House in November 1859, a resolution was passed to raise funds by public subscription. The inevitable list of subscribers was published and, Methodism notwithstanding, Zachariah was seen to be one of the major contributors to this Anglican fund. Holy Trinity Church was eventually restored – and Gilbert Scott would later go on to design the Albert Memorial for Queen Victoria and be knighted.

Another aspect of life in the mid-nineteenth century which was fundamentally important to Zachariah was the volunteer military force. After the Crimean War, much of the British army was garrisoned abroad, so the government encouraged the establishment of civilians to train and be prepared, if necessary, to go into action for the defence of the country – a sort of precursor to the Territorial Army (now the Army Reserve). When the Hull Volunteer Artillery was established in 1860, Zachariah was its Major, becoming its Commandant a couple of years later. It was a considerable social cachet to be an officer in the Volunteer Force, but one needed to be well-heeled: uniforms were not cheap, and officers were expected to provide the men's uniforms as well as their own. The Hull Volunteer Force was apparently noted for its music: *'the brass band of this brigade is one of the best Volunteer bands in England. There is also a good fife and drum band.'*

When Zachariah had become Mayor for the first time in 1859, he felt the inconvenience of not having a suitable place where the Town Council could meet and entertain. While council-entertaining probably sounds like an extravagant use of taxes today, it was an age-old expectation that town officials would inevitably entertain; it came with the job. There are archive cases of Sheriffs who were fined for not giving elegant entertainments, and an Alderman who was fined for his inhospitality, at which stage (admittedly in the seventeenth century) Aldermen were *ordered* to provide feasts. With hospitality in mind, then, Zachariah was the first to start the wheels turning for better facilities. A new Town Hall would be built, one that would accommodate the Mayor and Corporation properly and do the town proud. He held a competition for the best design, and out of the 40-plus plans submitted by architects the contract was awarded to Cuthbert Brodrick. His resulting Town Hall opened to much acclaim in 1866, but its life was short: once Hull was awarded 'city' status, the building was replaced in 1897 by the much larger Guildhall of today.

The Town Hall was just one of the projects in a wide range of buildings and infrastructure improvements with which Zachariah was associated. The waterworks was another. With its rapid growth and industrialisation, Hull needed more water than ever before, and new sources of clean water were in demand. A decade or so earlier, a new way of using tidal water out of the Humber had been found

The new Town Hall which Zachariah initiated in his first term as Mayor. Designed by Cuthbert Brodrick, it opened in 1866, and provided space for the Town Council to meet and entertain comfortably. It did not have a long life, though: when Hull acquired city status in 1897 a larger building was needed, and the Town Hall was replaced by the current Guildhall which opened in 1907.

but this had proved unsuccessful. Despite safety-testing, the water tasted muddy and salty at various times but, more seriously, Hull's fatalities had trumped every other town in England during the cholera outbreak of 1849. The lethal concoction of brackish water and 'night waste' (raw sewage) being illegally dumped upstream provided the ideal environment for cholera bacteria to thrive. The public outcry to their Town Council for clean water became impossible to ignore and further investigations were made.

Several unproductive attempts to solve the problem had been made over the years, and the arguments were long and bitter, but Zachariah's council managed to break the deadlock, proposing the successful plan of using spring water from the west of the town. Having been filtered by the chalk, this artesian water supply was pure – and a whole lot more acceptable than drinking accumulated sewage from upstream towns. All they had to do was bring it from the spring to the town. After extensive boring and testing, the plan was put into action, and on 27th January 1862 Mayor Zachariah Pearson 'turned the first sod at Stone Ferry', where the reservoir would be constructed.

Trenches were dug, pipes were laid, and pumping engines were installed. Six months later, the water was turned on, with huge rejoicing. Church bells 'rung forth their merry peals', and crowds of people gathered around the engine house at the spring head borehole to hear bands of musicians. Zachariah's carriage arrived at the works at two o'clock, and such was the euphoria of the occasion that some of the workmen 'attempted to take the horses from the Mayor's carriage, and pull it themselves with ropes'. But this jolly jape failed, as, 'being accompanied by the Mayoress, his Worship refused to allow them'. It sounds as though the presence of Mary Ann, at this stage heavily pregnant with Eveline Rose, saved the day.

In order to divert the water into the pipes, and thus start filling up the reservoir, Zachariah presented the Chairman of the Waterworks Committee with a massive ceremonial three-foot gold electroplated key, weighing half a hundred-weight (25 kilos). As well as including the usual names of officials, the inscription ended with the Latin phrase: 'forma flos, fama flatus' (beauty is a flower, fame a puff of wind), although it's not immediately obvious why a Latin saying denoting the ephemeral nature of things should be apportioned to the new engineering works for a whole town's water supply.

Zachariah made a generous speech praising everyone involved, the water was officially turned on, and then the party, accompanied by the musicians, proceeded to Stoneferry to observe, with some satisfaction, that the water was now running into the reservoir. Having assured themselves that all was on track for a healthy water supply, the civic party *'partook of a luncheon'* in a marquee, whilst the workmen *'were regaled with an excellent repast'* in a nearby tent. Zachariah had added another Hull project to his CV.

As well as the big schemes, there were constant Mayoral duties to be carried out, and the local paper reported almost weekly on these. The Earl of Shaftesbury had initiated new dwellings for the Incorporated Society for Improving the Conditions of the Labouring Classes, and in the Earl's absence, Zachariah laid the foundation stone in 1862. When completed, 32 families were able to live there in perfect health and safety: they boasted that the building was fireproof as no timber was used in the division walls.

Another enlightened cause was the welfare of pregnant girls. Because of the considerable stigma attached to them, there was a modern move to look after them and then return them to their families rather than let them take their chances on the streets. A house on Nile Street was bought for £525, Zachariah having donated £50 towards this, and the 'Hull Temporary Home for Fallen Women' opened in 1861, admitting 61 girls during that year. It proved so valuable that an adjoining house was bought, and the expanded home could accommodate 50 girls at any given time. The success of the home over its first five years needs to be judged in its time: while 64 of the girls were restored to their families or friends, 54 were placed in service, a few ran away, but 20 were *'sent to the workhouse on account of the poor state of their health'* – although arguably the workhouse was the last place to cure poor health.

As he became more prominent, especially in the field of local politics, Zachariah's name was frequently to be found listed among the Directors of new ventures. Personal and business contacts would have been important here, though the link is sometimes hard to understand. It would be intriguing to know how he came to head the list of only five Directors of The Hafod Lead Mining Company Ltd., formed *'for the purpose of raising the rich silver-lead ore on the Hafod Estate, Cardiganshire. North of the river Ystwith, 12 miles from the seaport of Aberystwyth'*. In their announcement in the Times of December 1861, they were tempting prospective investors to raise capital of £50,000 through the sale of shares, and described the productive lodes in that area. They stated that operations had already commenced at the mines and that large amounts of the capital had already been subscribed. As this was taking place in Wales, and was hardly a shipping-related activity, Zachariah's interest presumably fell within the realm of a purely business speculation.

A more obviously sea-linked directorship around this time was The Universal Marine Insurance Company for which Zachariah and others placed adverts in *The Times*, hoping to raise the ambitious capital sum of £1,000,000 via shares. Yet another company was set up in August 1862 *'for the purpose of purchasing Dagenham Lake, and about 80 acres of land adjoining and converting the same into docks, wharfs, &c. for the accommodation of all classes of vessels entering the port of London'*. Zachariah was one of the eight Directors of the Dagenham (Thames) Dock Co. who sought to raise capital of £300,000. The 'fishing hook' for investors was the fact that this would be the second largest dock in London, and therefore well-used. A lot of coal – 3.3 million tons of it – was arriving at London each year, as were 250,000 head of cattle. If they arrived at this proposed dock, the cattle would be able to graze on the surrounding pastureland after their voyage *'so as to arrive at market in the best possible condition, to the advantage alike of the importer and the purchaser'*. As the new dock was close to the London, Tilbury and Southend Railway, dispersal of goods would be easy and efficient. Why wouldn't everyone invest in such a scheme?

By 1862, Zachariah had a finger in many pies with his civic responsibilities, his directorships, his international trading businesses and his interest in social welfare – but deeds alone do not provide insight into character, so in order to get a rounded view of the man, we need to view him through the lens of those around him at the time.

5

Zachariah, the Man

History tells us a great deal about Zachariah's steady-yet-meteoric career trajectory, but little about his private life. What was he like as a person? As a colleague? As a husband? As a father? How did he provide for his growing family? Who was 'Zachariah, the Man'?

As a family man, the increasingly more land-based career was an obvious advantage. There was no longer any need for Zachariah to abandon the family for long periods to earn a living at sea. Embarking on a voyage was now a choice, not a requirement, and this was a huge benefit to married life and fatherhood. By the end of the 1850s he and Mary Ann had five surviving children; his family had grown as fast as his wealth, and the Pearson housing trail tells a story of increasing prosperity. The progressive address changes from modest to grand houses indicate a family moving up in the world. It was far more common to rent property than to buy, and we only know for certain that one of the following houses was owned by Zachariah, but whether bought or rented, the scale of the houses nonetheless reflects both position and wealth.

After they were married in 1844, Zachariah and Mary Ann lived in a tiny house only half a mile north of Queen's Dock in Caroline Place, next door to a Robert Pearson. This may have been Zachariah's brother, the younger of his two older brothers who remained in their father's household after their mother had died. If so, this is the only time that any of Zachariah's siblings appear in this story. The young couple settled into married life, and Charles Edward arrived in 1846 – their first child in their first home.

Before long, Mary and James made their appearances into the world, and more living space was needed, so 1851 finds the Pearson family of five living at 11 Spring Street, a road of terraced houses just to the west of the Beverley Road. These dwellings were not very big, but they did have room to employ a 'house servant'. With all the work needed for a large family – the heating, cleaning, washing and cooking – those who could afford to do so bought in domestic help, and Rebecca, their 20-year-old maid, lived in the house with the family and looked after them as required. Mary Ann by this stage was pregnant again, but 1851 was to prove bitter-sweet: their third son, Alfred, was born, but soon afterwards two-year-old James succumbed to the 'slow fever' which killed him.

The Spring Street location was very handy for the docks, but it was soon too small for the family, and some time soon afterwards the Pearsons moved to a larger house a little further north up the Beverley Road – No. 3 in Scarborough Terrace, a row of three-story houses affording more space. But the 1850s were Zachariah's period of galloping success, and around 1856-58 he took his ultimate step up the property ladder by purchasing a 'desirable residence' just a little further up the Beverley Road: No. 1 Grosvenor Terrace. This house was the end one of four, with plenty of large rooms, three stories and a good sized garden. It was located in the north of the town, where there was more space and cleaner air than in the centre of Hull, which had by now become very crowded with all the mill and factory workers. It made sound sense to move further out – and Grosvenor Terrace was well-positioned for bringing up a healthy family. Alfred, Arthur, and Emma arrived in quick succession, and by 1861 the census reveals that Mary Ann was being offered plenty of domestic help, as the Pearson household now included three servants. The smaller rooms at the top of the house were designed for servant accommodation and this is where Caroline the housemaid, Esther the nursemaid and Emma the cook lived.

It was into a house like this in Scarborough Terrace, Beverley Road, which Zachariah moved in the mid-1850s. He could now afford to upgrade, as his business was taking off, and his rapidly-increasing family needed the extra space provided by this three-storey house.

The two oldest boys, Charles and Alfred, were not always in residence in Hull as they were studying at a naval school in Kent at this time. Their destinies were being shaped by their maritime environment, and Zachariah was making sure that they acquired the education they needed to make a success in life. Charles would go on to partner and then take over from his father as a shipping agent, and Alfred would become a coal merchant supplying fuel for steam ships. The third boy, Arthur, who missed out on the naval boarding school experience, ultimately followed in his father's footsteps by becoming a sea captain.

This was the grandest of all Zachariah's houses. In the late 1850s he moved further north up the Beverley Road to Grosvenor Terrace, a row of four good-sized houses with large gardens. Today only the southernmost two houses remain, and the Pearsons lived in No. 1, the left hand house here (today No. 95 Beverley Road). There was plenty of room for servants as well as family.

In building up a picture of Zachariah himself, we can glean some idea of his character as he became more visible in Hull. Some of the character sketches of him as he rose to public positions have already been cited, and from these we get a nuanced perspective of the man. But we can also hear his own voice down the ages, thanks to the tradition of the local newspapers to report verbatim on proceedings and debates – and Zachariah's speeches were often to be found quoted in the press.

Further colour to Zachariah's character is added by a certain Mr Whiting, a political sketchwriter of his day. Unlike the stylised Victorian manner in which local papers lauded and applauded, the refreshing tongue-in-cheek text of Mr Whiting gives a new perspective and helps to fill in some of the gaps. Whiting wrote in the 1850s, choosing as his subjects certain Hull figures in the public eye, and he also included some who, like Zachariah, were as yet still up-and-coming. He wrote as he observed, and did not mince his words, brightening up his copy with hyperbole for effect, and from his vivid collection *'Portraits of Public Men'* published in 1858 we get an illuminating insight into Zachariah's character. This particular sketch was written in 1857 when Zachariah was just bursting onto the public scene. At this stage, Councillor Pearson was yet to occupy the positions of Sheriff and Mayor, but already he merited the attention of Whiting, who must have perceived him to be a chap who would be going places in local government.

As with today's sketchwriters, this is clearly one person's idiosyncratic view, but compared with many of Whiting's other subjects in the same publication, Zachariah emerges extremely well – clearly a favourite, in fact. As this is virtually the only really 'warts and all' image we have of how Zachariah was perceived in Hull, quite a lot of the article has been quoted here, starting with Whiting classifying Zachariah as one of life's 'nice fellows':

> *There are, here and there, a few men, who seem as though Nature had made them her especial favourites. Adorned with no difficult accomplishments, endowed with no awe-inspiring intellect, fortified by no uncommon learning, and apparently destitute of even the elements out of which public characters are moulded, these men are known as 'nice fellows,' and by virtue of a certain charm of manner, they are in the counting house, the street, the drawing room, more respected than the wit, more sought after than the philosopher, more popular than the orator, and more favoured than the rest of mankind. A mysterious, indefinable attraction environs*

the person of him whom the many tongued multitude have dubbed 'nice fellow'.

And of this ancient order of nice fellows, Mr Councillor Pearson is undoubtedly one. He is so artlessly courteous, the shake of his hand has in it such cordial empressment, the tones of his voice are so mellow, so genial, and ring so like a welcome; his eye beams down upon you so kindly, and there is such a warmth of manner about him, that you chat with him forgetful of time, are quite sorry to leave him, and when you do leave him you inevitably ejaculate to yourself "what a nice fellow".

He goes on to compare Zachariah favourably with other sea captains who, when seen around town, were apparently pretty scary:

Were we to tell you that Mr Councillor Pearson was recently the Captain of a ship, you would scarcely believe us. His dialect smacks not of tar, but of rose water rather, and in his bearing you see no sign of the sea-calf. You shall find no trace of the gruff, surly sea-captain. No aroma of pitch and seaweed, or salt water, fumes up from his words. Unlike the majority of skippers, he does not roll along like a tall ship in a rolling sea. His colour is not that black red hue of the surly sea kings who throng our streets. There is, in short, no visible vestige of the hoarse ship-master about our Councillor. Mr Pearson has that blandness of manner, that suavity of speech, and that pleasant face, of which juveniles are so fond, while the orthodox Captain looks on the other hand as though he had breakfasted on babies and was prowling about in search of more.

In not breakfasting on babies, Zachariah was clearly thought to be avoiding the stereotypical reputation of sea captains ashore, and he was seen by Mr Whiting to be altogether more civilised:

So far from discovering any indication of his sea experiences, our Councillor looks the model man of a West-end club, and his manners are as courteous to all who approach him, as though he were a candidate for parliamentary honours and they the free and independent burgesses to whose sweet voices he aspired. Had we not known, that old father Ocean has before today produced many elegant and delicate personages, we would utterly discredit the story of Mr Pearson's early life. There is ample precedent however. Once on a time, the sea gave birth to the dainty goddess of love, and now after a rest of some centuries, the briny god has once more taken to the fine arts, and produced Mr Councillor Pearson.

The romanticism of Zachariah's stow-away adventure quoted earlier added spice to his character sketch, and he ends this part of his account with:

Some time after this short cruise, one of the same lads [...] strutted up to a ship captain and with school-book in one hand and cap in the other, cast his hopeful eyes upwards as he addressed a bluff skipper with "Please, sir, do you want a boy?" Soon he was bound apprentice.

Whiting goes on to summarise Zachariah's rapid rise, and his growing importance to the seaport of Hull:

We need not tell the reader that the lad was an obliging youth and a favourite with the men, for the reader will have guessed all that, and will have seen that even when a lad, Mr Pearson must have been a nice fellow. Before the boy was out of his time he was made first mate, and had no sooner concluded his apprenticeship than he became Captain. Once Captain, he instantly developed into a merchant, and full of the enterprise which first made him to say, "Please, sir, do you want a boy?" he exported and imported goods, very much to the profit of himself and the town. From sea-boy to merchant was a short skip, and now he is not only a merchant but a ship owner, and a splendid fleet of steamers carry his flag. The advance made by Mr Pearson is scarcely equalled in rapidity or extent, by that of any of our public men. He is yet a young man, and though it seems but yesterday since he ran away to sea, he is now one of those whose business is of the first importance to the trade of the port.

Zachariah's objectivity, independence and judgement are lauded: '*Loving work for its own sake, he has allowed himself to be made Town Councillor. As a Town Councillor, he has taken a strictly independent course. Biased by no party, and influenced by no cliques, he consults merely his own judgment in the course he takes.*' And Whiting notes how Zachariah had the capacity to charm – despite his not being a natural orator:

His friendly spirit disarms animosity, his gentlemanly deportment and appearance grace the Council, and as you view his fine figure and his face at once so animated and so good natured, you put up with his careless scrambling style of speech making, and confess that although no orator, he is a very good looking and gentlemanly man and a very nice fellow.

But on this subject of Zachariah's verbal skills in more formal settings, there was also some serious advice for Councillor Pearson's continuing personal and professional development:

If however, we may be permitted to offer our Councillor a word of well intentioned advice, we would recommend him never to occupy the time of a deliberative assembly with a speech unless he has first taken the trouble to prepare himself for the occasion. Speech making is not so much a gift as an acquirement, and no amount of sang froid in the speaker can compensate his hearers for having to listen to a gentleman whose syllables are yawned rather than spoken, and whose ideas decamp for a run while the speaker is groping about for words in which to clothe them. Mr Pearson can write down his thoughts in a lucid and well arranged manner, and the man who can write well can also, if he will be at the trouble, grow to speak as ably as he can write. The tongue is sooner disciplined than the pen, and if our Councillor will award to his organ of speech one tithe of the attention he has given to his quill, he may become as persuasive as he is popular, as prominent in the Council as in the Chamber of Commerce, and as agreeable as a public speaker as he is now as a private gentleman.

This contemporaneous sketch of Zachariah, then, describes a good-looking and courteous gentleman, warm, genial, friendly and thoughtful, but nevertheless with a *'careless, scrambling style of speech-making'* with syllables *'yawned rather than spoken'*. While we'll never know whether or not the columnist's top tips for public speaking were heeded by his subject, Whiting's observations on Zachariah's character, objectivity, handsome bearing and geniality complement what we already know about Zachariah, and indeed are borne out in other independent descriptions of him cutting a fine figure about town, so we can assume that he really was a 'nice fellow'.

As Whiting's sketch was written before Zachariah was rich enough to be philanthropic, we can assume that this was his genuine opinion, untainted by sycophancy. Later glimpses into what people thought of him can be gleaned from speeches, editorial comment and council minutes, but some of these were when he was being generous with his wealth, and will be quoted in context later.

Some evidence of personality comes from correspondence. Zachariah was a judicious Mayor, aiming to settle quarrels as peaceably as possible, acting as arbitrator when needed, even in his first term of office. In early 1860, after a particularly unpleasant and entrenched row between the clerk and a councillor, which threatened to show the council in a poor light, he poured much oil on the waters of dissent, writing to the councillor in question: *'I am most anxious that the unfortunate dispute [...] should be settled in satisfaction to you and all parties [...] I do hope, therefore, that you will allow me to be the means of settling the matter...'* After his intercession, harmony was restored, and the council could get on with its business without the distraction of personality clashes. Zachariah the Mayor had been Zachariah the Peacemaker.

We now pick up the story in 1860. Zachariah had a business partner, a number of agents, and a position in society. The money was rolling in. His family was thriving. He could now afford to use his increasing power, influence and wealth more philanthropically. It was time to make his 'grand gesture' – the one that was to benefit the people of Hull in perpetuity.

6

A park for the people

The Government had a problem. The Industrial Revolution was making money for the country – but at a cost. Textile production was central to Britain's wealth, and cotton bales from the southern states of America were being imported to Britain by the shipload. The raw fibre was turned into usable thread in mills using steam mechanisation – and this required manpower. People were flooding into the towns in huge numbers for the paid employment of spinning and weaving in cotton mills. To accommodate them, houses were being built faster than at any time in history but they still could not be provided rapidly enough to keep up with the influx of workers. A great deal of this housing was built in the centre of towns close to the mills, which meant that, as well as living in extremely crowded dwellings, workers had no escape from the noxious fumes being pumped out from the coal-powered factories around them. Clean air was in very short supply in town. There was an inevitable effect on health and thus productivity.

And the working environment was no better. The nature of mill work meant that women and children could do it as well as men, but ruthless employers kept them at the looms for horrifying amounts of time. Although Lord Shaftesbury's 1833 reform of the labour laws had improved factory conditions, children as young as nine years old could still be made to work in the mills for nine hours a day

– a considerable reduction from the previous 18 hours, but still an inhuman workload.

A further significant bone of contention was a perception of degenerating morals resulting from the social context. It was now possible for women to become more independent, and for the first time working women, who would previously have toiled in the fields, could now earn a private income which they did not always choose to share with the family. Some even left their family to set up home with other female friends, and this was definitely seen as the slippery slope to ruin in Victorian times. Add to this the workplace situation where men and women were alongside each other for hours on end, and it is possible to see why there was considerable concern over morality.

Social concerns notwithstanding, the cotton mills were here to stay, but once ministers realised the long-term danger to the economy, the poor health of the workforce could be ignored no longer. Apart from the humanitarian angle, healthy, happy workers were needed or work would not get done properly. The national challenge was how to provide fresh air, healthy exercise and relaxation to folk confined by their circumstances. Even as far back as 1833, a House of Commons Select Committee on Public Walks had been set up to examine this issue, and it had taken evidence from a variety of witnesses, some of whom were concerned about more than just the physical health of the workers on their day off with free time: *'On Sunday, the entire working population sinks into a state of sloth or listless apathy, or even into the more degrading condition of reckless sensuality'*.

This perceived need to manage the population in its free time was a common theme but posed a seemingly intractable dilemma for the Government. As one minister warned in 1856, in response to the suggestion of an 'early closing' day, *'the mere placing of time at the disposal of young men and young women is by no means sufficient to satisfy the aims of enlightened benevolence. Leisure may prove the opposite of a blessing. Monotonous employment is infinitely better than licentious relaxation'*, and he went on to suggest ways in which any spare time may be gainfully employed. Clearly, the masses had to be weaned onto leisure carefully.

The recommendation from the Commons Select Committee was for the provision of footpaths for the public, but in 1840 the *Westminster Review* made a case instead for green space rather than paths, on the basis that *'the foot is freer and the spirits more buoyant when treading the turf than the harsh gravel, and one game at cricket or football would, to the young and active, be worth more than fifty solemn walks on a path beyond which they must not tread, and beyond which they are perpetually thirsting to go. Public grounds, not walks, are the things wanted.'* So it was that the concept of People's Parks in industrial towns took off. Halifax was the first town to provide one in 1840, then twenty years later it was Hull's turn – and not before time.

The problems in Hull were as bad as, or worse than, any other northern industrial town. Most of the cotton mills were in Lancashire, the damp climate in the north-west providing an ideal moisture content for spinning the yarn, but Yorkshire in the east also had a few cotton mills and Hull at this stage had two. A tragic 2½% of the population had already been lost in the 1849 cholera epidemic, a larger percentage than in any other English town, and now with the national move towards 'people's parks', the council realised something radical needed to be done to improve the health of its working population. The middle classes could afford to pay to enjoy the open space and fresh air of the Zoological or the Botanic Gardens, but the poor could not afford the entrance charges. They needed their own open-access green space. The Local Board of Health searched for some time for suitable land, and several false starts were made, but each one ended in disappointment.

Once the idea had been floated, though, the pressure continued to build up, and the local press was littered with reasons why the park was needed. This extract from a lengthy but articulate piece written by 'A Peripatetic' for the *Hull Packet* in 1856 made the case for a park rather than 'a line of walks' on the grounds of sheer numbers, pointing out the multiple benefits to Hull which was *'destitute of both natural and artificial beauty, and also of social liveliness'*. He went on to argue:

> The truth is, that there is no such thing as a line of walks, or space of pleasure ground, in which ninety thousand people, who constitute the vast population of Hull, can obtain that solace to the mind, stimulus to the feelings, and auxiliary to the health, which pleasant exercise is intended by the Creator to furnish [...] A park is THE great desideratum in Hull. Such an appendage would soon procure for the town a better reputation than that which it now enjoys abroad; make it a more agreeable and respectable place of residence; elevate the general pitch of feeling [...] promote the cause of morality and social progress, by offering to the working classes a wholesome and acceptable substitute for places of resort of an unhealthy and contaminating nature; conduce greatly to the improvement of the general health, and, finally, would enhance in a very large degree the enjoyment by thousands of the lawful and contemplated pleasures of human life.

Was this the catalyst that spurred Zachariah into action? If a park could confer all those benefits to Hull, how could he *not* help? Whatever the stimulus, the issue was being debated publicly and expectations were building up, but while successive proposals were failing, behind the scenes Zachariah was doing his own research and secretly hatching a plan. He searched for some open space in the centre of the town which could be enjoyed by all, regardless of income or class, and in his first year as Mayor he purchased 37 acres (15 ha) of land to the west of Beverley Road. Before making the gift public, though, he engaged James Craig Niven, the curator of Hull's Botanic Gardens and formerly of Kew Gardens, to design a park to cover the 27 acres in the middle of this plot. Zachariah then offered the plot, together with the ready-made design, to the Board of Health. His offer was accepted with alacrity: money would not now have to be spent on purchasing land. A long-standing problem had been solved.

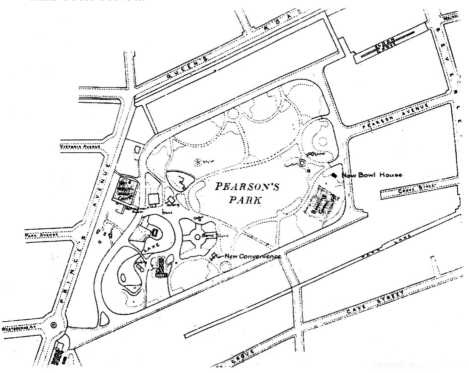

The layout of the park as planned by James Niven to Zachariah's specification – after some disagreement between the sculptor, Earle, and the garden designer, Niven, as to the position of Queen Victoria's statue. Niven had wanted it greeting visitors at the east entrance to the park, but Earle's preferred central spot won.

There were, inevitably, conditions, as Zachariah had a dual purpose in his action: to provide a green space for the workers to relax in, and at the same to create an attractive residential environment for Hull's wealth-earners. In a letter to the Parks Committee of the Local Board of Health, Zachariah set out his terms and conditions – his specifications for how the town council should lay out the park. The centre of the plot was for the public park, and the ten acres of ground that he had shrewdly retained around the edges would be sold privately for villas. In order to make this residential area attractive and safe to the inhabitants, Zachariah stipulated that *'a carriage road be made around the park [...] of not less than thirty-five feet in width'* and that the Board of Health should *'provide and fix an adequate number of gas lamps, and keep the same lighted with full lamps every night throughout the year from sunset to sunrise'*. The park itself also had conditions: Zachariah had a Methodist view as to what passed for appropriate behaviour on the Sabbath and so he specified: *'musicians shall not be allowed to play in the Park, nor shall refreshment stalls or public games be allowed therein upon a Sunday'*.

The gift was by any standards a generous and philanthropic gesture. Nevertheless, a qualm or two was expressed about how the Council would raise the £4,000 needed to lay out the park, and the estimated £200 per annum to maintain it. Anticipating this, the Mayor had already given the matter some thought, proposing such fundraising events as fetes and flower shows. He had also started a subscription list, setting an example with a personal donation of £100.

In the longer term, Zachariah's business plan stated that any excess profit from the eventual sale of the building plots would be donated to the park development: he only wished to cover the cost of his initial outlay. The plots should eventually sell for a good sum and generate a reasonable profit which would be ploughed back into the park budget. Under these conditions, the Council felt they could raise any interim costs (should there be any) through the rates. So with celebratory fervour, the precise finances were subjugated to the enthusiasm of the moment, 'carried unanimously' was recorded in the formal minutes, and a grand ceremony was planned for the 'turning of the first sod'.

Advertised as a 'Colossal Fete', this event was one of the most lavish that the North had ever seen and designed to attract multitudes from all sections of the community. It had originally been proposed to hold this on the 12th/13th August 1860, but the Fete Committee delayed the date by a fortnight in order not to clash with the opening of the grouse season on The Glorious Twelfth, which ensured that, in addition to the thousands of ordinary people expected to turn up (it was after all a *people*'s park'), the great and the good who were invited would also be free to attend.

We know a lot about these two days of festivities, as the local paper was packed with information. Zachariah declared a holiday for the Monday, urging *'the Owners of all such Establishments as can do so to close on that day, in order to give those in their employ an opportunity of witnessing the day's proceedings'*. A commemorative coin was struck to mark the event. There were limited editions of gold and silver medals reserved for important people, but for the price of three pence, a base metal version was available to everyone from booksellers, the station and stalls at the Fete.

There was no shortage of opportunists, from adverts to rent out rooms with a park view, to nursery-men selling plants. We are lucky to have a descriptive contemporaneous account of these two days, written by a Mr James Smith in his book *'Proceedings Relative to the Pearson's Park'*, and it is largely his words which are liberally quoted here, as they add colour to the event. Smith paints a picture of how the plot (not yet a park *per se*) was bedecked with calico, stands, tents, balconies and banners. However, the weather leading up to Monday 27th August had been appalling, and on the previous Saturday night *'a very heavy shower fell, followed by a violent wind, which dislocated the woodwork of the main entrance to the Park, carrying away the ornaments,*

PEARSON'S PARK,

KINGSTON-UPON-HULL.

THE PARK COMMITTEE HAVE MUCH PLEASURE IN SUBMITTING THE FOLLOWING PROGRAMME OF THE

COLOSSAL FETE!

To be held on the occasion of Planting the First Tree in the above-named Park, so nobly Presented to the People of Hull by their present Mayor, Z. C. Pearson, Esq., as a FREE GIFT.

On MONDAY & TUESDAY, August 27th & 28th, 1860.

The Mayor, Corporation, Magistrates, Wardens and Brethren of the Trinity House, Dock Company, Officers in H. M. ship Cornwallis, Foreign Consuls, Governor and Guardians of the Poor of Hull and Sculcoates, accompanied by Volunteer Artillery and Rifle Corps, the Benevolent Societies of Shipwrights, Manchester Unity of Odd Fellows, Foresters, Kingston Unity of Odd Fellows, Druids, Grand United Order of Odd Fellows, &c., &c., with their Splendid Flags, Banners, and Emblems, will leave the Mansion House, Lowgate, in

GRAND PROCESSION,

AT ONE O'CLOCK PRECISELY.

Upon the arrival of the Procession in the Park, the Mayor, Zachariah Charles Pearson, Esq., will formally convey the Deed of Grant of the Land to the Local Board of Health of the Borough of Kingston-upon-Hull, and afterwards

PLANT THE FIRST TREE.

Upon conclusion of these Ceremonies a

GRAND REVIEW OF VOLUNTEERS,

EMBRACING THE ARTILLERY AND RIFLE CORPS OF THE BOROUGH, AND THE COUNTIES OF YORKSHIRE AND LINCOLNSHIRE, WILL TAKE PLACE.

THE GENERAL ATTRACTIONS OF THE FETE WILL CONSIST OF

THE CELEBRATED

WOOLWICH ROYAL ARTILLERY BAND,

(By special Permission of General Sir Richard Dacres, Commandant) under the direction of Bandmaster, Mr. J. Smith; the

EAST YORK MILITIA BAND,

(By the kind permission of Lieut.-Colonel Thompson) Bandmaster Mr. Tabroell; and the

Bands of the Artillery and Rifle Corps.

ATTENDING THE REVIEW.

A VOCAL DEPARTMENT,

Under the direction of Mr. Alfred Mayward, of London, and Mr. Callister, of the Queen's Theatre.

AUSTRIAN SALAMANDER,

Who will Walk through an Avenue of Fire.

GRAND ASSAULT AT ARMS,

By Professor J. C. Gregory and Company.

AUNT SALLY,

The Ancient Game, superintended by Messrs. Wolfenden & Milbourne, Lessees Queen's Theatre.

MAY POLES AND GERMAN TREES,

Superintendent, Mr. Macarte.

RIFLE SHOOTING, &c., in retired part of the Park.

THE BROTHERS TALLEEN,

Gymnastic Artistes.

HERR EVANION,

Professor of Magic, Crystal Palace, Sydenham.

SIGNOR PIO WHAUTKINS,

Italian Juggler, Crystal Palace.

The POWELL FAMILY,

On the Corde Elastique and French Stilts.

MR. MACARTE, Grotesque Dancer.

ARCHERY AND CROSS BOW GROUNDS,

Superintendent, Mr. J. C. Gregory, of London.

A BALCONY,

Capable of accommodating 1,500 Persons, will be erected, the charge to which will be 2s. each.

AT DUSK, A BRILLIANT

TORCH LIGHT PROCESSION,

After the manner of the GREAT GERMAN FESTIVALS, Superintendent, Herr Schmidt.

Each Day's Fete will conclude with a Grand and Extensive Display of

FIREWORKS!

Embracing every Branch of the Pyrotechnic Art, by Mr. Seanon, of Hull.

DURING THE DISPLAY,

MADAME GENEAVE SAQUE

Will make her Terrific Ascent on the Fiery Rope, Sixty Feet in height, surrounded by prodigious Jets of Flame and Colored Fires.

AMPLE REFRESHMENTS WILL BE PROVIDED IN THE PARK, BY MR. GEO. HARTLEY, UPON A REASONABLE SCALE, ALSO LADIES' REFRESHMENT AND CLOAK ROOMS.

PARTICULARS OF ADMISSION.

MONDAY.

Admission for the Day, including Display of Fireworks - 2s. each.	Railway Passengers producing Trip Tickets - - - - 1s. each.
Tickets Purchased up to Saturday Night, August 25th - 1s. each.	Admission after Five o'Clock p.m. - - - - - 1s. each.

ON TUESDAY—ADMISSION TO ALL, 6d. EACH.

PASS-OUT CHECKS WILL NOT BE GIVEN.

CHEAP SPECIAL EXCURSION TRIPS.

Will be run on the Lancashire and Yorkshire Railway, under the management of Mr. Calverley, from Holmfirth, Honley, Huddersfield, Bradford, Low Moor, Cleckheaton, Heckmondwike, Mirfield, Todmorden, Sowerby Bridge, Halifax, Brighouse, Thornhill, Wakefield; Fares, (One Day) 3s.; (Two Days) 4s., leaving HULL at 7.0 p.m. Also from all Towns upon the North Eastern, Manchester, Sheffield, and Lincolnshire, Midland, and Great Northern Railways. For full Particulars of which see respective Companies' Bills.

Cash will not be taken at the Gates; Stands for the sale of Tickets will be fixed in various parts of the Town and the Beverley Road; To prevent confusion visitors are respectfully requested to procure their Tickets in the Town. Entrances to the Park will be from the Beverley Road and the Cemetery Lane. Children under Twelve Years of Age, Sixpence.

BY ORDER, **ENDERBY JACKSON.** GENERAL MANAGER, 24, Prospect-Street, Hull.

GODDARD, PRINTER & LITHOGRAPHER, HULL.

The poster advertising some of the entertainments in store for those attending the Colossal Fete at the handover of the deeds for the park. The event was designed to cater for everyone, and there were amusements to suit all tastes. It drew people from across the north of England, with special excursion trains being laid on.

and playing sad havoc with the calico barrier which had been stretched round the Park ground on three of its sides'.

This devastation had to be repaired before the Fete opened on Monday, so on the Sunday the place was buzzing with activity, *'a noticeable contrast to the usual pedestrianism of the Sabbath'.* Smith describes how *'vast booths were reared, as if by magic'* and that, in preparing to feed the hungry hoards, there was *'continuous importation of beef and beer'.* Zachariah would not have witnessed much of this industrious scene, as on that particular day he was just a little further south on Beverley Road, busy laying the foundation stone of the Wesleyan Chapel.

The 'Colossal Fete' had been widely advertised by posters which, alongside all the amusements on offer, listed special cheap excursion trips from across the north of England and the midlands. Trains from all the railway companies had been booked, and as they *'vomited forth their eager travellers, the density of crowds in the streets became for a few moments sensibly increased, until arrival after arrival was absorbed in the moving mass which occupied the thoroughfares down to the Park'.*

Some visitors arrived by river and sea: *'no fewer than nineteen packets [...] all crammed to excess, and conveying some 10,000 persons, landed their passengers at South end'.* In total, an estimated 40,000 people came, easily exceeding the attendance at Queen Victoria's visit to Hull six years earlier. In the town *'many shops were entirely closed; banners of device appropriate and inappropriate [...] were poked out of very many windows in the principal streets, or suspended across the thoroughfares'.* Everyone was looking forward to the festivities.

In the carnival atmosphere, there was something for everyone, starting with a two-mile procession, which *'occupied about three-quarters of an hour passing any particular point'.* The dignitaries set out from the Town Hall, where Zachariah *'had prepared refreshments preliminary to the proceedings'.* The carriage of His Worship, The Mayor, also conveyed Lord Wenlock and Lord Hotham, and all the symbols, organisations and representations of the ancient town of Hull were included in the procession: the Borough Mace and Ancient Sword, the Sheriff's Seal, two Halberdsmen, Town Council, magistrates, Trinity House, foreign consuls, guardians of the Workhouse, and the Ancient Orders of Foresters, Druids and Oddfellows.

The music for the procession was provided by the bands of 1600 Rifle and Artillery Corps of Volunteers from across the north of England. The Volunteers had only recently been formed and drilled, ready to be called up in an emergency, and this Colossal Fete would probably have been their largest gathering since their inception. Clearly they made a huge impact, advertising *'rifle shooting in [a] retired part of the Park'*.

Carnival-style floats offered a different style of entertainment. The local theatre's float had, to Mr Smith's mind, been *'the most attractive thing in the procession'*: a temple with the nine Muses, represented by children, and topped with *'a tableau of Shakespeare, being crowned by the Three Graces'*. Prior to the event, an 'ode competition' had been launched for the celebrations and a wagon, drawn by four horses, carried a printing press on which the Prize Ode was being continuously churned out for the delectation of the public.

The end of the procession gave ordinary people a space to parade: the fishermen's society, engineers, even the German Working Men's Society. All manner of tradesmen brought up the rear: this was, after all, to be the *people*'s park, and James Smith was moved to comment:

We venture to say that the sight presented by the latter part of the procession will never be forgotten by the thousands who witnessed it [...] It was an imposing thing to see so many thousands of earnest provident men, mainly mechanics and small tradesmen. The part which they took in the day's ceremonial augured well for the future of the Park.

The programme cover for the two days, embodying symbols of the event: shipping, an oak sapling, a VR monogram indicating the Queen 'Victoria Regina', the Pearson crest and motto, and the special medallion minted for the event – in gold, silver or base metal to suit all pockets.

Watching the procession all along its route were the avid spectators, their needs met, at a price, by the entrepreneurial:

Every window which commanded a view of the pageant was filled. Anxious spectators climbed onto lamp posts and the roofs of houses and sheds. Balconies (which looked in some cases rather frail) were erected whenever there was a vacant piece of ground, and the wise builders of these reaped a good harvest of silver in the sixpences, and shillings, and half-crowns which were paid for admission to them. Rickety old chairs and tables were in some places brought out, and commanded a high price.

And where side roads met the procession route,

waggons, cabs and omnibuses were drawn up behind the barricades which had been erected, and all these were covered with people in such a way that you were irresistibly driven to the conclusion that some of the spectators were like flies, and could hold their footing on the side of a wall.

Following the procession into the park, Mr Smith describes the *'really gay appearance'* of the rows of refreshment tents, the more peripheral amusements, and the dais for the formal part of the day, ready for Zachariah to hand over the Deeds of the park to the people. Although the ground *'was in many places quite a puddle'* due to the wet weekend, *'these discomforts were unheeded by those who had entered the park'*, and people took their place for the handover of Deeds. Seated next to Zachariah on the platform were Mary Ann and their children (though probably not the new-born baby, Beatrice). Naturally, no presentation was complete without speeches, and His Worship, The Mayor, rose to make his before signing the Deeds. Luckily for us, Mr Smith recorded verbatim what Zachariah said, so these extracts are Zachariah's voice.

He first outlined the social reason behind the park:

For a long period of my life, I felt that for Hull, a town of so much importance, and counting so large a population, a place of this kind was required, in order that the working classes might have an opportunity, when time suited them, of leaving the crowded thoroughfares and narrow lanes, and getting into a place which they might call their own, for the purposes of health and recreation [cheers].

Then he went on to say that '*by the aid of a kind and wise Providence*' he was now in a position to be able to do something about it. He had another motive, too – that of offering desirable housing inside Hull to those captains of industry who had made their fortunes:

Hull rising in importance as it is doing, and as it has done for some considerable time, I feel it is much to the interests of its inhabitants that we should improve as much as we can the architecture of its buildings, and the ornamentation of its ground, and its immediate neighbourhood, in order that those who, having obtained competency by industry, instead of leaving the town in which they have obtained that competency, to reside in a distant part of the country, may find in their native town such attractions as to induce them to reside in its immediate neighbourhood.

Having explained his rationale for the villa plots, he returned to the park itself, exhorting everyone to take some ownership of it: '*I consider it the duty of every inhabitant in the town to endeavour to ornament it so far as they can*'. He ended his speech to the people by emphasising the longer-term benefits to them, and to society, of having a place of their own:

*I have felt that the poorer part of the population – who
earn their livelihood by the sweat of their brow, and
who work from early morn till late at night – that it
was desirable on their part that they should have a
place which they might consider as their own. It will,
I trust, have a tendency, too, to elevate and raise their
minds, and until you can do that you can hardly expect
that the children will be properly attended to. The first
duty is to give the working classes of the community
an opportunity of raising themselves, and when that is
done, you have taken an important step in the advance
of the human race. They, feeling the benefit of the
progress they have made, will feel the desire for the
improvement of their children.*

Zachariah was enjoying the biggest party he would ever
hold in his life.

Then, to loud cheers, he handed over the Deeds to
Alderman Moss, the Chairman of the Park Committee,
who replied with a speech of gratitude, although mercifully
informing Zachariah that he was avoiding the traditional
'high eulogisms' which might *'offend the honest simplicity of
character which has marked [his] onward course throughout
life'*. He applauded Zachariah's intentions for the park as
a place where a working poor man *'may rest and amuse
himself'* but then, instead of reflecting on the outcomes for
future generations of children, he went on to moralise that
this place of rest and amusement for the workers would
thus *'avoid that dreadful and pernicious practice of spending
[their] time and money in the beer shop and dram house'*.

Moss' response continued to extol Zachariah, saying that
he was different from most benefactors who were:

*Inheritors of wealth, either by descent, or by some
way other than by their own exertions [...] You were
born to no hereditary rank; you acquired no hereditary
property. You are the architect of your own fortune [...]*

And when I look on the bench to the right, I find your lady and numerous family, and remember you are not yet in the noontide of life. Under circumstances like these it seems to me that the obligation to you is far greater than when a gift is made by landowners in districts in which they hold land. These are peculiar features in your gift which ought to make us the more truly grateful for the boon.

The speeches continued in this vein, ending with a call for *'three cheers for Mr Pearson, the working man's friend and benefactor.'* And three cheers there were – followed by three more for *'Mrs. Pearson and the Mayor's family'*.

Zachariah now, with a specially inscribed silver spade, ceremonially planted a *Wellingtonia gigantea* (now renamed *Sequoiadendron giganteum*). Seeds of this monstrous tree, 'discovered' in California, had only been brought into England seven years earlier, and the saplings were much sought-after. They had become a status symbol, so it was only to be expected that Zachariah (or more probably Niven) would choose, as the symbolic first tree in the park, one of the earliest Wellingtonia saplings ever to be raised in England.

Once the tree was planted, the Vicar of Sculcoates Church offered up a prayer, pleading that: *'This work, so auspiciously inaugurated, be fraught with blessings, both to this town and neighbourhood, in the prevention of vice and the encouragement of all manly virtues, that our youth of both sexes, and our adult population, may here taste those pure pleasures and innocent recreations which Thou, the benignant Father of Mankind, doth so willingly concede to us, Thy children'*.

Formalities over, Zachariah mounted his horse, still enjoying his party enormously. Atop his steed as he rode amongst the people, he must have cut quite a dashing figure in his bright Mayoral robes and ceremonial chain. This was the signal for the festivities to begin in earnest. The Artillery Bands took their place for a review, which went off well despite the muddy terrain. There were exotic sideshows, games, and competitions as well as a motley collection of intriguing acts, such as *'Mr Macarte, Grotesque Dancer'*, or Madame Geneave Saque's *'Terrific Ascent on the Fiery Rope, Sixty Feet in height, surrounded by Prodigious Jets of Flame and 'Coloured Fires'*. There were jugglers, musicians, gymnasts and an *'Austrian Salamander'* who walked through fire. The refreshment tents did a brisk trade, and the day ended with a torch-lit parade and huge firework display; visitors were certainly getting good value for their two-shillings' worth of entry fee (well, only a shilling if they had bought tickets in advance).

One of the Fete medallions, a rare family artefact to have survived from 1860. Zachariah is wearing his Mayoral chains, and is depicted here inside a laurel wreath. This was one of the cheap versions struck for the masses from base metal – which is possibly why Zachariah's nose has been disfiguringly worn away over the years.

The obverse of the medallion celebrates Hull with its coat of arms of the three coronets. This is surrounded by a laurel branch on the left and an oak one on the right. The caption above is 'Pearson Park for the People'.

The day ended for the key players somewhat differently. Zachariah had invited over 200 guests to a sumptuous dinner at the Royal Station Hotel. His long guest-list of gentlemen included MPs, Mayors and senior figures in the army and navy. By today's standards, the extensive banquet menu looks spectacular: turtle soup, turbot, salmon, whiting, sole; mutton, quail, pigeon, lobster, chicken, lamb, turtle, veal, grouse, venison, beef, duck, leverets, turkey, gosling – and an endless list of the moulded jellies with fruit so popular at Victorian tables. Any vegetarians may have taken less pleasure in the feast: apart from the desserts, there was apparently nothing on the menu for non-carnivores. The original menu itself could be found until very recently framed on the hotel wall (now the Mercure Hull Royal Hotel).

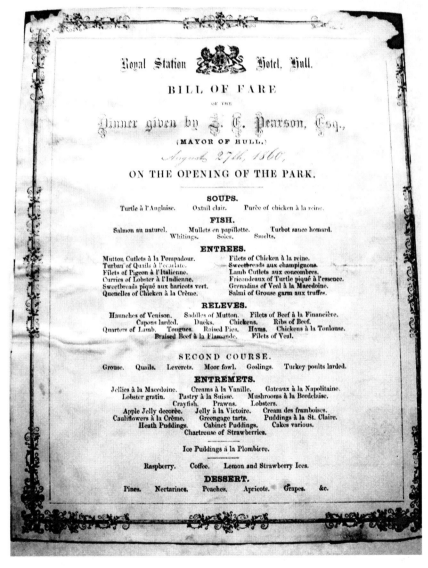

The menu as presented to Zachariah's guests for his sumptuous supper at the Station Hotel after he had presented the deeds for the park.

Royal Station ♛ Hotel, Hull

BILL OF FARE

of the

Dinner given by Z. C. Pearson, Esq.,

August 27th, 1860

ON THE OPENING OF THE PARK

SOUPS

Turtle à l'Anglais.   Oxtail clair.   Purèe of chicken à la reine.

FISH

Salmon au naturel.   Mullets en papillotte.   Turbot sauce homard.
Whitings.   Soles.   Smelts.

ENTREES

Mutton Cutlets à la Pompadour.   Filets of Chicken à la reine.
Turban of Quails à l'ecarlate.   Sweetbreads aux champignons.
Filets of Pigeon à l'Italienne.   Lamb cutlets aux concombres.
Curries of Lobster à l'Indienne.   Fricondeaux of Turtle piqué à l'essence.
Sweetbreads piqué aux haricots vert.   Grenadins of Veal à la Macedoine.
Quenelles of Chicken à la Crème.   Salmi of Grouse garm aux truffes.

RELEVES

SECOND COURSE

Grouse.   Quails.   Leverets.   Moor fowl.   Goslings.   Turkey poults larded.

ENTREMETS

Jellies à la Macedoine.   Creams à la Vanilla.   Gateaux à la Napolitaine.
Lobster gratin. Pastry à la Suisse.   Mushrooms à la Bordelaise.
Crayfish. Prawns. Lobsters.
Apple Jelly decoree.   Jelly à la Victoire.   Cream des Framboises.
Caulflowers à la Crème. Greengage tarts.   Puddings à la St. Claire.
Heath Puddings.   Cabinet Puddings.   Cakes various.
Chartreuse of Strawberries

Ice Pudding à la Plombiere

Raspberry.   Coffee.   Lemon and Strawberry Ices.

DESSERT

Pines.   Nectarines.   Peaches.   Apricots.   Grapes.   &c.

*To appreciate fully the dishes served up on 27th August 1860, the menu
has been transcribed. As was common practice on Victorian menus, the
descriptions are written in an early form of Franglais!*

Although there are no wines listed, given the numerous toasts proposed, we must assume their presence. Whether Zachariah himself, as a committed Methodist, was a partaker of alcoholic beverages, we do not know. A correspondent to *Private Eye* in 2012 described him as a *'city benefactor and famous abstinent'*, but this may well be deductive rather than evidential. In any case, whether or not he drank, at least it looks as though he knew how to throw a decent party!

Many speeches were made, toasts proposed, political points aired and compliments paid. Zachariah toasted the Queen, the Prince Consort, the Archbishop of York, and finally the *Navy* and Army – in that order, which caused some consternation as, being a man of the sea, he had reversed the conventional way of toasting the forces. Among generals and other officials, five MPs stood up to make speeches, the MP for Beverley even suggesting that Zachariah should be honoured *'by erecting a statue to his memory in marble (applause)'*. There were more and more toasts, and the surfeit of bonhomie finally ended with the sentiment that *'from this day forward the name of Z. C. Pearson would become a household word in Hull'*. It was – but not always in the context intended here.

The next day, 28th August, was Zachariah's 39th birthday, and the park was open for its second day of festivities with free admission for the poor. The entertainments now were *'principally for the juvenile portion of the community. By the kindness of the Park committee, the children of the Hull Workhouse, the Sculcoates Union, the Sailors' Orphans' Institution, and the Hull Ragged and Industrial Schools were admitted gratis.'* They were also fed: Mr Wallett, the 'Queen's Jester', a well-known clown, treated the destitute children to whatever they fancied to eat from the refreshment booth.

At four o'clock in the afternoon, Zachariah arrived back in the park with his older two children, Charles (aged 14), who planted another *Wellingtonia,* and Mary (11), who completed the ceremony with a *Thujopsis borealis* (a yellow cypress).

Zachariah told all the children present that he hoped they would live to see these saplings grow into mature trees one day. The evening festivities in the park followed the same pattern as the night before, ending again with fireworks.

It would be an omission to end the report of the Colossal Fete without including a few excerpts from the Prize Ode, which won Sergeant Wightman of the Volunteer Rifles the competition's £5 prize. This ode was epic, and truly of its time, painting a picture of what the park would mean to people in the future:

> 'Here shall the pale mechanic, when at last
> Toil's myriad hands have roll'd the labouring Sun
> Out through the western gate of Day, and rest
> Falls on the city like a wearied one –
> Here shall the pale mechanic gladly hie
> (With her the faithful partner of his care)
> Rejoicing in a good day's labour done,
> Drink in the blessing of the purer air...'

Childhood would benefit too:
> 'And here shall Childhood weave its daisy chain
> The livelong day, knee deep in waving flowers...'

Not forgetting the older generation:
> 'And here shall Age lean on his crazy staff
> And bask him in the restful summer sun,
> Glad at his heart to hear the children laugh...'

Or the sporty youth:
> 'Here shall the town's Olympics be
> And youthful athletes win nightly bays
> In well-matched games the pliant limbs be free...'

And on like this for several more flowery stanzas, describing the Volunteers and the bands drilling in the park, and ending with thanks to the benefactor (and an assumption that he would be memorialised with a monument):

'All honour to the kindly heart
Unbounded as its kindred brain –
To him who, tho' all unallied
Through paths of danger and of pain
He scaled Wealth's stronghold at the mountain side,
Forgets not those he left upon the plain...

This day is reared the crowning battlement
Of his good fame: his townsmen's love and praise
The lasting structure of the monument
On which tis memory stands for other days;
Whereof th' inscription carved about the base,
Through many generations handed down,
From sire to son
Shall ever run:
"The benefactor of his race"-
"The glory of his town!"'

Once Zachariah's party-of-a-lifetime was over, the real work started on the park, and the following three years saw landscaping and planting with nine thousand trees and bushes. The designer, Niven, had to turn a flat field of mud into a park with variety and interest at low cost. Inspired by the layout of Hyde Park, he designed a serpentine lake, limiting its depth to four feet, assuming it would be *'highly appreciated for the purposes of skating during the winter'*.

Paths and walks were laid out to achieve views around and across the lake, and the planting was done to Niven's specification; the park should contain *'variety in growth and foliage of trees and shrubs'*, and eventually become an arboretum. We can see from the park minutes that Niven was enthusiastic and knowledgeable, sending his gardener *'into the country for a few days to obtain briars for grafting roses'*. Niven's hope was that the 'genial shade' from his trees would be enjoyed by those spared to live another 50 years, and indeed it is a credit to his skill that his original planting framework and layout survives today. Although a severe drought in 1861 killed off huge numbers of the newly-planted saplings, many of the original trees have become today's mature horse chestnuts, poplars, willows, limes, copper beeches, and evergreen oaks. Sadly, the *Wellingtonia* planted by Zachariah died – though it was to be replaced, courtesy of Hull City Council's Wyke Area Committee, acting as The Pearson Park Trust, in 2010 at a ceremony where Zachariah's descendants from across the world gathered to celebrate the 150th anniversary of his gift of the park to the people of Hull. At the time of writing, the tree still survives.

This was the twentieth People's Park in England, and during its creation the park attracted much sponsorship. Ordinary folk had not had such an amenity before, and everyone wanted to be associated with it, so the subscription fund took off. After Zachariah had urged the people in his speech to make the park their own and ornament it, numerous miscellaneous donations were made – some of more suitability than others, requiring a degree of discretion as to which were acceptable. In addition to special plants and trees, donations included swans and geese to adorn the lake, rocks caught by trawlermen in their nets to edge the lake, and a massive 19-ton pillar of Cleveland ferruginous oolitic limestone, or ironstone, presented by Bolckow and Vaughan, local iron producers. Over the years, many of the donated items fell by the wayside, but not this pillar, which was later to bear Zachariah's commemoration plaque. There were also some architectural relics: a 'folly' from the closing Zoological Gardens and, much later, the cupola from 'Zachariah's' Town Hall after it had been replaced by the larger Guildhall, positioned today on a bank overlooking the children's playground.

Over the next few years, an iron bridge over the lake and an ornate bandstand were added – and later removed. Its conservatory was replaced in 1930 and today boasts exotic plants, an aquarium and a reptile house. A beautiful cast iron drinking fountain is one of the park's seven Grade II listed features – another donation at the park's inception. Over the years, the park has adapted to changing times, being a wartime home to Nissen huts and air-raid shelters, and a place to line up the barrage balloons, but it has never lost the purpose for which it was created: a park for all the people.

A post card of Pearson Park shortly after the bandstand was installed in 1908. It was removed later.

The politics of the gift were interesting. While the donation saved the council a great deal of money, Zachariah's business plan to finance the park's laying out through the sale of the building plots was initially derailed because sales of the building plots were slow: potential buyers wanted a better idea of how the park would evolve before committing to living there. This led to a degree of infighting among Councillors during the year after the gift had been made.

The question was how to raise the money in the interim to finish laying out the park according to Zachariah's specifications? Should they borrow £4,000 or increase the rates by twopence? One faction even wanted to simplify the design to reduce the cost – but the plans had already been adopted by the Council as a condition of the gift, and they were committed to the original design.

As he handed over the park to the people of Hull, Zachariah invited them all 'to ornament it as far as they can', and this lovely bright blue drinking fountain was one of the gifts, donated by Mr. Atkinson. It is one of several listed features of Pearson Park.

In a Council meeting things became acrimonious, and Zachariah was obliged to spell out how the delay and argument was running up costs. The *Hull Packet* reported him trying to clarify the situation, saying he had:

> purchased the land, paid for it, and submitted to them a plan by which he gave them a certain number of acres, and told them that if there was a profit on the sale of the other land [the building plots] he would hand it over to them, and if there was a loss, he would bear it [...] He said half of the surplus had been sold, and the remaining portion he intended to hold over until the park had been completed, when he had no doubt its value would be increased from 3s to 5s [from three shillings to five shillings] per yard.

In other words, once buyers could see what a pleasant environment the park was going to be, the plots would fetch a higher price than buying a plot on the edge of a muddy field buzzing with men digging and tree-planting. In the meantime, they needed to borrow the money rather than raise the rates by an extra 2d, which would have been very unpopular – this would look as though the people were paying for their own park. After a heated debate, a division was forced, and they voted to borrow the money.

With over a third of the cost of laying out the park being raised by public subscription, and the majority of the building plots eventually being sold for £9,800, the park was ultimately laid out just as Zachariah had specified and, as historian Sheahan summarised it: *'the cost of the park, both to the donor and the recipients, has been so arranged as to have been felt in the least burthensome manner by either party'*.

The broad lamplit carriageway which Zachariah had specified, separating the park from the building plots, was designed to service the potential villas, and Niven lined it with horse chestnuts, which he said combined *'beauty of flower with elegance of foliage'*; today we can still enjoy his elegant row of ancient trees around the sides of the park. It was all part of Zachariah's scheme to tempt the wealth-creators to remain living in Hull by creating an elegant environment. With this in mind, when the forty three building plots were put up for auction as *'suitable for villa residences'*, bearing in mind the sensibilities of its future residents, there were stringent specifications about what the plots could *not* be used for: *'No Slaughter-house, Tallow Chandler's Melting-house, Soap Manufactory, or Blacksmith's Shop, or any other building or erection shall hereafter be built or erected upon any such Lots, nor shall any noisome, offensive, or any other trade, business, or employment whatsoever be carried on in or upon any of the said Lots or in or upon any Villa'*.

PARTICULARS AND CONDITIONS OF SALE

OF

VALUABLE FREEHOLD LAND

(ADMIRABLY ADAPTED FOR BUILDING SITES)

Situate in and adjoining to the intended New Park, at Stepney,

IN THE BOROUGH OF KINGSTON-UPON-HULL,

AND DENOTED IN THE PLAN ANNEXED TO THESE PARTICULARS.

TO BE SOLD BY AUCTION,

BY MR. ROBERT CHATTAM,

AT THE KINGSTON HOTEL, IN HULL,

ON WEDNESDAY, THE 5TH DAY OF DECEMBER, 1860,

AT THREE O'CLOCK IN THE AFTERNOON,

In the following Lots (Subject to the annexed Conditions of Sale.)

PARTICULARS.
LOT 1.
Has been disposed of.

Building plots around the edge of the park were auctioned off, but they had strict conditions attached to them. This was to be a smart residential development: a tasteful villa would be encouraged, but a slaughterhouse was out of the question.

112

The elaborate ceremonial arch in Pearson Avenue is another of the park's listed features, and made entirely of iron. Created by local specialists Young and Pool, it originally had gates, but residents tired of opening them when they arrived back in their carriages after curfew and the gates were removed.

No doubt the latter-day uses to which these villas, or their successors, were put would have been met with Zachariah's approval: flats, residences for the elderly, a mosque, a police station, a poet's residence (Philip Larkin lived here for eighteen years), a vicarage and the Pearson Park Hotel (recently converted to flats) – and not a slaughter-house in sight!

Entering the park from the Beverley Road, via what is today Pearson Avenue, a wrought-iron ceremonial arch and gateway, bearing the symbols of maritime Hull, gave a sense of occasion, and these remain today. On the gates, which no longer exist, was a family crest: a *'demi-lion rampant holding a mullet'* (a six-pointed star). Whether this was Zachariah's idea or not, we do not know. As far as we can ascertain, there was no family crest prior to this – why would a humble family have had one? It looks as though it was probably designed for the occasion. It exists today only as a blueprint in the city archives, with its Latin motto 'Providentia fido' – I trust in Providence (or God).

When the Guildhall was built, it replaced the Town Hall that Zachariah had instigated while he was Mayor. The building was demolished, but its cupola was saved and installed in the park in 1912 near the children's' playground, where it still stands today.

One of the villas built around the periphery of the park in the 1860s. It is glimpsed here between some of the original trees from Niven's planting which have survived to this day.

No Victorian park was complete without statuary, and so Zachariah commissioned a well-known Hull sculptor, Thomas Earle, to make a statue of Queen Victoria in commemoration of her visit to the town in 1854. He paid Earle a deposit of £100, and then wrote to inform the council:

> *I beg to inform you that I have made an arrangement with our townsman Mr Thomas Earle, the eminent sculptor of London, for a full-sized marble statue of Her Most Gracious Majesty the Queen, which, when completed, I propose presenting to the Local Board of Health, to be placed by them in some conspicuous and suitable position in the park, there to remain an ornament to the town, and a first class specimen of a work of art by a native of our ancient and loyal borough. I shall be glad if you obtain the approval and sanction to this from the board at their next meeting.*

In characteristic style, Zachariah had once more informed the council after he had commissioned the work. The reference to the 'suitable position' was one of tact: there had been a standoff between the sculptor and the landscape artist, Niven designating a statue location near the entrance of the park, but Earle feeling that a more central position was appropriate.

The Queen granted Earle two live sittings at Windsor Castle where, apparently, the Royal Family took an interest in his work, as described in 1862 by the *Hull Packet*:

> The late Prince Consort was then in strong and vigorous health, and together with Princess Alice made suggestions to the sculptor, and even put into the clay touches of his own. A week or two afterwards, his Royal Highness was stricken with his fatal illness.

Earle carved the Queen in his London studio in Vincent Street from a 12-ton *'flawless block of Carrara marble'*, and the result was widely reckoned to be one of the finest statues of her at the time. When it was eventually unveiled (in Earle's preferred location, not Niven's) in 1863, the Queen herself was said to be delighted with it, and Sheahan describes it as *'a beautiful work of art which it is a great distinction to possess, and it is one of the finest figures of the Queen in the country. The effigy is seated in a chair of Greek form, and vested in a robe of state. The likeness is perfect. The countenance is beaming with intellectual expression.'*

To add to the ornamentation of the park, and to commemorate the death of Prince Albert, in his second term as Mayor, Zachariah started a public subscription to raise funds for Earle to carve Albert. He himself set an example by donating £50 – more than twice any other donation – and the resulting Prince Consort today stands a short distance away from his wife.

The completed Pearson Park was opened to the public three years later, and survives to this day, evolving as needed by a changing society, but still true to the original design, thanks to the vigilance of those on successive Parks Committees of the City Council. The Park was arguably Zachariah's grandest gesture, but even if it was not, it was certainly the one to survive as his legacy.

This, the mid-nineteenth century was an exciting time to be alive. Blessed by peace and prosperity, life in England was innovative and vibrant. In 1859, when Zachariah was ascending to the Mayoralty and secretly planning the park, Darwin was publishing his *Origin of Species*, and Mrs. Beeton was starting to serialise what was to become her *Book of Household Management*. As long as one had enough money, life was good. And Zachariah still seemed to have the 'Midas touch'. His businesses continued to make him money, enabling him to continue to play the high-profile and philanthropic role which he had now established at home.

But he was out of his depth when he naïvely got himself entangled with the political affairs of foreign governments...

7

The Garibaldi incident

Stepping aside for the moment from Zachariah's life in the spotlight, this chapter is peripheral to the rest of the book, but it describes an incident which lends colour to the story of the Mayor of Hull. It was notorious at the time, generating a lengthy debate in the House of Commons and questions being asked in the House of Lords. It is well documented with contemporaneous verbatim accounts, bringing the characters to life in a way which becomes lost down the years when historians tell and retell their own versions of events. Family folklore alleged that Zachariah had in some way helped Garibaldi near Naples. No details – just the rumour, relayed down the generations. Then a booklet of correspondence was a serendipitous find on eBay; it was the brief for a Parliamentary debate about the seizure of Zachariah's vessel, the *Orwell*. It included letters from such notaries as Lord Russell (ex-Prime Minister, then Foreign Secretary in Palmerston's government), Lord Wodehouse (Under-Secretary of State for Foreign Affairs), General Giuseppe Garibaldi, and of course Zachariah Pearson, Mayor of Hull. As well as the letters, the account of the debate itself is found in Hansard, the official verbatim records of the proceedings of Parliament. These two sources furnish all the quotations used in this chapter.

Before Zachariah's part in the story unfolds, the background political context of Europe needs to be sketched in. Prior to 1861, the Italian peninsula had been a patchwork of independent kingdoms, variously invaded and controlled at different times by the Bourbons and Napoleon. The situation was not to everyone's liking; while it suited Austria and the Pope, among others, to keep it fragmented, there was a growing movement towards a unified peninsula. After assorted struggles, exiles, punishments and fleeings, strong leaders such as General Giuseppe Garibaldi eventually emerged to lead the campaign to unite Italy.

By 1860, the Kingdom of Sardinia had already merged with Tuscany and other sections in the north, and in the May of 1861, continuing the movement of joining regions together, Garibaldi assembled men in the south to unite Sicily and the Neapolitan region with the rest of the peninsula. Under the Sardinian flag, Garibaldi and his army of red-shirted volunteers (known as the *Mille,* or 'the Thousand') landed at Marsala in the west of Sicily.

Britain did not want to be seen actively joining Garibaldi, but while she officially maintained a neutral position she was nevertheless quite pro-unification in the interests of regional stability. It would be better for Britain if the strategic ports in the Mediterranean were used by the 'right' people. In any case, Britain wanted to keep access to Sicily's rich sulphur deposits – not to mention her delicious Marsala wine.

When Garibaldi landed in Sicily in May 1860, British ships were among those in the harbour to help deter the Bourbon vessels. Within three months, he had taken the Island of Sicily, and new supporters were joining him daily, augmented by the hordes of locals who were deserting the rule of the Bourbons to join the unification process. Garibaldi's main aim was to capture the strategic city of Naples and, helped by British ships, his army of volunteers crossed to the Italian mainland in August and moved north. They reached Naples and joined it, with Sicily, to the Kingdom of Sardinia. The *Risorgimento* (the 'rising again') was well under way – and Zachariah's accidental role in it can now be told.

The life of a well-known shipowner was anything but hum-drum: one never knew what was just around the corner, from news of a ship being wrecked on a reef on some far-flung coast, to a request for a very unusual commission. A staid man would probably be inclined to play safe in choosing his business opportunities, and restrict his risks to manageable proportions. But a man of more entrepreneurial spirit faced with some new venture might be tempted to 'give it a go' – and Zachariah fell into this category when, with huge personal loss, he inadvertently played a tiny role in the unification of Italy. By 1860 he had perfected the knack of capitalising on business opportunities as they arose. He had an extensive network of contacts to enable him to operate successfully around the world: ship-brokers to act as intermediaries if vessels were being chartered, and agents to deal with the locals when buying and selling cargoes. They understood how Zachariah did business, and – possibly more crucially in an age before emails, texts and telephones – they also took the initiative and made decisions on Zachariah's behalf. Appointing the 'right' men to these positions was critical to his business.

Mr Henry Bake was one such trusted agent. He was a partner in a firm of shipbrokers from London, and acted as Zachariah's attorney in the matter of handling ships. He was sympathetic with Garibaldi's aims for the *Risorgimento*, and had been organising ships to carry volunteer reinforcements to assemble in Sicily. By mid-1860, he was on the lookout for appropriate vessels to transport supporters across the Straits of Messina to the mainland for the final push to unify Italy, and he spotted an opportunity that he thought would be profitable for both himself and Zachariah. Knowing Zachariah's ships, and aware that Garibaldi needed '*a paddle steamer of good power and speed, under the British flag*', he felt that either the *Orwell* or the *Amazon* would fit Garibaldi's requirements, and Garibaldi's instructions, written in July 1860, were fairly vague:

'Io autorizzo il Signor Pilotti di noleggiare 'I'Amazon' od un altro vapore per quindici giorni: qualunque condizione che egli faccia sarà da me approvata.'
[I authorise Signor Pilotti to charter the 'Amazon', or some other steamer, for fifteen days; whatever condition he may make shall be approved by me.]

This was ostensibly signed by Garibaldi, but Bake, familiar with the deceptions of warring factions, wanted to ensure that all was above board, and so he sent the letter to the Garibaldi Committee in Genoa to *'test the genuineness of the signature'*. Satisfied that the signature was authentic, he drew up a contract with Pilotti, Garibaldi's representative, for chartering the *Orwell* – the *Amazon* was not available. The *Orwell* was a relatively small wooden paddle steamer with a female figurehead and a speed of 10 knots. As the ship was needed at once, Zachariah sent her out from Hull – at high cost to himself as she was 'in ballast' (without any cargo to offset the coal bill).

The contract caused Mr Bake a degree of nervousness; knowing that the *Orwell* was entering into a war zone and working through interpreters and different cultures must all have added extra layers of complication to an already fraught situation. The agreement was to transport 100 men from Genoa direct to Messina in Sicily, with the charterers feeding the men and providing 50-60 tons of coal. In the enquiry that followed, though, it appeared that Bake had misgivings, as his own perception was that *'the object of the movement was stated to be that there were about 100 men, of questionable though resolute character, who were wanted in Sicily on some dangerous enterprise'*. Bake, presumably under Zachariah's instructions, also therefore inserted a clause in the contract which read: *'it is further provided and agreed, that no forceful possession will be taken of the steamer, so as to deviate from the direct course to Messina, under a penalty of 5,000l. sterling [£5,000] for the value of the said 'Orwell', besides becoming liable for other contingencies'*.

The penalty clause was inserted for sound business reasons: the *Orwell* had been on the market for £5,000, and she was now about to embark on an uncertain adventure in a politically tense part of the world. The clause made logical sense, but at the time only Bake and Zachariah knew why it was in the contract, and later, after the *Orwell* had met disaster, the clause gave rise to the suspicion that the agent, the captain, or possibly even Zachariah, were operating some form of swindle to make £5,000.

Over the next few days, Garibaldi's agent prepared the *Orwell* for her voyage from Genoa. She was loaded with coal, food, firearms, gunpowder and finally the men: 85 'passengers' under the direction of Captain Paulo Pilotti and his Lieutenant, Settembrini. These men were an assorted bunch from all over the world, the only element in common being that they were all seamen volunteering to support Garibaldi's quest for a united Italy and, suspiciously, they all had crew functions allocated to them: officers, midshipmen, engineers and firemen.

The *Orwell* herself was under the command of Zachariah's employees, Captain Sutton and his crew of 11. She had been due to leave Genoa harbour late on the evening of 22nd August 1860, but departure was delayed until the next morning. Pilotti, however, had different ideas: he had a crew-in-waiting and was determined to leave port as soon as possible, with or without permission.

At five o'clock that evening, when Captain Sutton had gone ashore with the ship's papers in his pocket, possibly to finalise the paperwork with the authorities in Genoa, Pilotti came on board and told the Mate that Captain Sutton *'desired that the fires should be lighted and steam ready by 7'*. Being a steam-driven vessel, there was inevitably a long lead time between giving orders and being ready to leave; the coal fires needed to be lit, and these would heat the boilers, but only when the water was boiling and generating steam could the engines be put to work. Pilotti wanted the process started at once. Captain Sutton knew nothing about this order – official departure time was set for the next morning.

Giuseppe Garibaldi, to whom Zachariah chartered his vessel Orwell to assist in the Risorgimento. Garibaldi organised thousands to gather in Sicily before crossing into the mainland. The Orwell was hijacked by a crew of desperadoes, who wrecked the engines. Zachariah was never compensated, and reckoned to have lost £7,500 in supporting the Italian cause.

Nonetheless, at this stage the Mate did not suspect Pilotti of deception. He took him at his word, not realising that the ship's Master had *not* issued the order. Accordingly, he passed the message down to the firemen, and the fires were started. But Captain Sutton was furious when he came back on board, and gave counter orders to extinguish the fires forthwith. For reasons unknown, particularly after this initial deception by Pilotti, the Captain left the ship again, and a prolonged battle of wills then ensued between Pilotti, who was determined to leave port imminently, and the *Orwell's* crew, who were equally determined to foil him. To be fair to Pilotti, he did try persuasion and deception before resorting to force, but when a pistol was put to the engineer's head, unsurprisingly this did the trick. In the engineer's own words: '*I was ordered away from the engines, which were taken charge of by two passengers (Italians) who were on board.*' With his life in danger, the engineer had no choice: he handed over the engines to Pilotti's own engineers and firemen.

The hi-jacking was complete. The crew-in-waiting now sprang into action to operate the *Orwell*. Pilotti had secured Zachariah's ship for his own dark purposes. With the 'passengers' now in control of the *Orwell*, her original British crew members, Zachariah's seamen, were overpowered and kept out of action below decks. Although they requested a boat to land them ashore, they were forced to join in the adventure against their will. Thus it was that Pilotti illegally set forth in the *Orwell* from Genoa, ostensibly to carry troops to join those in the south.

In keeping with a true adventure story, one of the seamen during this hijacking managed to slide overboard down the anchor chute, and swim to an English vessel nearby where he raised the alarm. The next day, this man, together with Captain Sutton, who had been blissfully unaware of the turn of events until that morning, went to the British Consul in Genoa to report the seizure of the *Orwell*. In his statement, the seaman said that around 6 pm *'two small barrels containing cutlasses were brought aboard'*, and that the crew had been *'clapped in irons'*. This was hyperbole, no doubt due to his traumatic experience. The crew, it emerged later, had actually been well-treated, though the escapee's version of events made Pilotti's men sound like a bunch of dangerous desperados. And it was on this one man's evidence that the British Consul sprang into action.

He sent a telegram to Rear-Admiral Mundy, who was on a British ship near Naples, to put him on the alert for the *Orwell*, and taking at face value the exaggerated account of the escaped seaman, the Consul also wrote to the British Minister in Naples, who acted as the local branch of the Foreign Office. Given that it sounded as though British seamen had been severely maltreated and were in danger, the tone of his letter was uncompromising. He blackened Settembrini's name, describing him as *'the son of Signor Settembrini, who was for a long time in prison at Naples'*, and repeated the inaccurate clapping-in-irons story, talking about *'the piratical seizure of the vessel'*.

At this stage, Consul Brown exonerated Zachariah: *'I believe the owner of the* Orwell *(who is Mayor of Hull) to have been totally ignorant of the description of persons who were passengers by his vessel, and he certainly had no suspicion of the possibility of any such events as those which occurred taking place'*. He was clearly less confident in Captain Sutton, though: *'the master of the vessel, on the other hand, who is still in Genoa having left the vessel but two hours before the seizure, and remained on shore all night, may, perhaps, be implicated in the affair. At any rate, if not culpable, his conduct appears to have been highly discreditable and careless in the extreme, and demands further investigation.'* Presumably his opinion referred to the way Captain Sutton had left the ship and not returned all night – even after Pilotti's deception had come to light.

The Consul at once fired off telegrams to everyone: the Foreign Secretary (Lord Russell), to Zachariah, and to Sir

James Hudson, the British Ambassador based in Turin. Now, Hudson was fiercely pro-unification, and this may have swayed his interpretation of the Consul's letter, as his own message to Lord Russell firms up the suspicion around the Captain: *'There appears to be good ground for suspecting complicity in this plot on the part of the captain, for Her Majesty's Consul was not informed of the seizure of the* 'Orwell' *until thirteen hours after it happened'*.

Does the Consul's phraseology here indicate a touch of impatience that the seizure of the *Orwell* was muddying the waters of the great Italian cause that he believed in so fervently? Whatever his agenda, we can see how rumour, suspicion and ideology all built on each other, for Rear-Admiral Mundy picked up this theme, reinforcing the conspiracy theory even further: *'It will therefore probably appear that the seizure of the* 'Orwell' *was not so lawless an act as was at first believed to be the case.'*

While the story is told here in some semblance of chronological order, this logic was not apparent to the key players at the time. Events unfolded in a much more jumbled order due to the many confusion-factors. Chief among these was the opaque environment of warring revolutionaries, where one thing was said while quite another was being secretly planned. An added complication was the communications system. While essential urgent information could be transmitted fast by telegrams, which were new and very expensive, the written follow-up letters didn't reach their destination across Europe until days or weeks later – sometimes when action had already been taken on a minimalist and inaccurate telegram message. And perhaps even more challenging was the question of what to do once information had been received. Diplomats saw intelligence through one lens, while the Navy used another. Whitehall had yet a different perspective (well, in reality it had several different perspectives). Zachariah, operating from Hull, was caught in the cross-fire of all the above, and just wanted to be re-paid for his losses at the hands of Garibaldi and the pirates.

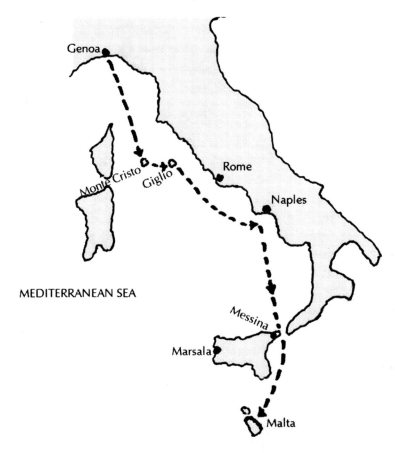

The Orwell's *route after she was hijacked in Genoa harbour. She steamed south, raiding two islands en route to 'capturing a Neapolitan ship of war', but plans in war are constantly being thwarted, and she was eventually recaptured by the Royal Navy off Messina. She limped to Malta where there was an argument about how to deal with a ship full of pirates.*

With successive telegrams arriving days or weeks ahead of the written depositions, and with the biased slants on the wording, the *Orwell's* story was morphing into something more deliberative. The hijacking now looked less sinister, and more like a planned event in cahoots with the captain.

And this ambiguity may have introduced a degree of prevarication in sorting it out. In any event, and leaving all recriminations aside, the *Orwell* needed to be found urgently. Given her head-start, rather than send a ship to chase after her, British naval vessels along the western coast of Italy were sent a description of her. Despite these alerts, though, nothing was seen of Zachariah's purloined property for several days.

Whilst all this diplomatic and Royal Navy activity was taking place across the Mediterranean, back on the *Orwell* – still flying the British flag – Pilotti was putting his dubious plans into action. The contract had been to take men to Messina, and not to deviate *en route*, but Pilotti had, in fact, chartered the vessel with other ideas in mind. He had a secret agenda: in his legal deposition much later, Pilotti revealed that his ultimate purpose in chartering the *Orwell* was actually to '*go to Naples for the purposes of capturing a Neapolitan ship of war*'. But, as events turned out, the only ship he could lay hands on had a built-in penalty of £5,000, which, in his words, '*placed me in a situation in which I must make a choice, either to incur a penalty by taking forcible possession of the vessel, or to lose entirely all hopes of my expedition*'. Clearly, Pilotti had felt it acceptable within the political constraints and the secrecy of war to take the risk of deceiving the owner in order to get hold of a vessel which would carry out his purposes. Zachariah just happened to be his victim.

Pilotti reckoned he would have got away with it, too, had he not left the *Orwell* in the charge of Settembrini, his second-in-command. Pilotti himself went ashore at Livorno (Leghorn) to travel down to Naples by land, and what happened next appears to have been a lapse of judgement which sparked off a new diplomatic incident and put Zachariah seriously out of pocket. Once Settembrini was in charge, instead of steaming directly south to intercept the vessel off Naples, he put ashore at Monte Cristo, a tiny island off the coast of Tuscany. This island was owned by a British subject, Mr Watson-Taylor, but as it had come under Sardinian control the previous year, the Watson-Taylor family had fled back to Britain for safety, which is where they were when the *Orwell* arrived searching for provisions. Settembrini's men first disarmed the guards and, in the account by one of his men, Settembrini then *'gave orders for the house to be searched, breaking open all doors which he found locked; also all the outstables etc. In the afternoon of the same day I was sent on shore with men, to shoot the bullocks, and bring them on board with poultry, flour, potatoes and all the firewood we could find.'*

It seems that either they were planning for a longer period aboard the *Orwell* than they had admitted to when they stocked up in Genoa, or that they had originally failed to take on board enough food for the men. Whatever the reason, they ransacked the house, and topped up their supplies on Monte Cristo – and all this time the *Orwell* continued to fly the British flag. But still they needed more, and the next raid was on the nearby Island of Giglio, where they forcefully took some extra firearms and ammunition. And this was where they acquired a new disguise: they stole a Sardinian flag and hoisted it forthwith, changing Zachariah's vessel from 'British' to 'Sardinian' at a stroke. Their piratical adventures accomplished, they now careered off south down the Mediterranean to meet Captain Pilotti and take possession of the designated warship in the Bay of Naples. But while the *Orwell* was awaiting the pre-arranged signal for action, *five* enemy Neapolitan war-steamers appeared, thwarting Pilotti's plan – and the *Orwell* changed course and continued south towards Sicily.

And this was where – at last – she was recaptured by the Royal Navy.

A week after leaving Genoa, and within half an hour of arrival in Messina, the Commander of *HMS Scilla*, who had been on the lookout for her, boarded the *Orwell* and took control of her and all the men, once again placing her back under British command. Undoubtedly, this would have been a huge relief for the *Orwell*'s real crew after a week of being kept below decks during all the Mediterranean adventures.

The British Navy now had to make a swift decision. Piracy was a serious issue – but what was the 'right' thing to do with 85 pirates and their leaders under these complex circumstances? Britain was, officially at least, neutral to the Italian cause, so the men could not become her 'prisoners of war'. One option was to hand them over to the local authority, but in its current state of flux Rear-Admiral Mundy pronounced this to be *'an unrecognized government'*. In any case, the local Sicilian military officer refused to take charge of them ashore – the men were from so many nations that he was worried about the potential for stirring up trouble. It was clearly going to be far easier to 'contain' them if he kept them on the ship, so Settembrini and his piratical crew were accordingly detained on board *HMS Scilla*. Mundy, though, did not really know what to do with them. In the end, he let someone else make the decision; it was his Pontius Pilate moment. He sent the *Orwell,* with all hands and prisoners, to the Governor in Malta *'in order that the case may be disposed of by the competent authorities'*.

On arrival in Malta, the *Orwell* was found to be in a very poor condition. Her hull had been damaged and her engines had been virtually wrecked; Settembrini's crew had badly over-exerted her, and she was pronounced to be *'of very little value'*. So now the accusations and recriminations started – and each party viewed the situation through a different lens.

The owner, Zachariah, focused on the business angle. He had a legal contract and would be seeking compensation. His main interest was in recouping the value of the *Orwell*, and the chief job of Bake, his agent, was to collect sufficient evidence to ensure this. Zachariah had no interest in pursuing prosecutions of the whole crew. He only wanted Pilotti – the man who signed the contract and then stole his ship – punished, and perhaps Settembrini, as he had been the one to misuse his property so atrociously. Zachariah was shrewd enough to concentrate his efforts where it mattered to him and he pragmatically accepted that if he sent a vessel into a war zone he would not realistically succeed in prosecuting a shipful of pirates.

The Governor of Malta had a different perspective. Having been placed in the uncomfortable position of dealing with a crew of miscreants, he was inclined to release the men. He had been in touch with the Crown Advocate to consult on the legality of detaining them and concluded that, while the problem between Pilotti and Zachariah needed to be sorted out, they should nevertheless set at liberty the foreign men *as being liable to no criminal proceedings in the British dominions'*.

At a higher level of authority, however, Rear-Admiral Codrington was utterly incensed, and he wrote an impassioned letter to the Governor's secretary: *'After maturely reconsidering the subject, I regret that I cannot join in the conclusion that the persons should be released without trial'*. He brought up the subject of force being used, but homed in on the issue which really vexed him. This was a *British* ship, not only *'navigating under the control of those who forcefully seized and abstracted her from the owners'*, but then *'committing a piratical act under cover of the British flag'*. He went on: *'the purity of our national flag is of supreme importance'* and Britain needed to do *'her best to prevent her flag from being prostituted for illegal purposes'*.

In his mind, this was a double crime: piracy was bad enough, but honour was doubly at stake with the 'flag-prostitution'. Retribution was essential, and in his letter to the Governor of Malta he made it perfectly clear that he was in favour of prosecuting *all* the men, ending his missive by appealing to the Government back home.

The battle between diplomat and rear-admiral raged on, each attempting to trump the other by applying to a higher authority. The Governor of Malta did as Codrington had ordered; he sent all the relevant papers to Her Majesty's Government for a final decision, but he made very sure that his own views were clear, convincingly slanting the argument as he saw it from a liberal perspective. His accompanying letter to the Colonial Office outlined the reasons why taking all the passengers to trial would be futile under the complicated circumstances: (a) the seizure was in a foreign port (Genoa); (b) the capture had been in a different foreign port (Messina); (c) there was the suspicion that the master had 'consented to, or connived at, the departure from Genoa without him', and (d) the prisoners were 'much aggravated by the political object for which the seizure had taken place, and by the present state of the political affairs in Europe'. He felt prosecution would be a waste of time and in any case, *he* was the one left with the prisoners in the meantime. Clearly, here was a man who didn't need all these complications; why not simply set the men free and focus on the ring-leaders?

The letter did the trick, and the Colonial Office agreed with the Governor of Malta. A letter from Lord Wodehouse to the Admiralty confirmed that instructions to release the prisoners would be sent at once. They were, and the matter was resolved – but Codrington remained outraged.

Zachariah, being far more concerned with his *Orwell* than with revenge, contacted the British Ambassador in Turin, Sir James Hudson, immediately after the piratical seizure to seek help. Hudson, remember, was pro-unification, and Zachariah suspected the Ambassador of dragging his feet for diplomatic reasons. He then wrote requesting a bit of Foreign Office leverage. Zachariah's letter in September 1860 was curt and to the point: *'I have the honour to request that you favour me with a letter to the British Ambassador at Turin, that his Excellency may assist my agent, Mr Henry Bake [...] who holds my power of attorney in all matters concerning the vessel 'Orwell' '.* He spelt out why pressure now needed to be put on the Ambassador on his behalf, and urged the Foreign Office to get on with it urgently: *'as the monetary interest to me now extends to some thousands of pounds, I should feel greatly obliged if you would favour me with the letter in question [...] without reference to the Foreign Minister [Ld Russell], who, I learn, is absent in Scotland'.* Clearly, it was useful to have friends in high places (even if some of them might be shooting in Scotland at the time) and to know the protocols of whom to contact about which matters.

Nevertheless, time dragged on, and there was no sign of recompense – only promises. By early 1861, Italy was settling down after the fighting, and most regions were now united. Garibaldi, having achieved his aim of linking all the regions under one flag, had handed over his dictatorial power to King Victor Emmanuel to form a government for the whole of Italy. However, with territory and power came responsibility, and the new king had to take on the liabilities of the provinces as well. He appointed his Prime Minister to carry out the tricky job of adjudicating these, but it was extremely challenging trying to sort out the aftermath of the *Risorgimento*, as everyone was pushing for a result.

Zachariah's case was luckily supported by plenty of evidential and legal documentation, and in Naples in May 1861 a tribunal agreed that he *was* due compensation for the loss of the *Orwell* and associated expenses, as the memo from Fabrizzi, the Military Commander of Messina, notes:

'Dichiaro che assumo officiale responsibilitata a guarantire il contratto stipulato dallo stesso Signor Pilotti col proprietatario Signor N. Bake'
[I declare that I take upon myself the official responsibility of guaranteeing the contract made by the Signor Pilotti with the owner [sic] Mr N Bake.]

This was the unambiguous declaration of rock-solid evidence that upheld Zachariah's case. All the same, still no money materialised and Zachariah was forced to exert even more pressure on his influential contacts. On his behalf, a question was asked in the House of Lords by the Earl of Malmesbury (recently in the Foreign Office), who asked Lord

Wodehouse (Under-Secretary of State for Foreign Affairs) what was being done to recompense Pearson. Wodehouse replied that *'Mr Pearson, the owner, has applied to the Foreign Office; and that instructions had been to Sir James Hudson to afford him all the assistance he could properly give'*. This was a partial success for Zachariah – with endorsement from the House of Lords, he had now got an even higher authority to lean on the reluctant Ambassador to push the Italians for his compensation.

In the meantime Bake, the loyal employee, was tireless in fighting Zachariah's corner: *'Mr Pearson feels he has double difficulty from the fact that more than one British Government official has insinuated that there was collusion between the captain and the charterer. This I emphatically and most unqualifiedly deny.'*

Despite all the solid evidence and friends in high places, the outcome for Zachariah was not good. Although the King of Italy had now taken over the liabilities of Garibaldi, and although recompense to him had officially been agreed, the Prime Minister charged with sorting out all these claims died within weeks of taking up office, and Zachariah never received his compensation. He calculated that he was £7,500 out of pocket – £5,000 being the value of the *Orwell*, and £2,500 being the expenses that the Italian Government still owed him.

To wrap up the remaining loose ends of this complex episode of Zachariah's life, Captain Sutton, with the cloud of uncertainty hanging over him, had undergone a tribunal before a Naval Court of Inquiry at Genoa only a few days after the seizure, and was declared innocent of complicity in the seizure of the *Orwell*. Nevertheless, despite his post hoc exoneration, the initial rumours about 'conniving' still echoed around the corridors of Whitehall, and were repeated whenever the conditions of the seizure were discussed. And discussion there was, for although the Navy was mainly concerned with what to do with the prisoners and how to get

Zachariah compensated, the whole question of the 'sacking of Monte Cristo' was much talked about.

Mr Watson-Taylor, the aggrieved owner of Monte Cristo, had also used his Whitehall contacts, and he leant on Her Majesty's Government to intervene on his behalf. He sought compensation from the newly-formed Italian Government for damages sustained to his property resulting from the seizure of the *Orwell*. Although, like Zachariah, he ultimately failed in this quest, his efforts stimulated a high-profile debate in the House of Commons on 13th June 1862. The great and the good were all involved, including, among others, Prime Minister Palmerston, Chancellor Gladstone, and Leader of the Opposition Disraeli. There was a strong sentiment of 'civis Romanum sum' [I am a Roman citizen] – the maxim that if a foreign power had mistreated a citizen, that person had a right to be protected by his own state. The circumstances of the *Orwell*'s misfortunes got a good airing, and Rear-Admiral Codrington's ferociously patriotic defence of the Honour of the British Flag drew particular praise in the Commons.

The debate was impassioned, and the views, as ever, reflected both personal and party allegiances. In his summary, Palmerston made the extraordinary suggestion that Watson-Taylor should perhaps have applied to the *Orwell*'s owner for compensation, on the grounds that if Zachariah had not chartered his vessel to Garibaldi in the first place, the whole incident could not possibly have happened! All the same, he ended his speech by agreeing to make friendly approaches to the new King of Italy on Watson-Taylor's behalf; in the event, however, even if he did so, nothing ever came of his efforts.

This ends the story of the *Orwell*, a British ship, chartered to a revolutionary cause, hijacked by the revolutionaries, taken on a piratical tour of islands, and finally recaptured by the British Navy. The repercussions echoed around Whitehall, the Mediterranean and Hull. Both Watson-Taylor and Pearson were the losers, and the case was prominently reported. It actually became rather notorious at the time, even being tangentially referred to the following month in a letter to Charles Darwin. The rights and wrongs and the derring-do of the affair had certainly struck a chord with the cognoscenti of the day.

No doubt the men who were released from the *Orwell* in Malta eventually found their way to join Garibaldi's forces, and three years later Garibaldi himself came to England to express his personal thanks to the British for their unofficial support. And perhaps Zachariah, licking his wounds in later years, might have satisfied himself that he had contributed in a tiny way towards the successful unification of Italy.

This incident, whilst being a sideshow in the story of Zachariah, demonstrates how geopolitical upheavals can shape the fortunes of those who stand on the sidelines, with little or no nod to fairness – hardly surprising under the circumstances, as Disraeli's comment summarising the Parliamentary debate succinctly points out:

> *When a country is in a state of revolution, everything relating to it is political, and it is ridiculous and mere pedantry to talk about having recourse to courts of justice.*

8

The Greek connection

Zachariah's Italian adventure needs to be seen in the context of the other things going on in his life at that period. The timing of any hijack could never be ideal, but this one came at a particularly inopportune moment. Zachariah had received the telegram about Pilotti making off with the *Orwell* on 23rd August 1860 – only three days before laying the foundation stone of the chapel, and four days before the Colossal Fete for Pearson Park. Just as he needed to be putting together some statesman-like speeches in preparation for his high profile roles in the imminent festivities, his focus was derailed by Garibaldi. We know little about Zachariah's ability to handle stress, but this must have tested him sorely. With his moral sense of right and wrong, he was incensed by anything that seemed to him to be unfair. He had hired out his ship in good faith to help a just cause, but when things went wrong no-one honoured the contract. He was no stranger to losing vessels, but this one fell into a different category of loss: people had broken their word.

The Italian affair, though, was merely the first of the international exchanges that Zachariah fell foul of, although this part of his story starts on the other side of Europe four years earlier, just as the Crimean War was ending in 1856. The war had taken a heavy toll on the finances of Greece, resulting in a knock-on effect on the fortunes of some of the Greeks trading in the City of London. Greek merchants were borrowing heavily and trading increasingly in paper receipts in an effort to stay solvent. These were often not honoured, though, and the practice soon tarred all their compatriots with the same brush: every Greek was generally considered to have a murky reputation, regardless of whether or not he deserved it. One such merchant was a flamboyant shipowner called Stefanos Xenos, and it was he who unwittingly contributed to Zachariah's downfall.

Stefanos Xenos, the colourful shipowner who had mortgaged a number of his vessels to the bank Overend, Gurney & Co. after the Crimean War. It was six of these steamers that Zachariah was sweet-talked by the bank into buying on credit, even though he did not have enough work for them – and this marked the beginning of his downfall.

An understanding of how business was conducted will help to contextualise the next phase in the Rise and Fall of Zachariah Pearson. A frequent form of currency was the 'Bill of Exchange', a sort of fixed-term IOU which could not only be renewed, accumulating interest each time, but which could also be sold on to a third party (or fourth, or fifth). These pieces of paper were often circulated so many times that the value of the original merchandise bore little relation to the inflated selling price of the bills. If the holders of these devalued 'bills of accommodation' were unshackled by delicate consciences, they might sell the bills on, knowing they were virtually worthless. Financially savvy dealers such as bankers and financiers were keen not to retain potential liabilities, and they aimed to shift such bills out of their own portfolios, preferably at a profit. But to do this, they needed to know how safe the bills were – in other words, to understand how solid and reliable the holders were. One's livelihood depended on this; intelligence was all.

Acquiring the relevant intelligence, though, was an increasingly specialised activity in the hothouse climate of the great London 'discount market', as it was known, and those who, like Zachariah, were left on the outside were readily taken advantage of. By virtue of being Greek, Stefanos Xenos was regarded with some suspicion in financial circles. He was a colourful figure, who owned the Greek and Oriental Steam Navigation Company, but for various financial reasons he had mortgaged a number of his steam ships to the eminent city bankers, Overend, Gurney and Co. Although this bank's spectacular crash and trial only five years later was to rock the City of London to its core, a feat not to be repeated until the Northern Rock crisis of 2007, back in 1860 this firm was still regarded with the utmost respect, its sound Quaker credentials belying the questionable morals of some of its principal players.

Now, fearing for their security, the bank wished to limit their risk of holding a number of ships mortgaged to them from a Greek; the question was, how could they ensure the safety of their investment? The answer was: find a buyer gullible enough, and pass the risk on to him. They needed someone safe and well-known, and Zachariah Pearson fitted their requirements perfectly. He was a renowned figure of impeccable reputation in the shipping business, and what's more he was crucially naïve in the machinations of the banking world. Zachariah would be ideal for their manipulative purposes. The next question was how to lure and land their squeaky-clean fish with the right bait and enough skill.

Xenos tells the story in his 1869 autobiography, *Depredations*, and describes how the labyrinthine financial transactions of Overend, Gurney & Co. completely lost him in their complexity, and had him questioning the integrity of the processes of banking and lending. And he paints a vivid picture of how *'poor Zachariah'* was stitched up in a sort of internal pincer movement.

Overend, Gurney & Co. had certainly done their homework to target the right prey. They knew that Zachariah paid his debts: they had already lent him money to buy the vessel *Cheronese*, which was now paid off. So in April 1860 they set out to persuade him to buy on credit six of Xenos' largest steamers – but Zachariah, whilst being canny in the world of shipping, proved to be no match for the wily bankers. Xenos relates how Zachariah told him the story of how he got ensnared in the trap of the London bankers, 'the great capitalists':

> *Knowing that his credit was good at Hull, with Smith Brothers, his bankers, the great capitalists sent for and asked him to buy a portion of my [Xenos'] fleet.*
> *"I cannot," said Mr Pearson.*
> *"You will not be asked to pay any cash," said Edwards; "you need only give your acceptances."*
> *"I am already overworked," said Pearson [fully committed financially].*
> *"It will be a good thing for you, Pearson," said the official assignee.*
> *Mr Pearson still hesitated. In fact, he did not like to enter into the transaction at all.*

Zachariah was nevertheless sweet-talked into agreeing, and marched off by Edwards, the main procurer for the bank, to see the bank's solicitor. But before he reached the lawyer's office his misgivings apparently got the better of him, and he told them he had changed his mind. Edwards, though, desperate not to lose his prey, managed to persuade Zachariah to return with him to the bank in Lombard Street, where Mr Gurney himself would talk with him. Once in the lair, the full charm offensive was switched on, the trap was sprung, and flattery-with-sweeteners won the day. Gurney gave Zachariah a cheque on the spot for £500 and his word of honour that all would be well. The deed was done. Zachariah signed the mortgages and accepted the bills – which immediately entered the discount market.

Apparently he was still filled with misgivings and a sense of doom: in Xenos' words:

"This is my death-warrant," sighed poor Pearson.
"Not at all. It's all right," said Edwards, his smooth face irradiated with a smile.

Even allowing for the melodramatic dialogue with which the Greek brings his narrative alive, this was nonetheless a reported conversation between Xenos and Zachariah. To add insult to injury, Edwards then extorted a dealer's fee. He

called into play all his eloquence and logic to prove to Zachariah Pearson that his share of the transaction was worth £1000. Poor Zachariah Pearson! I have it from his own lips that the same day he gave Edwards a cheque for £1000, double the bonus he himself had received. Verily, verily, Mr Edwards knew how to trim his sails so as to catch the wind from whatever point it blew.

Zachariah, without the benefit of insider knowledge of how the discount market might entrap him, had been cynically seduced into buying six large steamers on credit for £80,000 – and then paying heavily for the privilege. What did he plan to use them for? At that time he did not have enough trade to employ an extra fleet of six ships. Presumably, with his track record of successful shipping business, and his continuing 'Midas touch', he optimistically felt that he would be able to put them good use somehow, buying and selling even more cargoes around the world – but precisely *how* was not yet clear to him. Nevertheless, he had a huge amount invested in them now, and they needed to earn their keep – make sufficient money for the firm of Z. C. Pearson, Coleman and Co. to discharge its massive mortgage.

But now there was a new glitch: James Coleman, his partner. Zachariah was clearly the senior of the two, but what was James doing while his business colleague was in London making the worst decision of his life, and getting stitched up? Was he consulted? Did James, in fact, have any say whatsoever in their firm taking on such a huge debt? There are no records, only conjecture, but it seems reasonable to assume they had a considerable 'difference of opinion' on the matter, for this was the moment that James decided to break their partnership and bale out.

We know that they were still in partnership on 23rd April 1860, because a letter of that date to Xenos is signed *Z. C. Pearson, Coleman and Co.,* but only six weeks later their partnership was 'dissolved by mutual consent', as announced in *The London Gazette* of 29th June:

Notice is hereby given, that the Copartnership heretofore subsisting between us the undersigned, Zachariah Charles Pearson and James Coleman, carrying on business at Kingston-upon-Hull, and in the city of London, and elsewhere, as Merchants and Ship Owners, Ship Brokers, and General Commission Agents, under the style or firm of Z. C. Pearson, Coleman, and Co, has been dissolved by mutual consent, from the 9th day of June, 1860;

and that in future the said business will be carried on by the said Zachariah Charles Pearson, by whom all debts due to or owing by the said copartnership will be paid.
As witness our hands this 22nd day of June, 1860.
Z. C. Pearson
J. Coleman

Perhaps James left for pragmatic purposes, foreseeing that Zachariah was heading for the rocks with this massive debt? Or maybe he thought his brother-in-law had completely lost his usually-sound judgement? Or he may have been genuinely angry with Zachariah for going ahead in London without his agreement? Possibly all of the above. Whatever the reason, split they did, Zachariah buying out James for a quarter of the business. We have no way of telling, but it may well have been James who ensured, with considerable insight, that the clause about Zachariah being responsible for all debts was inserted into the official notice. The writing on the wall was more visible to him than to Zachariah.

It would be interesting to know how the repercussions affected the family. There would surely have been shock waves – this was, after all, a public declaration of division inside the family: his wife's brother had visibly distanced himself. The waves created by this split, though, were as nothing compared with the ensuing tsunami when the 'Greek Connection' was disastrously followed by the start of the American Civil War.

Apart from his unfortunate encounter with the warring Italians, most of Zachariah's entrepreneurial ventures had hitherto been successful. Whether this had led him to believe in his own invulnerability, or whether his customary sound judgement abandoned him, we shall never know. Zachariah, remember, was one of life's 'nice fellows', and had operated until now in the trusting environment of gentlemen's agreements. But this transaction with Overend,

Gurney & Co. fell into a different category, and it turned out to be only the first of two outrageous risks that he took. Having bought on credit more ships than he needed or could afford, he then did something with them that was, in the words of the Bankruptcy Commissioner, incredibly 'rash and hazardous'. One might imagine that, had it not been for yet another war, he could have survived the first of these ill-judged decisions, but the Americans went into battle against each other just at the right (well, wrong, as it happened) moment for Zachariah to play a pivotal role with his newly acquired vessels.

As soon as he had made the decision to buy the surplus steamers, his fate was sealed, although he did not yet know it. At this stage, life still looked good. He started a chapel, donated a park, and completed his highly-successful year as Mayor. Twelve months later he was re-elected to the Mayoralty in the autumn of 1861, embarking upon – but not completing – his second term of office.

9

Zachariah's nemesis – the American Civil War

Now the tale acquires an even more international dimension – and the second incredible risk. In a curious juxtaposition of circumstances, just at the critical time when Zachariah found himself with more ships than he knew what to do with, the Southern American States decided they had had enough of rule from Washington. They had grown rich by exporting their plentiful supply of cotton to Europe, and by 1860 as much as 78% of this cotton crop was coming to England to supply her highly successful textile industry. Cotton had brought huge wealth to the Southern States but they had few other resources, relying on the Northern States to supply them with all their other goods. In return, they paid taxes to the North.

While the causes of the American Civil War are complex and much debated, the key issue at the time was the amount of this cotton tax levied by Washington. With the cotton trade worth $2.6 million by 1860, (about $75 million today) the Federal government could see the plantation owners getting ever richer, and they wanted a slice of this, which they took by steeply raising the taxes. The South was outraged. They felt the North was getting far too greedy.

A second factor was slavery, although this was to emerge more visibly as a critical issue later on in the war, when Abraham Lincoln needed to win the hearts and minds of the English. While England had abolished slavery in 1833, America was ambivalent, and had not yet passed anti-slavery laws. Most of the plantations were in the South where the climate was better for the cotton plant, but owners here depended on slaves to cultivate and harvest their crops. Less cotton was grown in the North, which in any case had plenty of alternative resources. As a result, the growing anti-slavery movement in the North did not extend to the South. Cotton was all these folk had and, while the world needed their cotton, they needed their workforce.

It all came to a head when seven of the Southern states decided that independence from the greedy North would be the best way forward. If they broke away, they would be able to keep both their taxes and their slaves, and therefore their comfortable way of life. The Declaration of Independence had, on paper at least, given states the right to secede, but President Lincoln was afraid of fragmentation, and so he opposed the South splitting away. Peace negotiations were attempted but failed, and in 1861 the government of the Confederate States of America was set up under Jefferson Davis. Abraham Lincoln accordingly strengthened his army, requiring 75,000 men from the other states to join him. This was the last straw for some of the Southern states who could not stomach fighting against their neighbours, and now another four states joined the initial seven. The Confederacy now consisted of eleven states.

In order to make the South see sense, President Lincoln cut off their supplies, both by land and sea, in the hope that, without their living essentials, they would have to capitulate. As well as denying access by rail and road, the Southern ports were also blockaded – ships were unable either to enter or to leave their ports. The Confederates, in desperate need of everyday goods, were in dire straits, and they needed allies. Knowing how much the English economy relied on their raw cotton, they restricted the supply, and even burnt some of their own cotton stores, hoping to encourage the English to enter the war on their side. But this ruse backfired; there had been a bumper crop in 1860, and the English mills had stockpiled cotton. In 1861, though, the cotton yield was half the size of the previous year's crop, and cotton production dropped even further when plantation owners started to use their land to grow food crops to feed their families. With the reduced cotton supply, mill-owners in England were getting jumpy. Operatives were already being laid off, and they could see a time when production would completely grind to a halt – which in 1862 it did.

Alternative sources of cotton were sought so that mills could be kept open. Cotton from India was a theoretical possibility, but there was not enough of it; the supply line was not fast enough to meet the need. So with English cotton merchants looking for ways of obtaining a cotton supply, and the Confederates having a desperate need for imported goods, the risk-taking shipowners of Britain entered the gambling den of the American Civil War with zeal. The Confederates were grateful enough to pay well over the odds for cargoes of desirable goods, and huge profits were available to those vessels which got through to Southern ports.

In the meantime, back home the 'cotton famine' was starting to bite. One fifth of the entire population of England was dependent on cotton, and the local papers were getting gloomier in each edition: *'The suffering is real, widespread, undeserved and likely to be long-enduring'*. They gave horrifying descriptions of life on the street in a society without a social services safety net; the work-less had to resort to begging, prostitution or living in the workhouse. In the words of one letter to the *Hull Times* in October 1862, soliciting donations for the distressed cotton operatives, *'Winter, cheerless and cold, is marching on [...] the little ones cry for bread'*.

When things became really grim, the government put in place a help-programme to support the mill-workers in Lancashire, where most of the cotton was processed.

The few east coast mills, though, such as Hull's two, the Kingston Cotton Mill and the New Hull Flax Mill, were outside this scheme and received no government support. These mills were situated in the area where Zachariah had grown up. And now, with 1,500 people starving on Hull's streets, Zachariah was in his second term as Mayor – what could he do?

The Kingston Cotton Mill in Cumberland Street, one of the two cotton mills in Hull in 1861 when the American Civil War started. When they ran out of cotton owing to the blockade of the Confederate ports they had to close, forcing mill workers, many of them women and children, onto the streets or into the workhouse.

There was one obvious answer. He had spare vessels, the need to restore a cotton supply to the mills, an adventurous spirit and a nose for business. He would, of course, send some of his ships across the Atlantic laden with goods desperately needed by the Confederates, sell his cargoes, buy cotton bales, load his vessels, then bring these back to Hull and restart the mills. And this was how Zachariah, savvy at trading around the world, but naïve in the art of blockade-running, entered the American Civil War – his nemesis.

The key threat was President Lincoln's blockading squadron, the naval ships which were determined to stop the Confederates from topping up on essential supplies from overseas. These Union 'blockaders' patrolled the coast line of the Southern States, resolved on preventing any vessels with cargoes of supplies for the enemy from entering Southern ports – or leaving, laden with cotton to sell across the Atlantic.

The earliest English shipowners to try their luck in getting through the blockades with their 'blockade-runners' met with considerable success, with eight out of nine reaching port in 1861. Tales of triumph and profit circulated. Merchants were buying cotton really cheaply in the South, and selling it at vast return in England. The lure of such fortunes outweighed the risk of capture and it also encouraged more shipowners to do the same. With profits of up to £30,000 in each direction, it was reckoned that a shipowner could afford to lose a vessel to President Lincoln's navy after two successful trips.

Encouraged by these tales of derring-do and success in the early stages of the war, Zachariah entered the 'business' late in 1861. No doubt his motive was a double one: in addition to restarting the cotton mills, he must have hoped for a decent profit. His was, after all, an *entrepreneurial philanthropy*. He was a merchant and it was making money that allowed him to be generous with it.

Once the decision was made, anything that the South might need, Zachariah attempted to supply, and with his broad experience of selling goods world-wide he was well-positioned to buy the right cargoes and dispatch them to Charleston, Savannah, Wilmington, New Orleans or Mobile. Provisions needed by the South fell into several categories. Plantation owners and their families had been accustomed to living well, so doing without champagne, brandy, perfume and lace represented real hardship, and these luxury products were very popular imports during the early stages of the war. But the Confederates were also deprived of everyday commodities like clothing, iron, salt and tools, previously supplied by the North, so any of these items that they could buy from abroad would be most welcome.

Another group of desperately-needed goods was arms and gunpowder, as the Confederate government could not now manage to supply its soldiers with the artillery needed to defend their territory. And as the conflict progressed, and injuries mounted up, the emphasis shifted again. Luxuries now seemed less imperative, but pharmaceutical products were increasingly needed. The broken supply chain from the North made the situation increasingly serious. Deprived of drugs such as morphine and chloroform, limbs had to be amputated without anaesthetic, and the annals are full of grisly descriptions of primitive and agonising field treatments.

As ever in history, what was a tragedy to one nation was an opportunity to another. The entrepreneurial saw their chance. Zachariah was not one to let such a challenge go.

Needless to say, there was no official encouragement by the British government in this enterprise. Britain did not wish to be regarded as supporting one side or the other in America's own civil war, so a diplomatically neutral stance was taken by Queen Victoria and Parliament towards the American 'War Between the States'. It was made perfectly clear that neither help nor sympathy would be forthcoming, either to the warring parties themselves, or to any merchant who attempted to break the blockade by selling arms. That was the official stance.

Unofficially, though, despite being anti-slavery, Prime Minister Palmerston was pro-Confederate. He feared that the American nation, fast growing in power, might eventually threaten the British Empire, and he felt that

Britain's best commercial future lay in a secessionist South. If slavery were ever brought into the equation, it was subsumed to the commercial imperative to acquire cotton to supply Britain's main industry; it is easy to be blind to something one does not wish to confront. We have no way of knowing what Zachariah's personal views were but with his firm Methodist values and his principles of fairness he would almost certainly have been anti-slavery, had it surfaced as an issue – which it should have done, cotton being produced through slavery. But there were other more urgent and important national concerns at the time, and there is no evidence of pro-slavery sentiment in the press at the start of the war.

There were, on the other hand, many column inches devoted to admiration for entrepreneurs such as Zachariah. The public desperately needed their jobs in the mills back, and they hailed as heroes the men who took the risk of running the blockade to bring cotton back to England and keep the economy going. With the destitute on the streets, the cotton famine hardship had fanned the flames of British opinion, and leading articles in newspapers in the early stages of the war show that the majority of public sympathy lay with the Confederates. It has ever been a very British trait to empathise with the underdog, and the average man-in-the-street did not like to see Washington being the bully.

As the war dragged on, though, President Lincoln became increasingly disturbed by this informal pro-Confederacy stance adopted by the British press. He needed to gain support for his war, and so eventually he was moved to mount a charm offensive in England. He tapped into slavery as a weapon – this would surely sway opinion in liberal England with her anti-slavery laws? His tactics worked. Slave awareness grew, opinion gradually changed, and the press columns in the second part of the war veered towards support for the North.

Returning to the start of the war, there were practical challenges to be surmounted in the blockade-running business. Buying appropriate goods to sell to the Confederates was the easy part of the transaction. The real challenge was the cat-and-mouse game: getting ships past Lincoln's blockading squadron into port, and then out again loaded with cotton. Dodging the blockade was paramount. No shipowner wanted to see his vessel captured, his cargo confiscated and his ship then turned into one of Lincoln's patrolling vessels. With a coastline of 3,600 miles to guard, the odds were initially stacked on the side of the blockade-runners, but as the war progressed the blockading fleet grew bigger and more skilful, and the odds shortened. By the end of the war a blockade-runner stood a 50:50 chance of being caught. One of the challenges was unequal fire-power: while vessels belonging to the American navy were fully armed, blockade-runners, being merchant ships, were unarmed. They could not return fire. Their only strategy was to outwit the Union navy by not being seen. If they *were* seen, however, the Union ships had the clear advantage.

The blockade-runners' art of deception evolved as the war progressed. One ruse used was to load the ships' cargoes carefully, disguising the fact that they contained contraband goods such as armaments (enigmatically labelled 'hardware' on the bill of lading). This was in contravention of the neutral position declared, and so the legitimate goods, such as clothing or brandy, were arranged on top. But the Americans had spies – the consuls positioned around the coast of England – who kept a keen eye on what the ships were loading, and reported all the details to their masters in Washington. Skilful deception was needed, involving feint and counter feint. Sometimes a ship's paperwork disguised the real destination in order to confuse the spies, and occasionally even the names of vessels might be changed as well. The outcome was the same, though: all the shipping intelligence gleaned by the spies – name, description, cargo and likely destination – was passed on to Washington, whose ships would be on the alert, poised to intercept the blockade-runners before they could slip into port and discharge their cargo.

With luck on their side, the US Navy would be able to capture a British ship either entering or leaving a port, and this blockade-runner would later morph into a blockader. This added insult to injury. In its new livery, the British vessel would then have to go to work on behalf of President Lincoln, capturing other British ships. There were huge incentives for a US vessel to capture a blockade-runner. If successful, and especially if she was carrying a valuable cargo, the captain and crew stood to gain vast rewards from the Prize Courts. But this also meant that the crews of naval vessels were effectively competing against each other for the 'prizes', and the records are full of conflicting accounts of who was where, who fired and made a vessel alter course, who chased, and how the British vessel was finally apprehended. These narratives are heartfelt: a captain who could prove that his was the sole ship to capture the blockade-runner would get a far larger pay-out than one who was obliged to share the booty with another ship's crew.

If capture was impossible, the Union navy would at least try to prevent the Confederates getting their hands on the cargo, and so a second-best option was to sink the ship, together with its cargo. Complete defeat, of course, was allowing a ship into port to trade goods, and the Union ships and their captains were severely held to account for such carelessness.

With a finite chance of being captured, one might wonder why any seaman would want to work on a vessel that was heading into a wartime situation – albeit unofficially. But crew members were commonly paid three times more than they would earn for a regular job, and with the incentive of a possible bonus for making a successful run, it certainly appealed to a certain category of man. For some, the risk and the thrill of the chase were sufficient in themselves: in the words of Thomas Taylor, an English captain who sailed in and out of Wilmington many times during the Civil War, *'Hunting, pig-sticking, steeple-chasing, big-game shooting, polo – I have done a little of each – all have their thrilling moments, but none can approach running a blockade'.* Shipowners, of course, employed the most skilful men they could get to lead their vessels through the hazards of the Confederate coastline, and the *crème de la crème* were experienced officers on leave from the Royal Navy; they could command huge payments.

Once Abraham Lincoln had sealed off access to and from the Southern States, the lifeline for the Confederates became the largely British ships that could break through the naval blockade and get into one of these ports with their cargoes of luxury goods, medications, clothing and arms. A good deal of subterfuge was needed, and the islands of Bermuda and The Bahamas were critical, both for their intelligence and their transshipping. Zachariah had agents in Bermuda.

From the perspective of those masterminding the blockade-runners, intelligence was all. They needed to know which ports were safe to enter at any given time, and where the Union ships were. Without today's communication systems, they relied on local intelligence via their own spies, particularly in the British outposts of Bermuda and The Bahamas. While the latter islands lie quite close to the Florida coast, Bermuda lies north east of them, so they were both ideal for transshipment: the transatlantic vessels could off-load their cargos here into warehouses until they could be loaded onto ships more suitable for slipping unseen into Confederate ports at the right time.

An industrious trade sprang up in handling cargoes – expenses, of course, being paid by the shipowners. The islands were notoriously pro-Confederate, and became a busy centre for intelligence, with agents passing on up-to-date observations from east-bound vessels about the latest coastal activities of Lincoln's navy, and advising how individual ships might change destination to a more suitable port. In these hitherto-sleepy islands, a profitable industry now sprang up around the servicing of blockade-running: refuelling, transshipping cargoes, and generally providing intelligence. America's Civil War represented boom-time for the inhabitants of Bermuda and The Bahamas.

Zachariah, too, had agents in Bermuda, one of whom was an Edward Coleman, though it is not clear which Edward this was. Father-in-law Edward had been holding up the antipodean end of the Intercolonial Royal Mail Steam Packet Company, though it is perfectly feasible that, once he had got the business in The Colonies organised, he was shipped over to Bermuda to handle Zachariah's blockade-running business there. While it is just possible that the Edward in Bermuda was the younger brother of Mary Ann and James, another of Zachariah's brothers-in-law, given the complex and secretive nature of the Bermudan job, it is more likely that the more experienced older Edward would have been used to manage the delicate negotiations required.

Another agent that Zachariah used was John T. Bourne, whose prolific correspondence has survived for publication. His letters give us an insight into how the island business worked. Here, he is writing directly and cautiously to Zachariah:

St. George, 23 April 1862
Zachariah C. Pearson and Co, London
Gentlemen:- Enclosed I beg leave to hand you copy of disbursements of steamer Stettin Capt Johnston who arrived into port this port in want of coals she left this morning all well for her destination.
John T. Bourne

He was sending an expenses invoice for getting Zachariah's steamer *Stettin* re-fuelled – and at the same time being enigmatically cagy about where she was heading. 'Her destination' was actually Charleston, South Carolina, but Bourne was careful not to state this in case the information got into the wrong hands, so a neutrally-worded phrase imparted to Zachariah the reassuring message that she was safely *en route* as intended.

Zachariah was naïvely enthusiastic about his new enterprise, sending ten vessels over several months loaded with cargoes to the Southern ports – but all was to end in tears. Was he simply unlucky? Or did a combination of poor judgement, bad luck and inadequate equipment all conspire to bring him to his knees? He had ventured into blockade-running opportunistically, using the vessels he had to hand. Perhaps he didn't realise what he was getting into. While he knew all about what made a good cargo vessel, the extra requirements of a successful blockade-runner were probably obscure to him. There's no way of knowing how much homework he did, and he no longer had a business partner with whom to plan strategically and make decisions. Was it his imperative to put his newly-acquired, unused Greek ships to work? Or was he so desperate to restock the cotton mills that he could ignore the risk? Or was he keen to capture a slice of the huge rewards sitting there for the taking? Or maybe his love of adventure got the better of him? Possibly any or all of the above.

In any event, the vessels in Zachariah's existing fleet were not cut out for the task; they were cumbersome, slow, and drew too much water. They were fine for the main transatlantic run, with which Zachariah and his captains were already familiar, but they were less suitable for that tricky last leg of secretly sneaking into port. The navigational criteria for successful merchant trading were quite different from those needed to dodge Federal blockaders in coastal shallows.

Ideal 'designer' blockade-runners were sleek, grey, and lay low in the water so they were virtually invisible when the look-outs on the Union ships scanned the horizon. Their shallow draft meant they were less likely to get stranded on the coastal sandbanks, or shoals. They were longer and narrower than the conventional steamer, so they could put on a spurt of speed when they needed to, out-running the blockaders. And so as not to advertise their presence with plumes of black smoke, they burnt anthracite, a virtually smokeless fuel. The more 'bespoke' vessels were designed with a telescopic funnel which could be collapsed when necessary to escape detection close in to port. For the final critical approach to the port, some ships even had an adaptation which allowed steam to be discharged invisibly under water. When they 'ran in' on a dark, moonless night, such vessels stood a very good chance of escaping detection on their approach to the port.

Although Zachariah commissioned one vessel especially for the purpose, there is little evidence that he made many modifications to his commercial ships apart from getting them painted 'Atlantic grey'. This would have been fine if they had merely plied between Britain and the islands, and if the cargoes had been transferred to more specialised blockade-runners for the final leg of the journey, but there is no evidence of this happening. Bourne's letter made it clear that the *Stettin*, having crossed the Atlantic, was continuing to carry her cargo herself onwards from Bermuda to the coast – and the information about his other vessels led to the same conclusion: Zachariah's cargoes were intended to arrive at Confederate ports in the ships they had left Britain in. But these vessels simply did not cut the mustard; they would probably be easier to spot than the bespoke models – and so, disastrously, they were.

In deference to the official neutrality between America and Britain, Abraham Lincoln spelled out what would happen if any vessel tried to enter or leave the blockaded ports. In his proclamation of 19th April 1861, he said that such ships would first be *'warned by the Commander of one of the blockading vessels, who will endorse on her register the fact and date of such warning, and if the same vessel shall again attempt to enter or leave the blockaded port, she will be captured'*. In other words, ships supplying Confederates with goods would be given a sporting chance. But if handing out a public warning sounds too gentlemanly to be true in a war situation, so it proved as, unsurprisingly under the circumstances, none of the accounts of capture indicate any such polite warning. In any case, captains and crews of blockaders were only too keen to reap their due rewards: they would gain nothing by warning off a ship that was clearly up to no good.

In the event, a good number of British ships did succeed in getting through the blockade with essential supplies, and by doing so they managed to keep the South going; they were the 'Lifeline of the Confederacy'. And it was this success, together with the public pro-Confederacy stance in England, that made President Lincoln press the anti-slavery button half way through the war to change the mood of sympathy in England.

No doubt Zachariah would like a veil drawn over the next chapter, as in an extremely short space of time his entire empire collapsed, and his vessels were either sunk, captured, or sold off with their cargoes to settle financial claims against him. His trail of disasters can be pieced together from the many volumes of 'Official Records' of the progress of the War Between the States. This meticulous source comprises verbatim letters between the US Navy HQ and their ships' captains giving, in effect, a detailed blow-by-blow record of what was happening at the time. It is equivalent in today's terms of having access to personal emails, texts and phone calls. It describes how vessels were captured or sunk, how they were adapted for the task of blockade-running, and what their cargoes were. It shows how captains thought, and it describes their strategies – and the repercussions from Washington when they got it wrong.

It is from this detailed record that we can piece together the episodes which constitute Zachariah's complete downfall. The irony is that if Zachariah had been successful, very little evidence would exist of his role in the American Civil War…

10

Thrills and spills: Zachariah's blockade-runners

Zachariah has been described as being one of the most unlucky shipowners in the blockade-running business. Six of his vessels were captured by Abraham Lincoln's navy, one was sunk after coming under Federal attack, and three were sold on behalf of the creditors after Zachariah had ceased trading in August 1862. His total loss to the war was all ten of his vessels – together with their valuable cargoes. His mammoth empire collapsed like a pack of cards. How did it happen?

The detailed accounts in the Official Records, together with the letters to and from agents in Bermuda, paint a fairly thorough picture of the 'unravelling of Zachariah'. Needless to say, there was also extensive coverage in the Hull local press, who were particularly interested in the exploits of their eminent Mayor. A couple of his vessel losses became notorious and generated considerable media attention, and later, when the details of Zachariah's finances were pored over publicly during his complex bankruptcy proceedings, even more details could be added to the story of his downfall.

At this distance from the events, we only know about those ships of Zachariah that became visible due to disaster befalling them. We have no idea whether any others got through unrecorded, although none are listed in the Civil War annals or the Bankruptcy papers, so it is fair to assume that there were no successes. While Zachariah was engaging in his American project, his other businesses – the mail service in Australia and New Zealand, and the timber trade in the Baltic – were carrying on as normal, although by now this latter route was starting to look less profitable. Running these businesses generated the 'normal' shipping losses that seemed to be almost expected with steam ships, but these would all have been covered, at least to some extent, by insurance policies.

The problem with losing ships to blockade-running was that these disasters really hurt. Once Lloyds of London realised that the American government was picking off any foreign vessel appearing in their waters, the cost of premiums rocketed astronomically. Lloyds did not pay out on ships that were being adjudicated in the Prize Courts; these fell officially inside the American jurisdiction, and there was always the hope, however remote, that the shipowner might be compensated for the loss of his ship in the US if he could prove that it had been captured illegally. But this was war...

We have here a snapshot of how one man's fate was sealed. Every vessel had its own tale of disaster to tell – and each must have been individually agonising for Zachariah. Quotations from the Official Records are liberally included as they bring the scenes alive with the words and arguments that were used 150 years ago, and now the sad tale opens in 1861 with the *Empress*. Unlike all of Zachariah's other blockade-runners, she was a barque, not a steamer; she was the vessel which had received notoriety and praise for achieving a record-breaking journey of 27 days to Constantinople in 1855. Probably the first of the Pearson ships to attempt to run through the blockade, she was certainly the first to be recorded as captured.

An American spy in England had alerted his masters in Washington that the *Empress* was suspected of heading to a Southern port, although she did not sail there directly; she first visited Rio de Janeiro to load up with a cargo of Brazilian coffee, and then ostensibly set out for New York.

Now, although coffee *per se* was not an embargoed cargo, her next move was actually to sail up the Mississippi, heading towards New Orleans. This counted as suspicious behaviour, and was considered to be breaking the blockade. So when the *USS Vincennes* challenged and captured her in December 1861, the paperwork found on board confirmed their misgivings: *'the captain's letter of instruction tells him that in the event of the port of New Orleans being blockaded, he will be warned off, and will then proceed to New York'*.

This was quite early in the war, only a few months after President Lincoln had decreed that a warning would be issued before capture, and so it's probable that the *Empress* captain, perhaps naïvely, had every expectation that the captain of the *Vincennes* would caution her before boarding her. But he did not, and once aboard, the *Vincennes* captain noted in his dispatches that the *Empress* did not have sufficient water or food to reach New York. This was the final bit of evidence needed to convince him that she was certainly heading for New Orleans – especially as she was running in at night.

Interestingly, the other English ship spotted at the same time as the *Empress* was released with a warning because, instead of ignoring the *Vincennes* when challenged, she *'stood boldly in, in broad daylight, making no effort to avoid the blockading vessels'*. In other words, Lincoln's proclamation promise was being applied selectively: if a ship did not seem to have something to hide, she was given the benefit of doubt, and the warning was issued. If her behaviour gave rise to suspicion, she was captured forthwith.

The men from the *Empress* were arrested and sent to New York for imprisonment. But this was in the early stages of the war, and it was fast becoming clear to Washington that if the gaols were filled up with unimportant seamen there would soon be no space for the main protagonists. So the New York marshal guarding the crew was ordered to release the men and to retain only the captain and a couple of officers to give evidence in the Prize Court. He was incensed, complaining that all the lawbreakers should remain imprisoned, but he reluctantly complied.

The Prize Court was the place where a judgement was given on whether or not a vessel had been taken lawfully. If a ship was 'condemned' in this court, it meant that the capture was legal, and she was now the lawful property of the US Government. She could then be used as they saw fit – either redeployed as a gunboat in the Union navy or, if unsuitable for blockading duty, she would be sold. Zachariah's *Empress* was condemned, taken as a lawful prize, converted into the *USS Empress*, and she was then used as a supply vessel to the blockading squadron during 1862. Zachariah disputed the legality of her capture, but like all cases in the Prize Court, this was to drag on for a couple of years. In yet another role-reversal, she was recaptured in 1863, this time by the Confederates, and used by them to supply – once more – the Southern ports.

Zachariah spent the early months of 1862 organising his transatlantic missions. Behind the scenes he and his agents were occupied buying cargoes and loading up vessels to carry them to the Confederates. We know this because in May of that year three of his ships were captured before they reached their Southern destination. With the promise of prize money, the US navy went about their blockading business with gusto; mere suspicion was sufficient cause to apprehend a vessel. Unlike the situation in criminal law, the Prize Courts demanded proof of innocence rather than proof of guilt, so it was very difficult for an English owner to succeed in these courts, as the case of the *Circassian* showed.

Circassian was a large screw steamer, one of the Xenos fleet that Zachariah had been seduced into buying on credit, and the US spies were watching her even in December 1861 when she left Constantinople *'under suspicious circumstances'* with a cargo of saltpetre, a component of gunpowder. However, she did nothing more untoward than bring this cargo back to England, where she loaded up with tea, coffee, tools and other household goods, and departed in February 1862 for Bordeaux. Zachariah in the meantime chartered her to a Frenchman, Soubry, who topped up her cargo in Bordeaux with wines and spirits. Crossing the Atlantic, she refuelled in the West Indies in April before heading towards Havana in Cuba.

The Circassian, *one of the vessels Zachariah acquired from Xenos, was a 1750 ton screw steamer. Whilst being used as a blockade-runner, she had a yellow stripe around her black hull, a white figurehead and a pink chimney – hardly cryptic colouration, although she did not, in fact, carry contraband goods. Her heading towards New Orleans was suspicious, although she was only planning to collect a cargo of cotton, and she was captured off Havana. In this sketch she is flying the US flag, showing that she is now the* USS Circassian, *part of Lincoln's blockading force which intercepted British vessels trying to run through the blockade.*

The spies were watching and the word was out. The blockading force was briefed that they would be able to recognise her from her size, her black hull and her *'female figurehead, painted white'*. It was probably not the tasteful figurehead, though, that advertised her presence to the *USS Somerset*. This blockader was patrolling the seas north of Cuba when she challenged an unknown vessel in her patch, but the *Circassian* did not stop – until compelled to do so by a shot through her rigging. It was an inspired hunch by the US navy: *Circassian* was not in forbidden waters, nor heading towards an embargoed port, nor even carrying any contraband goods – but not stopping was her fatal error. This raised suspicion. The Master swore he knew nothing about any destination other than Havana – but he was nevertheless said to have burnt some of the ship's papers before she was boarded. This was not, perhaps, the most innocent of actions, particularly when other papers contained more damning evidence: Zachariah had apparently agreed that she should '*proceed to Havana, Nassau or Bermuda, as ordered on sailing, and thence to proceed to a port of America, and to run the blockade, if so ordered by the freighters*'.

In other words, Zachariah was handing over responsibility to Soubry for making the decision. The description of the instructions from Soubry himself were more explicit: '*the merchandise shall not be disembarked but at the port of New Orleans, and to this effect he engages to force the blockade, for account and with authority of J. Soubry*'. This, together with some letters in French addressed to merchants in New Orleans, was enough for them to believe that the *Circassian* was eventually heading into an embargoed port. After capture, she was sent to the Prize Court and condemned. Later, as the *USS Circassian,* she became a very successful member of the blockading squadron, ironically preventing several British blockade-runners from entering Southern ports.

But the story of the *Circassian* did not stop here. This was Zachariah's first huge loss, and he must have felt it sorely, especially as the press reported that the Mayor of Hull had been set on trading illicit goods (not true) in an illicit port (true). Zachariah wrote a letter to *The Times* (6th June 1862) to clear his name. The argument lay in whether or not the capture of his ship had been legally made – and he claimed it was not. She had, after all, been heading to a neutral port with a legal cargo. As a clincher, he added: '*If this were not sufficient to prove her destination, the fact that her draught of water is upwards of 20ft., and that there is no harbour in the Confederate States capable of receiving such a vessel, ought to be conclusive on the point*'.

Although he must have expected some losses in his 'American adventures', as he later called them, Zachariah at least hoped for a bit of fair play, and he appealed to the American Supreme Court to overturn this 'unlawful' verdict. The case was not heard until 1864, but at that stage another point of law emerged. While the Chief Justice agreed with the Prize Court that there was sufficient circumstantial evidence to condemn the *Circassian*, there was an anomaly in the dates which threw doubt on the judgement. She had been captured on 4th May, but only two days previously New Orleans had been taken by the Federal forces, and was thus, at the precise moment of the *Circassian*'s capture, a US port, not a Confederate one. This meant that even if she had been intending to dock at New Orleans, she could not legally be accused of breaking the blockade as this was now no longer an embargoed port. It was a legal nicety, and Zachariah attempted to exploit the technicality, but it made no difference in the end. He failed to get any compensation from the American government for losing his largest ship and one of his most valuable cargoes.

The case of the *Circassian* also entered the English courts. Being relatively early in the war, the legal system was still working out how to compensate seamen who claimed they had lost wages due to the time spent getting back home after their vessel had been captured. A few brought their grievances to court, and in October 1862 such a sailor claimed against Zachariah for £10 in what was to become a test case. But the defence counsel maintained that Zachariah was not liable since the ship had been taken illegally: '*the Federal government had no more right to seize the* Circassian *when they did than they would have to have done so in the British Channel [...] We look at this seizure in the light of piracy.'* The judge, realising that this would become a test case, sympathised with all seamen in such situations, only reserving judgement in this particular case because of the 'piracy' question.

Another of Zachariah's May victims to the blockading force was the *Patras*, also one of the Xenos steamers. She had been logged by a US consul leaving Falmouth in April, and the spies kept an eye on her progress as she left Havana. She headed towards Charleston, but before she reached that port she gave herself away by *'emitting black smoke from her funnel'*. The USS *Bienville* spotted her, and sent a boat with an officer and an armed guard to question Captain Elliott of the *Patras,* and to examine her papers. But the officer returned to the *Bienville* saying that Elliott denied having any papers and that he was just *'coasting along'*. This only fanned the flames of mistrust, so the *Patras* was boarded and captured, where she was found to have on board quinine, coffee, arms and gunpowder – and her papers.

The case of this ship nicely illustrates the competition between the vessels of the blockading force. There are many pages of letters in the Official Records from captains of other ships who were patrolling in the vicinity at the time, each describing how they had played a key role in enabling the *Bienville* to capture the *Patras*, thus aiming to have her recorded as a joint capture. Naturally, there were counterclaims from the *Bienville*'s captain, who was determined to claim sole capture and secure the prize money for his own crew.

The case of the *Patras* also gives us an example of how blockade-running captains might go into denial. One assumes that Zachariah's agents would have been careful to appoint Masters who were experienced, and who stood the best possible chance of dodging the blockade, so these men must have keenly felt the failure and ignominy of being caught. Merchant ships not being armed, the game was up as soon as they were approached by a blockader, but probably from the perspective of the *Patras'* captain there was no harm in trying to continue the deceit for a little longer: he *'had no papers'* and he was not heading anywhere in particular, he was just *'coasting along'...*

Captain Elliott, the carpenter and the cook were sent to New York on another US vessel 'to assist in the Prize Court'. They were not formally arrested and locked below during this voyage, but allowed to remain on deck – but only if they promised not to talk to any of the US seamen. The story was rounded off from the crew's perspective in *The Times* six weeks later when the remaining 18 men from the *Patras* arrived back home. They described a tortuous journey, having been kept in unsavoury conditions aboard various ships, sent on a train to New York, and finally put on a Royal Navy ship bound for Liverpool. Probably because she was too small to be a blockader, the *Patras* was sold to a private company rather than incorporated into the US navy.

Another of the disastrous May losses was the *Stettin,* the screw steamer built for Zachariah in 1861 for £17,000. She was loaded with a huge mixed cargo that the crew, under interrogation, said had cost Zachariah over £100,000: she carried saltpetre, lead, quinine, tea, coffee, brandy, gin, champagne, clothing, tin plates, and 'boxes and kegs' (arms and powder). Like the *Patras*, she also left England in April, then refuelled in Madeira, and went on to Bermuda and Nassau in the Bahamas. Had she succeeded in getting into Charleston, the officers would have received £100 each, the crew a bit less, and the captain much more. But she did not.

Perhaps it was a tactical error to send two vessels at the same time to the same port? Or was it just bad luck that the two ended up in the same place together? In either case, the *USS Bienville* was patrolling this section of the coast, and *Stettin's* fate was sealed. Both the *Stettin* and the *Patras*, with their valuable cargoes, were taken within three days of each other – and both by the *Bienville*. It was no wonder that the other US vessels were fighting for a share of the massive double prize claimed by the *Bienville's* captain...

Adding insult to injury, after being condemned in the Prize Court, Zachariah's vessel was converted into the gunboat *USS Stettin,* and went on to capture or sink four British ships which were attempting to run the blockade.

The following month, June, saw another double disaster, with the *Ann* and the *Modern Greece* being lost within two days of each other – though under very different circumstances. The *Ann* was a large screw steamer, only two years old, and she took a valuable cargo of coffee, tea, paper, muskets and gunpowder to Havana. When a buyer for her high-priced goods could not be found there, the Master decided to try to run her into Mobile, Alabama, a Confederate port on the Gulf of Mexico. Being rather heavily laden, she ran aground on her approach near the Confederate defence, Fort Morgan, and the Confederates soldiers quickly started removing her cargo. They had not succeeded in salvaging much, however, before the *USS Kanawha* appeared on the scene, and the men abandoned *Ann* to her fate. The commander of the fort was so furious at the prospect of losing a cargo that would have been invaluable to the Confederate cause that he sent a couple of vessels to try to collect the now-drifting *Ann* – only to discover that her boilers had gone out.

With the *Kanawha* coming up fast, there was no time to rekindle the boilers, so they decided to scuttle the *Ann*: if they couldn't have the cargo, at least they could sink her to prevent the Union from profiting from her. But the *Ann* had been too well built. Although they managed to flood one compartment, the others proved to be too watertight, and she refused to sink. In the end, the *Kanawha* did capture her, and took the substantial remains of her cargo as a prize. Although 400 muskets, together with 30,000 pounds of gunpowder, had gone to defend Port Morgan, far more went to the US navy. And *Ann* entered the history books as being the first vessel to test the blockade at Mobile – a dubious distinction which would have afforded Zachariah very little consolation.

A painting of the Modern Greece *after she had been fired on by Lincoln's blockaders and run aground. She was a 753 ton single screw steamer with a draft of 17 feet – far too deep to survive the shoals around the mouth of Cape Fear River. This ship settled into the sands and, like the Sleeping Beauty, she lay dormant for 100 years, being awakened not by a handsome prince but by a hurricane. Her artefacts are today on display in the museum at Fort Fisher.*

The *Modern Greece* became famous in history due to a peculiar combination of events, and we know far more about her than any of Zachariah's other vessels. In essence, only two days after the *Ann* had been captured, the *Modern Greece* was seen and chased into the shallows of a river mouth, where a few days later she settled into the sands, completely out of reach of all parties. But in 1962, exactly 100 years after she sank, a fierce storm exposed the wreck, and after some initial trophy-seeking by divers, she became one of the most famous Civil War archaeological naval sites. As the owner of the vessel which was so helpfully mothballed for 100 years, Zachariah had inadvertently supplied the world with an extremely valuable historical resource, a time capsule which even today is still being productive. The details of the demise of the *Modern Greece* are worth the telling because, with so many sources of information, they shine a light on the human reality of the Civil War and its blockade-running.

An article of white porcelain recovered from the Modern Greece, *tastefully adorned with blue lettering. It demonstrates the high standard which Xenos had specified for this top-of-the-range passenger ship in his fleet.*

The *Modern Greece* had been made in Stockton-on-Tees in 1859 and was only two years old when Zachariah bought her on credit from the bank. She was a 1000 ton, single screw iron steamer, and must have been top-of-the-range in Xenos' fleet. She had been beautifully appointed, as we can tell from the exhibits on display today in the Fort Fisher museum: etched glass for her wall lights, monogrammed blue-and-white porcelain tableware, and a great many other personal touches. Ready for her new role, she had been painted slate-grey, loaded with cargo, both legitimate and contraband, and sent to try her luck in collecting cotton bales for Hull. She left Falmouth on 2nd April 1862, *'with a cargo, it is suspected, for the rebels'*, in the US Consul's words. Indeed, after she had been intercepted, his suspicions were verified, as *'her cargo consisted of 1000 tons of gunpowder, some rifled cannon and other arms and equipments [...] together with bales of clothing and spirituous liquors'*.

Some of the guns on display at the Fort Fisher museum. There were 20,000 Enfield rifles on board the Modern Greece *– two of them are shown at the top of this photo. Other plentiful artefacts retrieved from this vessel included Bowie knives, a type of fighting dagger, pen knives and other utensils.*

As she approached the coast of North Carolina on 27th June, masked by the early morning mists, the *Modern Greece* attempted to slide quietly into the Cape Fear River at Fort Fisher. She was heading for Wilmington, some 25 miles upstream. With its good rail and road connections, this town was an ideal distribution point for the Confederate States. Furthermore, being so far upstream, Wilmington was more successfully defended from Union attack than the other southern ports, and 'stayed open for business' later in the war than any other port. To get there, though, vessels first had to pass the treacherous sandbanks, or shoals, in the mouth of the river.

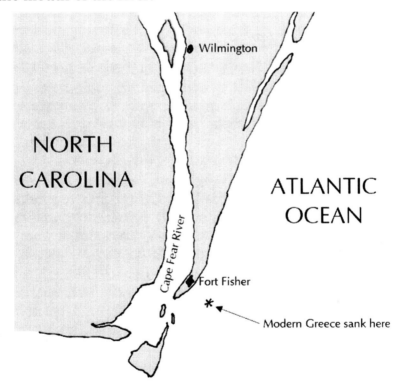

Situated 30 miles up the Cape Fear River, Wilmington was well-placed to avoid the attentions of Lincoln's forces. And as the estuary was well-defended by the Confederates posted at Fort Fisher, Lincoln's blockaders were held off. But the sandbanks were shallow, and treacherous, and this is where two of Zachariah's ships sank – the Modern Greece, *and much later the* Peterhoff .

Cape Fear River was guarded by Confederate soldiers who were stationed at Fort Fisher, a stronghold on a raised bank overlooking the estuary. From here they could protect the river from US ships, and try to clear a safe passage for blockade-runners heading to Wilmington. Approaching vessels nevertheless had to evade the North Atlantic Blockading Squadron and steer through the shifting, shallow sandbars before gaining the safety of the river. On this particular morning, as the *Modern Greece* slid silently in towards the river mouth, two blockaders were patrolling the area, and at 4.15 am the *USS Cambridge* spotted her and opened fire, soon joined by the *USS Stars and Stripes*. Not being armed, the *Modern Greece* could only try to outrun them and make for the safety of the river, relying on the fire power of Fort Fisher. To no avail. In the words of a US captain, she '*hoisted English colours and ran under a heavy press of steam toward the channel within half a mile of the fort, where she was necessarily beached, in consequence of our continually firing upon her, her crew leaving in boats for the shore*'.

Instead of capturing her, then, the blockaders had only succeeded in running her aground, her deep hull – not ideal for running the blockade – sinking into a sandbar. Paradoxically, the cannons at Fort Fisher were not only firing on the Union ships, but also – once the crew had left – on the *Modern Greece*. Only being half a mile off shore, the Confederates knew they would be able to salvage some of her valuable cargo, so they fired on her to submerge her enough to saturate the gunpowder that would be in her hold. They were desperate to ensure that this valuable prize did not explode under their noses.

The minutiae of her sinking are recorded in the Official Records, where the commanders of the blockaders provide some illuminating detail of the action. Neither wished to be blamed by Washington for losing the *Modern Greece,* so both captains had to cover their backs when writing the account of what had happened. Under fire from Fort Fisher, and unable to get close in to the *Modern Greece*, the Lieutenant commanding the *USS Stars and Stripes* wrote:

I used my rifled howitzer and 20-pound Parrott chiefly, but tried to get close enough to use my 8 inch guns. Finding I could not get close enough to use my broadside guns at direct firing without coming under the guns of the battery, I tried to ricochet my shells in. I think I succeeded in striking her twice this way.

The next part of his account paints a quaint insight into the workings of the blockading squadron: *'Fire was kept up from this vessel until almost 7.a.m., when Captain Parker ordered me to suspend firing until after breakfast. After breakfast both vessels stood in for the second time'.* One can envisage the irate cook in the galley stressing about the croissants getting cold...

The end of this particular report expresses solidarity, for once, between the two captains regarding the reason they left the scene without destroying the *Modern Greece:*

both Captain Parker and myself agreed that we could do no more with our vessels, that to send our light boats in to burn her, under the fire of two batteries, would only be to insure their destruction, without accomplishing the desired object.

After the blockaders had departed, the Confederate soldiers off-loaded goods to shore over several days before the ship settled too far into the sand to be accessible. The cargo having arrived somewhat unconventionally, and clearly unable to be sold through official channels to the intended Confederate buyers, the locals made good use of it. There were 20,000 Enfield rifles aboard, 500 of which were salvaged for active use against the North, together with a resource which turned out to be invaluable to the Confederates – four brass, breech-loading, Whitworth rifled cannons. At a less military level, the barrels of 'spirituous liquors' were put to good local use, apparently keeping the soldiers at Fort Fisher merry for a week!

One of the four Whitworth cannons that the Confederates salvaged off the Modern Greece before she sank into the sands in 1862 on display here at the Fort Fisher museum in 2005. These four guns were the envy of forts along the coast due to their accuracy and range. Their design represents a new generation of large guns: the barrel was rifled for more accurate and powerful projection, and the gun could be loaded rapidly from the rear.

A model of Confederate soldiers using the Whitworth cannon at Fort Fisher. With this gun they could fire on US blockaders up to five miles off coast, far better than the two mile range of conventional cannons. Some historians reckon they prolonged the war.

While this event was a windfall for the Confederates, the Secretary of the Navy in Washington DC, Gideon Welles, was furious with his blockaders for bungling the job. Not only had they failed to capture the steamer, but they had left the Confederates to get their hands on a good portion of the illicit cargo. His curt memo to the Flag Officer, *'This whole blockade is and has been unsatisfactory from the beginning'*, started the witch-hunt that ensued. So the captains of the two blockaders now tried to launch a damage-limitation offensive through their dispatches. Thus there is the vain assurance of the *Cambridge's* captain that although *'liquors and clothing [had] been saved...not one pound of powder nor a single cannon was saved'*. He went on to explain how they failed to blow the vessel up due to the fort firing *'solid shot to admit water into her and thus prevent our shells from exploding the large quantity of powder in her hold'*, but reassured Welles that: *'the present state of* Modern Greece *is a total wreck. Her spar deck is level with the water and her upper works have been washed away and removed. A bed of sand has formed around her so she will never float again, probably. Her masts and smokestack are still standing.'*

These verbatim accounts supply insight into the coastal defence process from the Union navy's perspective, but how about the Confederate's angle? Not having a navy *per se*, they relied on fire-power from their forts around the coast – and this, in turn, depended on the quality of guns they had. So when *Modern Greece* delivered to Fort Fisher four long-range guns representing a quantum leap in artillery design, Colonel Lamb, the Commander of Fort Fisher, sang their praises: *'Shortly after taking command of Fort Fisher, I recovered from the wreck of the* Modern Greece *four twelve-pounder Whitworth rifled cannons with a range of five miles. With these guns, we made the US blockading fleet remove their anchorage from two-and-a-half miles to five miles from the Fort. So many vessels were saved with these guns.'*

Until now, cannons had been loaded down the barrel from the front end, a time-consuming and dangerous process, but the Whitworth cannon were loaded from the back end (breech loaded) so that they could be refired quickly. And instead of using smooth, rounded cannonballs which were rather hit-and-miss, they fired shaped, precision bolts from a carefully engineered spiral 'rifled' barrel, as lauded by Captain W. Wheeler from North Carolina: *'The Whitworth Gun [...] was a terror for the enemy; its range was immense, its accuracy that of a sharp shooter [...] Our Whitworth would shoot clear through their vessels when they came in range. One of its projectiles cut the throat of a quartermaster as clean as if done by a razor.'*

With a reputation like this, these cannon were greatly coveted all along the coast, and battle-leaders everywhere wanted one – or preferably two: *'I beg that a couple of the Whitworth guns originally saved from the* Modern Greece *may be sent here at once. Their long range makes them most suitable for a seaboard position.'* (Major General Whiting writing to the Confederate Secretary of War, Seddon, on 24th August 1863).

Having arrived in Confederate possession relatively early in the war, these four Whitworths had several years to establish a fearsome reputation on both sides in the war. And being lighter than previous cannon, they were more mobile; hitched to horses, they could easily be moved around from one position to another. They were, in fact, reckoned by historians to have been a key factor in keeping the port of Wilmington active – some even saying they extended the war by keeping the 'Lifeline of the Confederacy' open.

The details of the *Modern Greece* are particularly colourful for several reasons: because of the blockader captains having to account for a failed capture; because of its Whitworth legacy in coastal defences; and because of the storm which exposed a buried time capsule to public scrutiny in 1962. Since then, thanks to the careful excavations of the Naval Archaeology department at Fort Fisher, a good deal more information has been gleaned. Zachariah's steamer has furnished the adjacent Civil War Museum with half of its public exhibits, and there are many more of her artefacts in store behind the scenes. On our visit there, we were granted privileged behind-the-scenes access to many of these items of cargo, and they are to this day still being examined and catalogued. The *Modern Greece,* caught literally in the crossfire between Unionists and Confederates, has added greatly to the history about blockade-running. In addition, she has become a laboratory on how to excavate a wreck and preserve its artefacts: scientific experiments on the stocks (handles) of some of her Enfield rifles have recently led to breakthrough discoveries about the best way to restore and preserve wooden structures after decades or centuries of immersion in the ocean. Who knows what may be revealed in the future from further detection work on the *Modern Greece?*

The Modern Greece *had several anchors. Here the author and her husband are demonstrating the scale of the main anchor on display at Fort Fisher.*

The May and June of 1862 had been a torrid time for Zachariah. Carried away with enthusiasm to participate, and sending so many ships west at the same time, it was inevitable that unspecialised vessels would be intercepted. In the space of only a few weeks Zachariah had lost five of his key vessels, together with their pricey cargoes.

By July, Zachariah's fate was sealed – he had lost far too many of ships to recover financially, several of them still being mortgaged to Overend, Gurney & Co.. He had spent a fortune on his cargoes, on none of which had he seen any return. He had failed to bring any cotton back home, and the mills still stood idle. So his *Indian Empire* disaster, the ship that burnt in the Thames just after Zachariah had paid for its refit, came as a crushing blow towards the end of July. It was yet another nail in Zachariah's coffin, albeit not of American making this time.

In the midst of the relentless and gloomy messages about his heavy losses, Zachariah clung desperately to the hope that one of the remaining vessels might be his salvation. Unlike all his other vessels, which were minimally-adapted commercial ships, he had built *Lodona* specifically for the purpose of evading the Union navy. Launched in 1862, she was long, low and fast, with a shallow draught and some other anti-capture adaptations.

She left Falmouth in June loaded with '*brandy, wines, tea, coffee, salt, clothing, boots, drugs, watches, figs, raisins, whisky, starch, soap, tin plates, soda, dry goods, paints, colors, quinine, etc.*', a mixed cargo worth a massive sum of money. She docked in Bermuda, went on to Nassau and then headed towards Savannah, Georgia. Her clever design, though, did her little good, as she was spotted by *USS Unadilla,* whose captain wrote in dispatches on 4th August:

> *upon her discovering us, she attempted to run through Hell Gate, where she grounded and hoisted the English ensign, union down, [signalling that she acknowledged capture] and a white flag at her mizzen. We ran down near her, hoisted our ensign, sent a boat on board, took possession of her, and soon succeeded in getting her afloat.*

U.S.Str.Lodona *&c...R. Cothoun...*

The Lodona, *the vessel which Zachariah had built especially for blockade-running in 1862. She had collapsible masts to reduce the chances of being seen, and quick-release plugs so that she could be scuttled fast rather than fall into the hands of the US navy. Sadly, none of her devices helped, and she was captured at Savannah. This sketch was drawn by her commander after she had been converted to the* USS Lodona.

It is also through these dispatches that we learn how *Lodona's* design was modified to avoid being captured:

> *It is said she has 6 screw plugs in her bottom, which, when taken out, will sink her in 20 minutes, and [...] her master has orders to sink her rather than let her fall into the hands of the United States. [...] To prevent being seen, the Lodona had all her yards and topmasts on deck when she was discovered and captured.*

Nevertheless, her commander, Captain Luckie, while ordering the masts to be folded flat on the deck so the *Lodona* was less visible, does not seem to have been able to bring himself to remove her plugs and scuttle her when the critical moment arrived – after all, how many captains could have deliberately sunk their own ship? So she was captured, adjudicated, condemned and sold in the Prize Court later in the month, and after being armed, became the *USS Lodona,* in which role she went on to work for the Union navy.

By the time news of the *Lodona* arrived back in England, Zachariah had pulled his own plug and been forced to cease trading. There was no way he could sustain losses of this nature. From mid-August 1862 onwards, all Zachariah's property was impounded. The other three vessels that were already on their way to the Southern states at this moment, the *Phoebe,* the *Merrimac* and the *Peterhoff,* together with their valuable cargoes, now became the property of the creditors, and were sold to help offset the massive debt.

The *Phoebe* (identified in dispatches as having at her prow a *'full-length figure of a woman, small and pretty')* and the larger steamer, the *Merrimac,* seemed to be working in tandem initially. Possibly in an attempt to throw the American spies off the trail, they met up at Sheppey in the Thames estuary and exchanged some of their cargoes. They then proceeded to Bermuda, where the lighter *Phoebe* arrived first and unloaded her cargo of arms and powder, but because Zachariah was no longer trading, this was impounded and stored in warehouses on the island until it could be sold on – at a good profit to the go-between agents. *Phoebe* was then sold privately to the Australian Steam Packet Co.

A similar fate awaited the *Merrimac* a little later. On the way from England to Bermuda, Zachariah had ostensibly sold her to the Confederates, agreeing a sum of £131,785 *'to be paid for in sterling at an English port'.* But the timing was disastrous. Before she arrived at St. George, Zachariah was not in business, so she was impounded on arrival. Her valuable cargo included three 8-inch Blakely rifled cannon and 1,100 barrels of gunpowder, but the vessel and cargo were seized by the creditors and the Confederates refused to honour their contract. The cargo was far more valuable than the vessel itself, but under the circumstances it was impossible to separate cargo and vessel, so eventually they were sold as one lot to an agent for the Confederate States, Caleb Huse, for a mere £7,000, a tiny fraction of the real value. Zachariah was in no position to bargain at this stage but he was reeling from the injustice of it all. Apart from losing a literal fortune on the *Merrimac* with such bad-luck timing, he had been hoping against hope that this might just be the vessel to bail him out. Behind the scenes he had been borrowing furiously against the chance that one of these late vessels would break the blockade and save his bacon.

Zachariah's loss was other people's gain, of course. Caleb Huse sold this windfall on to the Confederates for a great deal more than £7,000. The cannons were divided up, one going to defend Vicksburg, and two to defend Wilmington. John T. Bourne's commission for handling the sale was £400 – equivalent to a cut of £35,000 today. All were winners – except for Zachariah.

Now that the *Merrimac* was working for the 'Rebels' rather than for Z. C. Pearson and Co., and commanded by Confederates who understood the Southern ports, she was successful in breaking the blockade and getting into Wilmington, where Huse sold her at vast profit to the Confederates themselves. Her hold was then loaded with cotton bales, and she departed triumphantly for England, but it seems that, while the Confederate captain may have known more than his English counterparts about the tricks of breaking the blockade in local ports, he knew less about the best way to manage the vessel's engines, and on the way out of port the *Merrimac* was overtaken and captured by the far slower sloop *USS Iroquois,* sold to the Union navy – her third owner in a few months – and converted to a US gunboat.

The last of Zachariah's blockade-runners, the *Peterhoff,* was a screw steamer which Zachariah had ordered to be built originally for his Baltic trade. However, the shipbuilder had gone bankrupt before she was finished, which caused a delay, and by the time she was ready to go to sea it was 1862, so Zachariah had decided to use her instead for potentially greater profits in blockade-running. She was in Bermuda at the same time as *Phoebe* but, unlike that ship, she managed to continue her run into Charleston – and was successful! She sold her high-value cargo of *'artillery harness, boots, blankets, iron, steel, nails, leather, drugs: calomel, morphine, chloroform, quinine and wine'* to the locals, and loaded up with bales to bring home. She even succeeded in getting back through the blockade with her cotton cargo. But alas, this was too little too late for Zachariah...

How ironic! The only one of Zachariah's ships to make a completely successful round trip to the Confederate States – selling one cargo, loading with cotton, then returning safely to England – was seized immediately on arrival back home by the creditors and sold, no doubt at greatly devalued prices. If only she had managed this feat earlier, Zachariah might have survived financially.

It was probably of little comfort to Zachariah that *Peterhoff*'s new owner, Spence, also attempted to run the blockade with her, and that this time she was caught and sold in the Prize Court and converted to a gunboat. Spence brought an action in the Supreme Court to challenge the legality of the *Peterhoff*'s capture, and succeeded in getting the Prize Court ruling overturned, being paid compensation for the *Peterhoff*, something that Zachariah failed to achieve with the *Circassian.* To round off the story of this vessel's misadventures, in 1864, in what today would be called 'collateral damage', *USS Peterhoff* met her doom when mistaken for a blockade-runner by one of her own side, another Union vessel, and she sank just off Fort Fisher whilst defending access to Wilmington. Years later, like the *Modern Greece,* she became a dive site, with a number of *Peterhoff* artefacts, some of Zachariah's original property, being retrieved from her. Today she is merely known as a good place to fish for flounder.

This rounds off the sorry saga of Zachariah's blockade-running adventures. They had, of course, shaped his future by fundamentally altering the direction of his life and that of his family. In order to sort out his finances, his creditors needed to assess the value of his assets. With so many ships, and such complex international involvement, there were multitudinous loose ends to be picked up, with a great many traders and agents fighting to ensure that they got what they were owed before the formal valuation was made – and before the lawyers mopped up huge amounts of Zachariah's estate in fees.

John T. Bourne, the go-between in Bermuda, was a good example of this. He found himself in a tricky situation; expenses had been run up and he needed to know how he could be paid now that the creditors were claiming everything. A letter that Bourne wrote to Zachariah's own agent, Edward Coleman, on 26th December 1862, illustrates some of his concerns:

Edward Coleman Esquire, Present
Dear Sir:- I have to acknowledge the receipt of your letter of the 24th inst. with invoice, also Power of Attorney authorising me to get for you in certain goods warehoused and now lying in the Islands of Bermuda and in reply thereto beg to say that due attention will be given to the instructions therein contained.
With reference to the Gunpowder warehoused at Tuckers town I consider that as circumstances have now arisen I hold this powder liable for the monies advanced Messrs Z. C. Pearson and Co.'s ships who have passed through Bermuda some time since & that on 9th August when you endorsed the Bill of Lading for this powder to me you were acting as the Atty of Messrs Z. C. Pearson and Co, all of which I presume you understand.
John T Bourne

In other words, here is agent Bourne telling agent Coleman, in cautious language, that owner Zachariah owed him money for his services on handling several of his ships, but that, as he could see that he would never be paid now, rather than wait until the lawyers had finished arguing, he was holding the gunpowder from various of Zachariah's cargos as collateral – he was sure Coleman would understand why without having to spell it out. And no doubt he sold the powder at a very good price to ships heading into Confederate ports.

Certainly, being an agent in Bermuda at this time was a lucrative job – especially with clients like this to keep him in luxury. The world was avariciously cashing in on Zachariah's misfortune: vultures round the kill, competing to scavenge any scraps possible from the collapsed empire. The rules had suddenly changed.

11

Bankruptcy!

Back at home the rules had also changed. Someone who had overstepped his financial commitments while in the process of carrying out complex international business transactions did not now deserve the niceties of conventional trading. Gentlemen's handshakes and civilised invoicing were suddenly irrelevant. The vultures in England had the same appetites as the rest of the world, but the law intervened, and they were unable to feast off the scraps in the same way. The court had to decide who got which bits of the remains. Zachariah's life was now being diverted down a completely different path. Instead of being an objective tale of achievement, adventure and public duty, the focus had changed precipitously to the subjective. It was now all about him – and he found it extremely uncomfortable. This chapter documents how a prominent court case of an eminent figure turned increasingly nasty, and how a well-respected character was cynically blackened by copious mudslinging. But then, seismic events do tend to churn up the mud at the bottom of the pond...

Having ventured into the risky world of blockade-running, any shipowner might expect the odd loss, but as long as he could pull off the gamble of getting ships and cargoes through to the lucrative besieged Confederate Government, any shortfall would easily be covered. It was all a matter of holding one's nerve, and spinning the plates to balance disaster against success. All the same, once it became apparent that catastrophic news was arriving back in England far too fast to be manageable, the plates fell, and Zachariah's world collapsed. On one single day in July 1862 he received news of £85,000's worth of loss – the *Patras,* the *Modern Greece* and the *Indian Empire.* To put this in perspective, the losses on that day amounted to an unimaginable £7.4 million by today's standards.

This would certainly count as catastrophic by any measure and on 9th September the *York Gazette* announced, under the heading 'Failure of the Mayor of Hull':

for some days past rumours have been in circulation respecting Messrs. Z. C. Pearson and Co., steamship owners, of Hull, whose recent transactions with the Confederate States of America were believed to have involved the firm in somewhat serious difficulties. On Monday all doubt was removed by the formal announcement that Mr Pearson was unable to meet his acceptances. The total amount of his liabilities has not transpired, but though they are undoubtedly large, they are in a great measure secured.

There was still some optimism at this point:

though the cargoes were disposed of at immense profit, the remittances have not yet been able to reach this country. We understand, however, that arrangements are being made which will enable the firm to keep out of the Bankruptcy Court. As the embarrassment is occasioned by the non-receipt of remittances from America, it is confidently believed that when those remittances can be forwarded to England Mr Pearson will be able to meet all his liabilities, with a handsome surplus to spare.

And expectations were met when, few days later, an offer was made by the accountants to manage Zachariah out of bankruptcy by paying eight shillings in the pound to creditors:

> Messrs Pearson and Co's affairs, it is now generally believed, will be amicably arranged. Four fifths of the whole firm are due to creditors who are said to be secured. To the unsecured creditors, the cash payment of 40 per cent is to be made on the 1st October next, and there are remaining assets which, when realised, are expected fully to cover the balance and to leave a handsome surplus.
>
> (*Hull Times*, 20th September 1862).

In effect, once the Americans had paid up, everything would be fine – except they didn't and it wasn't: none of these vast sums of money ever crossed the Atlantic. But even before the realisation of this American non-payment, once the announcement had been made, rumour was rife, and all interested parties were intensely nervous. They needed what was owed to them before the estate trickled away, and it was 'snouts in the trough' time – every creditor for himself. It was inevitable that Zachariah eventually had to petition the Bankruptcy Court for his affairs to be examined publicly.

He was an upstanding member of the Hull public and commercial world; as well as holding the highest office in town, he was also that year the Commandant of the Hull Volunteers. He could not have had a taller pedestal from which to topple, and he was devastated and humiliated to find himself in this position. As well as resigning forthwith from his Mayoral role, honour demanded that he withdrew from all his charitable and trustee positions as well as from the Minerva Lodge and the Volunteers. As his case was being held in the London Bankruptcy Court, he now had to spend more time living in London than in Hull so that he could be on-the-spot and in touch with his lawyers and advisers. Considering the ignominy he must have felt among his own people in Hull, being in London may have come as a welcome relief to him.

There was nothing Zachariah could do to avoid humiliation. All was now out of his control. Every aspect of his private and public finances was about to be exposed for anyone, including his fellow townsmen, to trawl through. At the Bankruptcy Court, there would be national and Hull journalists present to make sure that the proceedings of a public figure in such a spectacularly sorry state were fully reported in the press. The best Zachariah could hope for was to be 'discharged', for the court to find that there was no case to answer – and it appears in the early stages that this might have been a possibility. The reports of the court proceedings in *The Times* and various Yorkshire local newspapers have been the main source of what follows, as the official court records of this case no longer exist. However, the journal coverage is almost as illuminating, as it reports the actual words spoken in court.

A bankruptcy case, of course, involved money, massive amounts of it, but it is hard to comprehend exactly how vast the sums were unless they are translated into today's values. An exact equivalent to what things might be worth today is difficult to assess, because the relative costs of services and prices of commodities differed considerably from modern day ones, but the inflation conversion algorithm which has been used gives £1 in 1862 a roughly equivalent value to £88 in 2015. While clearly only an approximation, it is helpful to contextualise what these figures would mean in today's terms.

The Bankruptcy Court worked liked this. A case was heard before a 'Commissioner', who sat in judgement on the 'bankrupt'. He listened to the evidence presented by lawyers who spoke on behalf of the 'creditors', the people who were owed money. Then the bankrupt's own advocate put forward the argument for the defence. All the financial details of the bankrupt's estate were assembled by a group called the 'assignees', and the accounts were on display to the whole court – and to any journalists present. Witnesses could be called on behalf of either side, but there was no jury; everything rested on the decision by the Commissioner.

How did this work for Zachariah? Before the case could be heard in court, his accounts had to be ready for examination, but this in itself proved to be problematic. It was very difficult to get to grips with the labyrinthine complexities of Zachariah's various businesses, not to mention the sheer size of his estate, with multiple ships and cargoes, and an apparently endless list of creditors. Another problem was the extraordinary challenge of extracting information from sources in recent war zones – the Confederate Government, the Federal US Government's Prize Courts, and the newly-unified Italian Government. And it did not help matters that the American court cases on Zachariah's ships were being carried on concurrently.

Zachariah's businesses had failed in the middle of 1862, and his case opened in October of that year at the London Bankruptcy Court. This initial meeting was to establish *'the proof of debts and a choice of assignees of the bankrupt'*, and the reason for his failure was given by Zachariah as his *'inability to meet his engagements to losses through the capture of steamers and goods by the Federal government of America, and the destruction of the steamer* Indian Empire *by fire'*.

The issues were so complex that an adjournment was requested at once so that the creditors could decide *'the mode in which the estates shall be administered'*. At this stage things still looked optimistic for Zachariah; the creditors, who were mainly his townsfolk, among whom Zachariah had grown up and worked, were sympathetic, and the *Hull Times* reported that in the court *'a strong feeling existed that the estate should be administered out of bankruptcy, and therefore the resolution had been adopted to appoint a committee to devise the best means of accomplishing that object'*. Here was a genuine attempt to avoid bankruptcy; Zachariah had the backing and goodwill of many colleagues and merchants in Hull, most of whom admired what he had achieved and what he had done for Hull.

After this opening bout, there were still difficulties in collecting all the figures, and this resulted in repeated adjournments over the next 10 months. During this time it was becoming increasingly obvious that since the initial meeting the atmosphere was turning sour. Attitudes were hardening, and things were now growing more polarised and confrontational. Was this triggered by a gradual awareness, during the compilation of the accounts, of the extent of Zachariah's debts? Or was it a build-up of resentment aimed at this 'nobody' who had risen so rapidly to success and then crashed? Whatever the reason, it became apparent that, while the majority of the creditors did not oppose Zachariah's discharge, there was a minority group of five or six antagonistic creditors who did – and they were vociferous. In these Victorian times, success was lauded and failure condemned. Those who failed were fed to the lions. People who had praised Zachariah for his philanthropy now chose to re-interpret his noble actions as self-aggrandisement, and in some circles, he became *persona non grata*. This group of lions – mixing their metaphors – threw the book at him, grinding his nose in his failings, and at the same time rubbing their hands together with a good degree of *schadenfreude*.

The accounts were finally ready to be presented on 1st August 1863 – but yet another adjournment was granted as the accounts *'were only filed on Saturday last, and [were] of a very voluminous character, occupying 120 sheets of paper'*. The Assignees had not been able to examine these complex accounts properly over the last few days, and they now wanted to scrutinise every last entry. As did the reporters. They pored over Zachariah's accounts presented at this hearing but, with 120 pages to analyse, the newspapers were only able to publish incomplete records, cherry-picking those entries which were likely to be of greatest interest to their readers and the overall picture has had to emerge from the comments and reactions in court alongside these entries. Regardless of detail, by the time the hawkish creditors had finished assembling the figures, Zachariah's debts were summarised by *The Times*: '*The aggregate liabilities have been hitherto stated in round numbers at upwards of half-a-million; the exact amount is now shown to be a £645,435.*' At today's values, Zachariah's liabilities would represent over £56 million pounds – a very scary sum indeed.

The figures were listed against who owed what to whom, and what Zachariah thought he was entitled to claim from the estate. Zachariah had also listed the claims he had against foreign governments, such as cargo payments from the Confederates, and the compensation claims he felt he was entitled to against the US Government. In his words:

By an agreement dated May, 1862, I sold to the Confederate government, through their authorised agent, S Ransom, Esq., the steamship Merrimac *and her cargo, for the sum of £131,785, to be paid for in sterling at an English port. The ship and cargo arrived at Bermuda, and the Confederate government when called upon failed to fulfil their contract. The mortgagees have since taken possession of and sold the ship and cargo. The estimated loss on non-fulfilment of contract is £90,000. The Federal government have, by their naval officers, captured the undermentioned steamships and cargoes; and I am advised that I am entitled to recover their full value, together with compensation for illegal detention, and proceedings are being taken in the law courts in America for that purpose:*

Patras, *cargo and freight, £15,378*

Stettin *£19,840*

Circassian *£35,000*

Empress *£3,003*

Lodona *£14,744.*

He added to this a claim on the Italian Government for the loss of the *Orwell* which he had chartered to Garibaldi and which had then been hijacked by the Mediterranean pirates. Again, in his words:

The steamship Orwell *was chartered in 1860 by Garibaldi to take passengers from Genoa to Messina; and a clause was inserted in the agreement that if the passengers took forcible possession of the vessel the charterer was to pay the owners the sum of £5,000. The charterers took possession of the vessel in the harbour of Genoa, and the said sum of £5,000 became due and payable by Garibaldi, whose liabilities have been adopted by the Italian government, who have admitted their liability, and have made an offer of compromise. The claim on the charter is £5,000; sundry expenses incurred in prosecuting the claim £2,500; total £7,500.*

His total loss of vessels was presented as:

8 ships lost at sea, partly insured, £24,276
6 ditto sold by me prior to the bankruptcy £11,520
1 ditto burnt in the Thames, £13,192
6 ditto captured by the Federal cruisers £34,223
10 ditto mortgaged to creditors £63,461
1 sloop given up to the assignees £50
1 yacht, ditto £103
Total 33 ships, £146,827

In giving evidence in court, Zachariah could not hide his bitterness about the vigilance with which he felt the blockading fleet had watched for his vessels: '*the Federals seized anything that had my name on it. They knew I was a sincere sympathiser with the Confederates*' – although, given the story behind each capture related in the last chapter, this perception may have been a touch paranoid...

In addition to the ships themselves, there were massive lists of what he owed in bills for fuelling them, insuring them, maintaining them, and then buying cargoes for them – all the paraphernalia of the shipping business. The accounts accordingly identify a plethora of traders and services to whom he owed money: clothing manufacturers, coal merchants, shipbuilders, gun makers, ship brokers, Lloyds' insurance, gunpowder makers, named captains of some of his vessels, solicitors, rope makers, tea merchants, ironmongers... the list goes on and on. The biggest creditors, well at the top of the list, were Overend, Gurney & Co. Not only had they been responsible for the six mortgaged Greek vessels they had foisted on Zachariah, but they had later apparently 'helped' him finance the massively-rising insurance premiums – all on credit, of course.

To add to the complexity of sorting Zachariah's estate, there were also claims in court by seamen who had been stranded for months when the vessels on which they had been serving were captured by the US navy. In finding their way back to England from America they had lost pay, as their route home could be quite complicated. Sometimes this was also compounded by quarantine rules. Just at the time when Zachariah was forced to abandon his blockade-running experiment in mid-1862, Wilmington was plagued by an epidemic of yellow fever. Every seaman from any vessel arriving in Wilmington was accordingly quarantined for 50 days – an added time of hardship for anyone trying to return to England. Those arriving home now wished to reclaim monies they were owed. Their families had suffered enough, and judges were largely sympathetic to them. So was Zachariah: the *Hull Times* in 1863 notes that *'Mr Pearson's carriage and horses and some furniture, were sold [...] requesting the agents to distribute the amount among the wives of the seamen'*. But there was no knowing how many such claims on his estate were lying hidden, ready to surface later, which made the accounts all the more treacherous.

Buried among the expected items of expenditure in these accounts were some intriguing little snippets, about which it would be interesting to know more. There was the £1,746 designated for the *Southampton Times*, but the only clarification is given as: *'for expenses in connection with this paper'*. Why? The reason is not stated. Certainly, as a port in southern England, some of his vessels were likely to have set out from here, and he would have run up port expenses and fuel bills, but not in the local paper. He possibly advertised for passengers in the *Southampton Times*, but surely not running up a bill which today would today represent £152,000. A possible link is the company he had been trying to set up in early 1862, *The United Kingdom Shipowning Company Ltd.*, where, together with the President of the Southampton Chamber of Commerce and six other directors, he had been trying to establish his fleet of iron sailing ships. Could the local newspaper have been part of this scheme? Could they, in fact, have been underwriting it? It is one of the many unsolved pieces of Zachariah's jigsaw.

A more informative piece of this gigantic jigsaw was the £4000 identified by Zachariah to buy James Coleman out of the business partnership in 1860. This represented a quarter-share of the company of Z. C. Pearson, Coleman and Co., which meant that the whole business enterprise must have been worth £16,000 at that time. In context, this would mean the company had been worth the equivalent of £1.4 million today. One assumes that James's quarter of this must had set him up in business nicely.

One of the items exempt from being included in the estate was £120 entered as a *'reversionary interest under the will of the late M. J. Harker'*. This was Mary Ann's grandfather, who had left to Zachariah the residue of some money after it had first been used for another family purpose. In the scale of the figures being bandied around in this particular court case, this legacy looks diminutive but it's the equivalent to being left more than £10,000 today – and Zachariah wanted to put it on record that it belonged to him, and not the general estate. It was an exacting task, listing all these small sums, but in the allocation of the spoils, every little helped.

During this initial sitting, where Zachariah had his financial affairs spread out on the table for all to see, another interesting facet of his life surfaced. In 1858, four years before any of his troubles started, Zachariah had drawn up a post-nuptial agreement, making over their house in Beverley Road, together with two other freehold houses and several insurance policies, to his wife, Mary Ann. He was at this stage at the peak of his success, and presumably wished – with some considerable prescience – to share out his assets and protect his family against future misfortune. There was later to be some argument in court as to whether at the time of this agreement he was worth £20,000 or £16,000, but in either case it was a *lot* of money (valued at £1.7 or £1.4 million today). The post-nuptial arrangement was later to be portrayed as highly sinister by the opposing creditors who attempted to pin as much as possible on Zachariah. But their accusation of cynically trying to hide assets was instantly dismissed by the Commissioner – it was clear that Zachariah had been rich and prosperous at the time of the agreement.

During the 18 months of adjournments, Zachariah's assets had been sold off by the assignees. In January 1863, for example, a 25,000 square yard plot of land to the east of Beverley Road was auctioned for a reserve of £5,760 in 1863. There is no record of when Zachariah bought this parcel of land, or why, but having been a Major in the Hull Volunteer Artillery Corps since its inception in 1860, and then its Commandant in 1862, it is likely that he purchased this space specifically for the Corps to use for parading and drilling. In any case, it was now sold off as one of his assets.

Regardless of the amount of money paid by asset-sales into the debt-relief pool, Zachariah's estate haemorrhaged money at an alarming rate to pay the legal and court fees each time the case was adjourned yet again, prompting the defence attorney to plead in January 1863 for matters to be speeded up on the grounds that *'the misfortune is that what is fun for the accountant is death to the bankrupt'*. The

Commissioner replied that it was to be regretted that an adjournment of sufficient length had not been taken in the first instant.

After the prolonged and costly lead-up, the actual hearing itself started in earnest in February 1864. The court cast was headed up by Commissioner Goulburn, who sat in judgement, and the other players in this legal drama were Mr Lewis, Zachariah's defence attorney, and Mr Bagley, representing the opposing creditors. The Assignees' counsel, Mr Laurance, remained neutral, as did Mr Linklater for the unopposing creditors. Zachariah now acquired the epithet of 'the bankrupt'.

The case started well, with Mr Laurance stating that he had no objection to Zachariah's discharge, adding that he *did not think that there was any point upon which the order of discharge could be successfully opposed. The assignees had been ready and willing at all times to receive information from any creditor as to any individual ground of any opposition, but no such information had been tendered to them in that respect.*' So far, so good. No objections had been registered, so Mr Laurance was unaware of any opposition to a discharge, and this sitting was the opportunity for various parties to clarify points of information for the Commissioner before the lawyers went into detail.

Zachariah was charged on four counts: with trading on fictitious capital; with rash and hazardous speculation; with contracting debts without any reasonable expectation of being able to pay them; and with extravagant personal expenditure. Mr Laurance explained the reasons for the Assignees' non-opposition to a discharge by saying that, considering his position in life, he was not spending unreasonably, and that *'it was difficult to say how any speculation was rash and hazardous unless goods were consigned to a desert island'.*

As the hearing drew on, though, things got more difficult. The Commissioner asked Zachariah to clarify his personal expenses, but he was in a tricky position; having been kept in the dark and denied access to his papers for 18 months, he had to rely on memory. He remarked: *'I have not seen the notes of my evidence at the last examination. I have only read the reports in the public papers.'* Nevertheless, when asked about financial details, his answer indicated that he had paid a less than meticulous attention to detail:

The bankrupt: *After the balance sheet of December 1858 I never made a balance sheet showing the state of my affairs, but I roughly estimated the result of my business from time to time. I had a partner up to 1860. Mr Coleman was the partner, having a 4th of my business. He was my brother-in-law. I think he retired in July. We then roughly estimated the state of affairs. All I know is, I gave him a sum of money to leave the partnership. At that time I considered I was flourishing. We must have made a balance sheet of some sort, but not a formal one. The books are in the hands of the assignees, and I cannot tell where balance sheets are.*
Mr Laurance: *There has been no balance sheet found amongst the books.*
The Commissioner: *Did you take stock at all?*
The bankrupt: *Yes, as recently as three months before the bankruptcy, and that shows a large balance in my favour.*
Mr Laurance: *We have not seen it.*
The Commissioner: *Such an account would be most important.*
The bankrupt: *I could find it if I had the opportunity.*

It reads like a scene from Alice in Wonderland. This passage is clearly a composite press report of Zachariah's response to several questions that we can only guess at. As the interrogation continued, Zachariah's answers were grouped together by the press, again leaving some of the precise questions to the imagination. A tale unfolds of a man who, having let his bookkeeping slip, and then being denied access to such figures as had been collected, was now being asked under oath to remember individual items when, with all the drama and excitement of the previous couple of years, and astronomical turnover, there must have been many items that escaped his memory. As he said, 'we were [at that time] paying in and out thousands of pounds a day'.

In this opening bout, where all the evidence was being laid out before being examined in detail, it became clear that Mr Bagley had been searching for anything which would blacken Zachariah's character and paint him in a poor light to the court. So having kept their ammunition dry, when they then pulled out new evidence in court, it came as a bombshell to Zachariah and to his counsel. It concerned an incident with a man called Brodrick, who had come to ask Zachariah to lend him money. Zachariah had said he could not lend him any as he was short of money himself, but Brodrick persuaded him to give him, in exchange for a consignment of wine, an accommodation bill. Brodrick immediately took this to the discount house – which morally obliged Zachariah to pay up at once. Clearly, this was impossible for him at that moment, and it thrust him immediately into debt. Zachariah maintained that this intervention of Brodrick's – or was it a trap? – was the catalyst that had derailed the early plan to pay creditors eight shillings in the pound, turning the small group of opposing creditors into hawks, and making bankruptcy inevitable. In Zachariah's words, 'Mr Brodrick was the very man who put an execution into my house – (the very man to whom I had given my acceptance to oblige) – and thereby compelled me to seek the protection of this court'.

Needless to say, Brodrick's version of the incident was different, and the issue had only been introduced by the opposing creditors to set the word of Brodrick against the word of Zachariah and prove what a villain the latter was. While it was all a bit of a sideshow as far as the court case itself was concerned, the story of Brodrick, lining up with the opposing creditors, really rankled with Zachariah, who felt deceived and let down by someone he thought had been a trusted friend.

Even so, whatever the cause of Zachariah being brought into bankruptcy, this was now history. Mr Bagley, having spent considerable time 'digging for dirt' with which to discredit Zachariah, now unleashed his second grenade: Zachariah had apparently been continuing to trade since he had entered bankruptcy proceedings – hiding under another name. He was accused of selling a ship, the *Rappahannock*, while officially not allowed to trade, but Zachariah emphatically denied this: *'I negotiated the sale of the vessel. I was purely a broker for Messrs Robert Gordon Coleman and Co.'*. This man, Robert, one of Mary Ann's brothers, was also part of the shipping family – but the Commissioner had had enough, and was starting to get lost in the complex details of all this mudslinging. So when Mr Lewis (for Zachariah) and Mr Bagley (for the opposing creditors) were crossing swords acrimoniously in the courtroom, Commissioner Goulburn had to knock heads together, saying he *'did not understand this mode of conducting a case',* and threatened to adjourn the examination if these expressions of feeling were not restrained.

One assumes that the lawyers behaved themselves after this, as the Commissioner went on to summarise what he considered to be his main task:

> *he considered it his duty to inquire into the transactions of the bankrupt before and after his bankruptcy. The speculations of the bankrupt were of vast magnitude, having 27 steam vessels going at one time. He had been raising money upon them, and endeavouring in any way to keep the thing going, but it had turned out to be a bubble.*

This session of the court set the scene for the main hearing, and by now there was no more talk of discharge being unopposed. Things were looking even bleaker for Zachariah, as during all this time he was given no allowance for daily living; the Assignees said there was no money to grant him one, and so he remained financially unsupported except for a few months. But the court was not without humour – albeit at Zachariah's expense; when Zachariah, denying that his speculation had been 'rash and hazardous', informed the Commissioner: '*My losses were occasioned by putting faith in the proclamation of the American President*', Mr Bagley quipped: '*That was rash and hazardous speculation (laughter)*'.

Before the case started in March, the opposing creditors bowled their last googly: Mr Bagley asked the Commissioner whether they could conduct the case in Hull on the grounds that some of the creditors were '*unable to leave or neglect their business to attend the court in London*'. Mr Lewis, on Zachariah's behalf, objected violently to this suggestion, as '*the object appeared to be to drag Mr Pearson down to Hull, and trail him through the mire for the purpose of degrading him in a place where he had occupied such an important position*'. The Commissioner agreed: he needed all witnesses in person in London. He wanted them to be seen in open court – they should be '*bound to come here and give their evidence fully and fairly. Much more is to be collected from the demeanour of a witness in the box than from what may fall from his lips*'. Here was a judge who knew the value of body language.

Once the 'trial' got under way, it took the form of three sessions: initially, the case for the opposing creditors, presented by Mr Bagley, secondly the case for Zachariah, presented by Mr Lewis, and finally the Commissioner's summing up and 'verdict'. As Mr Bagley '*delivered a speech of some four hours' duration*', the press had to do a good deal of summarising but the key point appeared to be predicated on his view that '*the system of blockade-running which the defendant had endeavoured to carry on was nothing better than gambling*'. He also said it was smuggling – but with other people's money, and thus a clear proof that this was 'rash and hazardous'. He listed some of Zachariah's debts, and concluded that he must have been trading *'not having reasonable or probable expectation of being able to meet the claim upon him when he incurred these debts'*.

When it came to proving that *'the personal expenditure of the bankrupt was unjustifiable and extravagant'*, he threw the book at him, and focused on character-assassination, asserting that all the charities and good works that Zachariah had supported from his own pocket were *'assumed by the bankrupt's own will for his own glorification'*. While a man of means would have been lauded, he said, *'this was one of the cases in which a man, from motives of ostentation, put himself forward as a person of great pretension, and gave, not from his own abundance, but from the hard earnings of others, obtaining a sham popularity by their spurious generosity'*.

Having set up Zachariah as seeking 'sham popularity' by his charitable giving, Bagley picked out the £1000 that Zachariah had contributed initially towards building the Methodist Chapel in Beverley Road. This was, indeed, a large sum – worth nearly £88,000 at today's values – but Mr Lewis could not let this preposterous slur on Zachariah's character pass, interrupting with: *'I am quite sure the learned counsel will like to know that the £1,000 donation to this chapel was given by the bankrupt at the end of the year 1860, long before the severe losses were incurred which brought him to the ground'*. The donation had been clearly documented as genuinely paid out of his own money well before Zachariah's current financial straits, but Mr Bagley had brought it up to discredit the bankrupt in the eyes of the court.

Still on the character-assassination theme, Mr Bagley next accused Zachariah of wilful lying about the circumstances in which Mr Brodrick had borrowed money from him and set in train the events which brought him into this court – but now he overdid it. The Commissioner, who in any case saw this as incidental to the key issues, intervened with '*this is, indeed, a most melancholy part of the case; but have we not heard enough of it?*' At the end of his four-hour marathon, two hours of which had been spent on trying to discredit Zachariah, Mr Bagley urged the court to refuse Zachariah's discharge on all counts.

The next hearing took place a few days later, when Mr Lewis stood up in court to defend Zachariah. His first job was to reinstate Zachariah's character by portraying his actions in a different light, and the first point he tackled was this discrepancy in the Brodrick-Pearson tale. After weighing the evidence on both sides, the report of his speech continued:

> *Did not these facts bear out the statement of the bankrupt that this was not an ordinary business transaction, but that it was an act of kindness and courtesy towards Mr Brodrick, and an accommodation? He contended that the balance of probability, and the balance of evidence, were strongly on the side of the bankrupt in this matter, and that throughout the whole of Mr Pearson's evidence, in the harassing and deplorable condition to which he had been reduced in the course of 18 months' proceedings, he had done nothing, and said nothing, to show that he was unworthy of belief.*

In any case, he ended, '*what earthly motive could the bankrupt have had for inventing a story of that kind?*'

The second false accusation he wished to address was that of Zachariah's personal overspending and using other people's money to do it: '*It had been said that the bankrupt, in the position he occupied at Hull, had been guilty of a sham liberality. Now he hoped that the time would never come when, in this court, an endeavour would be made to throw contempt upon municipal honours.*' The expenses he had incurred as Mayor and Sheriff were completely justified, and any personal pay-outs, such as the £1,000 gift to the chapel, were *bone fide* generosity, and to prove it, he gave the dates when the three tranches of the chapel gift were paid – all well before Zachariah had any financial problems.

Mr Lewis also sought to contextualise the bitter attacks on Zachariah by envy:

> *By the age of 39, the bankrupt, by his industry and commercial ability, found himself the Mayor of one of the first commercial ports in the kingdom. Was it unnatural to suppose, as the bankrupt did, that some of the opposition by which he had been pursued with so much bitterness in Hull, originated with the jealousy which lingered in the minds of some of his former colleagues at his occupying so early in life a situation which they had not? Let the court remember that these high positions were thrust upon the bankrupt by his high commercial status in Hull.*

He went on to berate the fact that, possibly because of this envy, the creditors were *'charging the bankrupt with all the offences contained in the criminal section of the act. "We had better fling all these charges at him," it appeared to be said; "we shall hit him somewhere"'*.

The last point on which he was determined to clear Zachariah's besmirched name was the size of his estate at the time of the post-nuptial agreement, as the Assignees had *'sought to impeach the settlement for the purpose of making the money available for the estate'*. Mr Lewis confirmed categorically that all was above board, and that Zachariah had been worth £20,000 in 1858 at the time of the settlement, although *'the bankrupt had since tumbled down'*.

Once he had dealt with the subplot of character-assassination, Mr Lewis turned to the real reason for Zachariah's downfall: his imprudent dealings with Overend, Gurney & Co. over the Greek ships. *'It might be that such prosperity as he had attained to was too much for Mr Pearson's prudence'*, he said, and went on to describe how Zachariah had been seduced by the over-favourable terms on which the bank had persuaded him to buy, on credit, six vessels that he could neither afford nor use. *'This was the key to the whole of Mr Pearson's subsequent misfortunes; and although he had steered through many other shoals, he did not know how to steer through the shoal of prosperity'*. Mr Lewis could clearly engage his audience, and even invoked Shakespeare to help him:

> *Well, then the Civil War broke out in America. The bankrupt had this large fleet of ships, and he thought he saw a market for them in America. The Baltic trade, in which he had been engaged, had become unprofitable; and unhappily for him he entered into a course of trading. Then began his losses which crowded quickly upon him, and his position soon resembled that of which Bassanio* [in The Merchant of Venice] *spoke:*
> *"Have all his ventures failed? What, not one hit*
> *From Tripolis, from Mexico and England?*
> *Has not one vessel 'scaped the dreadful touch*
> *Of merchant-warring rocks?"*

He defended the charge of 'trading on fictitious capital' by saying that the defaults were relatively small in the grand scale of things: *'The charge of trading on fictitious capital was based on his having issued some £12,000 or £15,000 of accommodation bills, as compared with transactions during the year to the amount of a million and a half money. This was indeed a small stain to fix upon the bankrupt.'*
Then he tackled the emotive accusation of smuggling, saying that while smuggling was illegal, the Queen's Proclamation did not make blockade-running illegal – just not officially approved of. He described the President's Proclamation as *'a Yankee trap'*, and suggested that on Lincoln's proclamation there *'might well be inscribed the lines "'Will you walk into my parlour? said the spider to the fly"'*.

He went on to parody the biblical saying, 'put not your trust in princes', as *'"put not your trust in Princes or in Presidents" (laughter in court)'*. He maintained that, if Zachariah had received what he was owed from the Prize Courts, and if the Confederates, on hearing about his bankruptcy, had not suspended the £100,000 they owed him for the *Merrimac*, he could easily have covered his debts. *'But the contract was broken up by Messrs. Overend and Gurney, upon what appeared to be conscientious scruples, there being some powder on board – (a laugh) – and thus £100,000 marched out of the balance sheet, because the bankruptcy intervened and prevented the execution of the contract.'*

Here was Mr Lewis using humour again, this time at the bankers' expense – Overend and Gurney being Quakers, he quipped that that was the reason they had disapproved of a cargo of gunpowder. Between the wisecracks – the psychology of a skilful barrister designed to bring the court on his side – Mr Lewis admitted and regretted that Zachariah had been unwise in some of the trading he did while things were falling apart, trying at all costs to keep up his credit against the odds. But he came back again to the way a very small group of creditors had turned against Zachariah, when they were only owed a mere £6,000-£7,000 between them – a tiny amount in proportion to the whole estate. When, back in 1862, the *Stettin* had erroneously been reported in the Hull press as having succeeded in running the blockade, there had been all-round rejoicing, with two of the main protagonists lauding him publicly at that stage,

But as soon as he became a bankrupt they got upon stilts – their commercial morality revolted at the spectacle and they called him a reckless speculator. If he had had good luck no amount of laudation would have been too much for both Mr Pease and Mr Bannister. But he became a ruined man, and then they called him a commercial delinquent. So in the history of nations a man is either a patriot or a rebel – he either swung or he reigned.

He also pointed out that Zachariah's creditors had extended credit to him, even while *'knowing the nature of the trade in which he was engaging, and could not therefore now come forward and say that he had been engaged rather a hazardous speculation'.*

Lastly, he returned to defending Zachariah against the accusation of sham liberality and spending too much personally, and *'he flung back with scorn and contempt to that corner of Hull where it had arisen, the charge that the bankrupt had been liberal in this instance with other people's money.'* He went into detail about Zachariah's accounts, and continued:

> *From a perusal of the charitable objects which he had assisted, it was evident that Mr Pearson, believing he had the money to spend, gave it away like a Christian giver. He had spent upon public entertainments, of which, no doubt, Mr Pease and Mr Brodrick* [two of the main protagonists] *had their fair share, £859 – a sum spread over three years – namely, £213 in 1859, when sheriff; £279 in 1860, when mayor; and in 1861, £365. Considering the bankrupt's position in Hull, this was not extravagant.*

But the Commissioner now interrupted: as this charge of overspending was clearly not going to stick, he did not need to hear any more about it. Mr Lewis concluded his defence by once more pointing out that the vast majority of the creditors had no problem with a discharge, but that the case was due to *'the opposition of five or six gentlemen from Hull, who had raised the great charges, but who really had no cause for complaint. There was not a particle of evidence of fraud against the bankrupt, though his transactions were so gigantic.'*

The day's hearing ended with the Commissioner commenting on the quality of Mr Lewis' argument: *'whatever Mr Pearson's misfortunes might have been, they did not extend to the choice of an advocate'.* Mr Lewis had indeed been a good choice of lawyer by Zachariah.

The cases for and against Zachariah being concluded, the final hearing took place a few weeks later in April 1864, when the Commissioner summed up and passed judgement. It seems that Zachariah's demeanour in court had impressed the judge from the beginning, commenting that the bankrupt *'has been able and willing at all times to afford all the assistance in his power to the assignees. He has been very much assisted by able accountants, and has done his best to explain a very serious state of things, to say no more.'* Commenting that this was a case that would probably be widely quoted, he summarised its unusual nature:

The case presents some features of a startling kind. The history of the bankrupt is in itself a somewhat extraordinary one, or at least a singular one. This Mr Pearson, it seems, began life in a very humble position – as a ship boy or cabin boy on board the vessel. Very much to his credit he soon began to rise out of that condition: by getting from the cabin to the quarter deck, obtaining the command of the ship, and then becoming her owner, and the owner of other vessels. Undoubtedly, we must assume that by diligence and good conduct he earned for himself a good reputation, and a considerable fortune besides, for we find that at the end of the year 1858, when he executed a post-nuptial settlement, he had a balance of £16,000 in hard money, which, to use a common expression, he had earned off his own bat, and which he had a right to employ as he pleased.

He then went on to say that he thought the beginning of Zachariah's downfall was his split from James Coleman in 1860.

When that partner withdrew in 1860, and he was left to himself, his downward career began. He bought his partner out. Perhaps he got impatient, as many men of a speculative turn do, and resolved, as the Americans say, to go fast a-head. Now, nothing is more troublesome to such a man than a partner who checks him in his adventures, and in the year 1860, as I have said, he much to his misfortune got rid of that partner, and from that time, as I have before intimated, I date his downward career.

He regretted the fact that this was conjecture, as *'it was a very melancholy fact'* that Zachariah did not seem to have kept proper accounts after the break-up. He pointed out that the opposing creditors were only owed £6,000-£7,000 between them, but discredited one of them (Mr Pease) as not being 'a *creditor by any actual transaction'.* In running through the four charges, he praised the performance of Mr Lewis: *'I must say that in the whole course of my experience I never heard a more able address on behalf of a client'.* Then he threw out the charge of excessive personal expenditure, while wishing at the same time that Zachariah had taken more care with his accounts:

He was a man who had risen, as many other men have done, from a humble position, and had attained a position which entitled him to the respect of those around him. Occupying such a position he was necessarily called upon to incur some expenditure. He could not fill the office of mayor without giving those entertainments which appertain to the office, and he kindly contributed to many of the charities of the town. I therefore say that I cannot attribute his failure to undue extravagance, although, looking at what followed, and the downward course he was taking, I think it would have been wiser and better if he had held his hand and looked more into his accounts. With these remarks I dismiss that point.

With that, the charge was dismissed – Zachariah was exonerated on excessive overspending.

He next addressed the charge of 'rash and hazardous speculation', concluding that this charge was justifiable. While he could not go so far as to agree with Mr Bagley that it was smuggling, he implied that he didn't think Zachariah could possibly have been taken in by the Presidential Proclamation: *'as to trusting to anything that the President said about vessels being warned off, I don't suppose anybody gave credit to that, and Mr Pearson is too wise a man to have lent himself to any such supposition'*.

He enumerated the disasters which had befallen Zachariah, but he explained that *'no man has a right to embark in a speculation unless he has, if the speculation fails, wherewith to pay every man his own'*. As Zachariah clearly did not have enough money to cover all debts in the event of failure, and as he had been embarking on a very large and risky venture, the Commissioner summarised by saying that *'the speculation was a rash and hazardous one, and that his failure is clearly owing to it'*.

On this charge, then, he was indicted – no discharge here.

On the third charge, that of trading on fictitious capital, Commissioner Goulburn, while empathising with Zachariah's increasingly desperate attempt at keeping afloat with more and more accommodation bills, reckoned that *'he ought to have said to himself, these adventures have failed – I am the most unlucky man, perhaps, that ever lived – the odds have turned up against me, and there is an end of the matter'*. But as it was, Zachariah did not stop; he paddled ever faster to stay afloat, and he was charged on this offence. The Commissioner explained carefully how he arrived at the conclusion that he did:

> *It appears that the bankrupt gave a commission to people to accept bills for him to keep him going, and that they had the disastrous effect of keeping him afloat much longer than was beneficent to his creditors and to himself. I have laid down the principle that if a*

*man when he is failing keeps himself afloat by means
of accommodation paper, that man by so doing is, in my
judgment, trading upon fictitious capital.*

On this third charge, then, Zachariah again did not
receive his discharge.

There was only one question left now – had Zachariah
been obtaining goods without reasonable expectation of
payment? Commissioner Goulburn seemed to be struggling
with this charge, putting forward two views:

*Suppose Mr Pearson had said – "If my ships break
the blockade and get into Nassau, I shall have more
than enough" – that is not a reasonable and probable
expectation. A man has no right, whilst engaged in a
gambling transaction, to run into debt, and say "If I win
I can pay you tomorrow morning." He has no right to
run into debt unless he has a reasonable and probable
expectation of paying his debt. That is my view of the
matter.*

Here he sounded unsupportive of what Zachariah did,
but next he cited a previous case, where a man deliberately
continued to run up debts after repeated discharges, and yet
was still given his discharge, and so Goulburn concluded:
'On the authority of that case [...] I shall not act in this, and I
still assume that Mr Pearson had a reasonable and probable
expectation of being able to pay, even up to the last, and
I don't think I am doing any injustice in expressing that
opinion'.

In other words, he gave Zachariah his discharge on this
final count.

Before pronouncing the 'sentence' the Commissioner
made some remarks that were supportive towards Zachariah:

*He has been remarkable for giving assistance to his
creditors, and for doing all that he could to help them
in the circumstances in which he is placed; and I think*

*that, as to punishment, the case is very nearly satisfied.
But I am more anxious to lay down my view of the law
on these two points than to inflict anything in the way
of punishment on Mr Pearson, for I think he has already
suffered greatly, very much.*

In addition, he pointed out that for 18 months Zachariah
had been obliged to live without any allowance. He brought
the case to an end by delivering his judgement:

*I have gone through it with the greatest care and anxiety,
and I may say, that there are two points on which I feel
discharged from giving a verdict. On the other two points
I am very anxious, and I think that with respect to them
he has brought himself within the section of the Act of
Parliament; but looking at what has passed, I think the
justice of the case will be quite met by giving Mr Pearson
his discharge at the end of six months from this day –
three months on each point – he having protection from
arrest in the meantime. I pass this sentence more for
the purpose of having the principle established than for
punishing Mr Pearson who has already undergone very
considerable privations.*

The Commissioner had cleared Zachariah on two charges:
he had not overspent while he was Mayor, and he had not
had any fraudulent intention of obtaining goods without a
reasonable expectation of being able to pay for them. But
he did judge that Zachariah had been 'rash and hazardous',
and that he had indeed 'traded on fictitious capital' in an
effort to stay solvent once things had started to implode.
On these two points, he would be given his discharge after
three month each – six months in all.

The time allotted for a discharge was normally related
to the seriousness of the bankruptcy, and it defined a
reasonable time in which a bankrupt would be able to pay
off his debts. After the end of the discharge period, the

bankrupt would be legally free from any remaining debts. In this complicated case, though, which had dragged on so long, practically everything Zachariah owned had already been sold, and Commissioner Goulburn now came over as rather sympathetic. He portrayed Zachariah as a gentleman who was somewhat confused as to how he had found himself in the position of trading beyond his means, and ever-hopeful of good fortune in breaking the blockade. He saw him, not as a man who had deliberately set out to swindle people, but more as a victim – a victim of Overend and Gurney, of the Italian Government, and of Abraham Lincoln and his broken promise to warn ships off. So, having dismissed two of the charges against Zachariah, he sounded mildly reluctant to be giving him two three-month discharges on the other counts – almost as though he needed to be seen to hold Zachariah up as an example rather than punish him.

Whether Zachariah felt relieved or unhappy about the verdict, we have no way of knowing, but whatever his feelings, he now had to pick himself up by his bootstraps and rebuild his life.

12

Schadenfreude: he had it coming!

The worst was over. Zachariah knew his fate. After waiting in dread and suspense for so long, he surfaced after the Bankruptcy Court verdict in the spring of 1864 and faced the future. There were wounds to be licked and injuries to be repaired, but he must had have been relieved when he found he had the sympathy of the local press in Hull, who echoed the kindly remarks of Commissioner Goulburn. The *Hull Packet* of 29th April pointed out that while there had been several recent bankrupts who had deliberately set out to live a life of grandeur, knowing that they did not have the funds to do so, Zachariah certainly did not fit into this category. By the time he had lost his money, he had already proved himself financially, although the *'enterprise and ambition which had pushed on the cabin boy until he became one of the leading shipowners, and then the Sheriff, and twice Mayor of Hull, unfortunately did not let him rest there'*.

This relentless drive to push himself also had the press both amused and dismissive of the Commissioner's attribution of the origin of Zachariah's troubles to the loss of his business partner. Having observed at first hand the way Zachariah operated in Hull, they knew that *'Mr Pearson had both the money and the brains of the firm, and that his partner would have soon as thought of trying to stop the flow of the Humber as of trying to arrest any of Mr Pearson's commercial operations'*. So much for young James Coleman's influence! Zachariah had clearly been seen as the dominant and headstrong partner in the business, determined to do whatever he felt was right, regardless of James' opinion.

The same article empathised with Zachariah's bad fortune in his dealings with the Confederates: it was a perfectly understandable business move to take. After all, as they somewhat tactlessly pointed out, one firm in Manchester had managed to net £2 million from successful blockade-running during exactly the same period when Zachariah lost everything. Then they went on to comment that the two counts of three months till Zachariah's discharge was negligible compared to his personal suffering during the process:

> Terrible [...] has been the punishment of his folly. Nobody who can think or feel can imagine that six month's suspension of certificate will be regarded by him as very great punishment. The real judgement had gone by before that judgement was pronounced. The resignation of his Mayoralty; his compulsory absence from the town where he had been so honoured an inhabitant; the eighteen months' suspension of business in the very prime of his manhood; the attendance at meeting after meeting in the Bankruptcy Court, and day after day in the official assignee's office; and the examinations and the cross-examinations to which he has been subjected – these must have constituted the real sufferings of our late Mayor. But those who remember his kindness of heart, his public spirit, the benefits that he has conferred upon the town, and those who recognise his ability as a merchant and shipowner, will be only too glad that within a very brief period Mr Pearson will be a free man again.

Here, then, was a positive public statement of support, and very comforting it must have been for Zachariah to realise that he had some compassion in his home town after his ordeal. Nevertheless, the turmoil and the depths of torture beneath the surface were only alluded to here. The paper glossed over the really hurtful stuff – the deep vindictiveness with which Zachariah had been remorselessly pursued in a public forum. The conclusion of the court case did not resolve the polarisation of emotions about him in Hull, even if the press was publicly very much on his side.

Where did this crusade against him spring from? Why was it apparently so sudden? Sure, he had let people down, and gone through a personal hell in dealing with the consequences, but was there anything that might have predicted the hostility that emerged in court? In exploring the roots of this vitriol we need to backtrack a few years to the time when everything Zachariah touched had turned to gold. In his charmed life, he had initiated a grand church one day, handed over the deeds to the park the next, and turned 39 the day after that. He was turning into a cult figure – and he was still a young man.

Did he ever look back at his humble roots, and reflect that he might be jumping over too many social and cultural barriers too fast? While society was changing rapidly, opening up opportunities for everyone to prosper, this did not stop the traditionalists harking back to a time when everyone knew their place. People were pigeonholed according to whether their money was old (inherited) or new (self-made), whether they were working, middle or upper class – or even whether they were young or old. There was tribalism in local politics, there were in-crowds and out-crowds, and there were professional jealousies in a town whose economy was based almost entirely on businesses associated with shipping, a town where everyone knew everyone and all their business.

Long before his fall was even hinted at, there were those who were looking sideways at Zachariah, the self-made, youthful nobody who was now in the centre of the in-crowd. Possibly they were even then biding their time to knock him down a peg or two when he put a foot wrong. In the meantime, everyone loved a winner; Zachariah's star was shining brightly – and there was glory to be had in associating with stars. Zachariah himself was probably oblivious. Things just kept getting better for him. He was being invited into inner circles he would not once have dreamed of joining, moving in levels of society to which he had not been born, and his largesse knew no bounds.

One of the events that demonstrated how Zachariah-worship was rising to fever-pitch occurred after the birth of their seventh child, and it could also have been perceived as yet another factor raising the height of the pedestal from which he could later be toppled. Mary Ann had given birth just before the Colossal Fete in the park, and the council had commissioned an extremely flashy gift to commemorate the occasion. The *Hull Packet* of 22nd February 1861 describes this as a table ornament of plate (silver), two-and-a-half feet in height, with four dolphins *'gracefully arranged'*, scrolls, foliage and vine stems *'embowering an infant in a golden cradle'*, and topped with festoons of flowers. Around the base the figure of Zachariah was depicted presenting the deeds of the park

accompanied by figures representing civic dignity and justice, and commercial prosperity. In the distance shipping and active commerce are represented as well as foliage of the park. In addition to the arms and crest of Mr Pearson there is the following inscription: *"Presented by the members and ex-members of the Council of the Borough of Kingston-upon-Hull, to Mrs Pearson, to commemorate the birth of a daughter during the mayoralty of her munificent and highly-esteemed husband, Zachariah Charles Pearson Esq. in the year 1860"*.

The baby, Beatrice, was seven months old by the time this magnificent gift was completed, and three members of the committee took it round to their house to present it to Mary Ann. Zachariah responded on behalf of his wife, *'expressing her gratification at the kind feeling manifested by the donors, and her admiration of the valuable and elegant piece of plate they had provided. The healths of Mrs Pearson, the infant and Mr Pearson were then drunk, and responded to by Mr Pearson, after which the deputation withdrew.'* If Mary Ann appears here to be a voiceless, passive recipient on an occasion dedicated specifically to her, this was the social expectation of how Victorian women would behave. After all, she was only singled out for the honour because of her 'munificent and highly-esteemed husband' – unless it was the custom to award such gifts to any Mayoress giving birth.

History does not tell us what Mary Ann thought about having such a huge and flamboyant ornament on her table. But the event was an indication of the Pearson family in the limelight, and honours like this splashed across the local paper may well have contributed towards the politics of envy, albeit latent at this stage.

Another potentially contentious issue was Zachariah's coat of arms. This had decorated the park gates, and now 'the arms and crest of Mr Pearson' were on the ostentatious ornament. But it is not clear where it came from. Did Zachariah request it, or was it awarded for public service? One assumes, since it was clearly in use in the early 1860s, that its design had been approved by the College of Arms, but a search through heraldry records has drawn a blank, and after his fall from grace we see nothing more of it. Could the Pearson crest have been a hubristic sign of Zachariah's ambition? Was this, perhaps, a clear indication that Zachariah was getting a bit too big for his boots – a humble chap made good and wanting his own coat of arms? Perhaps his motto, *'Providentia fido'* (I trust in Providence) was tempting fate a step too far...

And then there was the proposed knighthood, perhaps another nail in Zachariah's coffin. An undated 1862 newspaper article describes a plan by the Prince of Wales to celebrate his own coming-of-age on 9th November 1862 by conferring knighthoods upon all Mayors in post throughout England on that date. The local paper in Hull accordingly declared: *'under these circumstances, we may, with confidence, congratulate Mr Z. C. Pearson on the honours which await him. We believe it is the wish of the town that he who now fills the civic chair may be the man whom the Queen will honour, and we trust his life may be spared to enjoy the distinction.'*

Zachariah's coat of arms. This seems to have been created around 1860 at the time he gave the land for the park. It appears for the first time in this sketch from the Hull archive's blueprint for the park gates in the ceremonial arch. It is described as a 'lion demirampant holding a mullet' (star). Zachariah's motto, Providentia Fido, presumably celebrated his meteoric success in the first 39 years of his life, though it was less auspicious later.

Yes, his life was indeed spared – but not his mayoral seat, nor his reputation, and the knighthood never materialised, the date of the Prince's birthday coming after The Great Crash. However, between the announcement in the Court Circular and the financial collapse there may well have been those in Hull who saw this as yet another over-the-top honour about to be bestowed on Zachariah-the-Great. Were episodes like these contributory factors in understanding why, a year or so later, there might be a faction in Hull poised to give Zachariah his comeuppance at the first opportunity?

While overtly popular, successful and rich, then, the seeds of discontent had possibly been germinating under the surface for some time, and when Zachariah's dramatic fall came, it did not take much for the shoots to become visible. Victorians heaped scorn upon losers, and the small group of influential men who set up as opposing creditors were bitter and unforgiving. There was a good deal of *schadenfreude*: he'd had it coming, and he now deserved everything he got.

And now that 'it' had arrived, Zachariah had to manage the consequences. As soon as his dire situation became irreversible, his resignation letter to the Town Council of Kingston-upon-Hull on 24th September 1862, a few weeks before the end of his second term of office, was short and to the point:

Gentlemen,
I regret that circumstances connected with my business compel me to resign the offices of Mayor and Alderman which you confided to me. I beg sincerely to thank you for the support and confidence given me, as well as for the courtesy and kindness always manifested by the entire Council during the time I have had the honour to hold these offices.
I am, Gentlemen,
Yours faithfully,
Z. C. Pearson

The council accepted this resignation with regret, handing over the reins to Alderman Moss. When the new mayor, William Hodge, came into post he made a generous speech in council: '*a kinder-hearted gentleman has seldom sat in this chair. I repeat again that I regret the circumstances that have caused this. I sympathise with him, and though he is somewhat fallen, I respect him (hear, hear). I believe I express the feelings of every gentleman here present when I say this (hear, hear).*'

This warm vote of sympathy was given when things were still looking relatively rosy; Zachariah and his creditors were waiting for the Americans to pay up, and the knives of the hostile creditors, some of whom were on the council, were still sheathed – for the moment.

Resigning from all his roles in public life would have been deeply upsetting, but giving up his leadership position in the East York Artillery Volunteers would have been especially hurtful. Having nurtured the unit from its inception in 1860, and having been promoted to Lieutenant-Colonel only four months prior to his disaster, he was clearly very proud of 'his' corps. But the *London Gazette* announced: '*Her Majesty has been graciously pleased to accept the resignation of the commission held by Lieut.-Col. Z. C. Pearson*'.

Zachariah had now been toppled from each of the highest positions in Hull. But departing office so suddenly had left a lot of unfinished business, so while he was in London for the court case he was writing to Hull to tie off some of the loose ends. The Hull Archive has several of his letters written in the early 1860s, before and during the bankruptcy case, and these throw light on his dawning realisation of what was about to happen, and how the situation was affecting him psychologically.

Even before his crash, Zachariah had been spending a lot of his time in London as that was where his big new business, the Intercolonial Royal Mail Steam Packet Co. Ltd., was based. His dispatches to Yorkshire show that he was juggling his Hull commitments with his London businesses, touching base with the Town Clerk while he was commuting. His letters were short and business-like, usually apologising for being detained in London on business and therefore missing a meeting, a deputation, or a lunch the following day – the Victorian postal service clearly being far more reliable than ours today. He would then express a view about current council business: where cattle might or might not be allowed in the town, his preference on nominations for council positions, and in one letter, written on 2nd July 1862, he hoped that *'an address be voted to the Queen on the marriage of the "Princess Alice"'*.

After Zachariah's world had been rocked by the financial earthquake, though, the tone of his letters changed. On 6th August in 1862, the week after the grisly day when he had received the devastating news of the loss of ships to the value of £85,000, and just before he officially resigned from the Mayoralty, he fired off a quick message to Hull:

My Dear Mr Town Clerk,
I am very sorry that I shall not be able to be present at the Council Meeting tomorrow. I am unfortunately detained here much against my will.
Will you please arrange for the Presidentship of the Council tomorrow & apologise to the Council for my non-attendance.
Yours very truly...

The 'much against my will' said it all. He knew by now that he had no choice – he had to stay in London to try to salvage his affairs, even though this meant someone else had to chair the Council Meeting. Although at this stage Zachariah probably did not know it, two days earlier his valuable ship *Lodona* had been captured. In any case, when he wrote this letter he must have had a profound sense of doom about the fate of all of his remaining vessels and cargoes which he knew were, at that very moment, still steaming west across the Atlantic into the jaws of trouble.

Although he was hoping against hope that one of them might break the blockade and rescue his fortunes, he probably knew this was clutching at straws. He feared for the timing, knowing that to offset his losses they would be put up for sale, doubtlessly at well below their value.

This was the stage when he was still hoping to avoid bankruptcy and the dreadful social stigma associated with it, but once the small group of antagonistic creditors had unsheathed their knives, the writing was on the wall. One of the key figures playing a powerful role in leading the 'hawks' against Zachariah was Mr Samuelson. In fairness, Samuelson did have a right to feel aggrieved; he ran a major ship-building business, and had sold Zachariah several vessels, subsequently finding himself considerably out of pocket because of Zachariah's risky ventures, so he was understandably not greatly disposed to sympathise with this man.

Behind the scenes, as time dragged on, Zachariah recognised that people were positioning themselves: they were either for him or against him. On the one hand, Zachariah-the-Philanthropist had been generous with his riches; he was well-liked and popular. Instead of living a gentleman's life in the country, he stayed in Hull because he cared about it, and he used his wealth to try to improve conditions for the people and for the town's trade. This was well-appreciated – he was a benefactor to the town and to working people. On the other hand, Zachariah-the-Swindler had not only taken the risk of running the blockade, but he had done so with other people's money. The risk was 'rash and hazardous' and it was not surprising that he had failed. He was a crook, or a 'great kite-flier', and he deserved everything that was coming to him.

Zachariah, until this point in time, had been accustomed to the appreciation and the goodwill of his townsfolk, so this emerging hostility from certain quarters came as a severe blow to him. We know that he was extremely agitated, because this is the unique point in the whole of Zachariah's story where we do not have to surmise what he was thinking and feeling at the time: he himself committed it to paper. Zachariah wrote to Hull from his London address, where he was preparing papers and figures for the court. The letter was written to a Mr Richardson on the Hull council before the first court hearing in October, and the Hull History Archive has this letter – the only correspondence of personal nature that has been preserved.

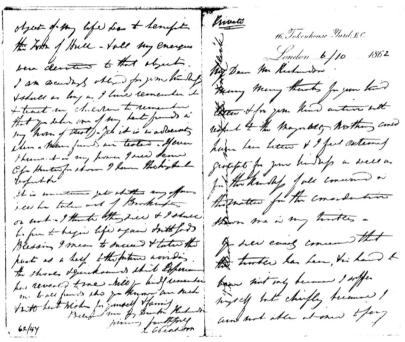

The first and last page of Zachariah's letter to Mr Richardson - the only personal latter that has survived. He wrote it from London when the enormity of his losses and the humiliation of his circumstances was just dawning on him. Mr Richardson had clearly been sympathetic, and Zachariah unburdened himself, adding the cross-written PS: 'Please remember me to the Town Clerk'.

The letter is remarkable in expressing Zachariah's inner feelings of remorse and sorrow to a fellow councillor in Hull. At a time when others were turning against him, Zachariah clearly valued his friendship with Richardson, and trusted him enough to express his fears. Because this is the only time that we can read Zachariah's raw emotions scribbled in a letter to a friend, instead of his official speechmaking or guarded court appearances, the whole of the letter is reproduced here.

Zachariah starts by acknowledging an empathetic (but unrecorded) letter that Mr Richardson had written to him:

Private

> *6, Tokenhouse Yard,*
> *London, E C 6/10/62*

My Dear Mr Richardson,
Many many thanks for your kind letter and for your kind action with regard to the Mayoralty. Nothing could have been better & I feel extremely grateful for your kinship as well as for the kinship of all concerned in this matter for the consideration shown me in my troubles.
You will easily perceive that the trouble has been, & is, hard to bear not only because I suffer myself but chiefly because I am not able at once to pay all claims upon me. I no doubt am censored by many & probably I deserve it. If I had seen the end from the beginning I should not probably have ventured so much. But on the other hand, how many of us are very wise after the facts have transpired & all is known. I am now the better for my experience as far as knowledge goes, but no prudence & no foresight ever provided against the series of bad luck & misfortune which followed me after the other. All will depend upon the course my affairs take as to my future plans. I am only afraid lest my estate is frittered away & goes into other hands but the creditors.
But I do resolve that if the estate does not pay 20/- in the pound I shall devote a portion of my future earnings to pay in full all the creditors in Hull. I have no doubt that I shall again rise, but whether Hull is then my future home all will depend upon the people themselves; if kinship and sympathy is shown me, that of course will

encourage me to come again and work for my family and the town. But it would be very unpleasant indeed for me to live among a people who had known me as prospering & who had no respect for me in adversity. Whether I have done right or not in the past, the thing I am sure of, and my family knows it, that the object of my life was to benefit this Town of Hull – & all my energies were devoted to that object.

I am exceedingly obliged for your kinship & shall as long as I live remember it & teach my children to remember that you were one of my best friends in my hour of trial. Yes it is in adversity when a man's friends are tested. If ever I have it in my power I will serve Cllr. Hunter for whom I have the highest respect.

It is uncertain yet whether my affairs will be taken into Bankruptcy or not. I think they will and I shall hope to begin life again & with Lord's Blessing I mean to succeed and take the past as a help to the future avoiding the shoals & quicksands which experience has revealed to me. Will you kindly remember me to all friends who you know are such, and with best wishes for yourself and family.

Believe me, My Dear Mr Richardson,
Yours faithfully,
Z. C. Pearson
P.S. Please remember me to the Town Clerk

He was agonising over not being able immediately to honour his debts, and while he was still hoping against hope that he would avoid bankruptcy, he made it clear that, whatever the outcome, he was determined to repay every penny of his debts eventually. He feared that his estate would be 'frittered away' from the people who were owed money, noting that hindsight was a wonderful thing, but nevertheless saw himself as victim of circumstance and bad luck. Having gone through so much in his life by the age of 41, he recognised that this experience had taught him a valuable lesson, and that with the Lord's help he hoped to avoid 'shoals and quicksands' in the future.

The deepest emotion was reserved for the realisation that previous friends and associates were rejecting him now that his fortunes had changed. He had written this letter before experiencing the cynical character-assassination by Bagley in court, but it shows that even then he was expecting the worst. The mood-music in Hull had changed, and the letter expressed his deep sense of distress. But at the same time, he was enormously grateful for the loyalty and friendship of Mr Richardson and those of his friends who had stuck by him in his hour of need.

His comment that Hull was at his heart was reinforced in another letter that he wrote a few days later. Even in the throes of trying to avoid the ignominy of bankruptcy, he still had time to articulate his fears about Hull and its Trade to Mr Richardson:

I hope you are well & please accept my warm thanks for your kinship in writing me. I am not without hope of some day being among you again. Hull wants pushing on – I fear much of its Trade will run away to Hartlepool and is owing to the want of push and energy among steam ship owners etc. etc. (18th October 1862)

It seems he was still seeing himself as having a future leadership role in promoting Hull's trade among other steamer owners. The Hartlepool comment probably referred to the lower rail freight charges and landing rates in that dock, making it more attractive to merchants and shipowners; Zachariah was worried about Hartlepool as a competitor to Hull. In the event, of course, being a bankrupt, he was allowed to be neither a shipowner nor a civic leader, although he did, even in his reduced circumstances, eventually go on to play a significant 'elder statesman' role in his later years.

The statue of Queen Victoria, a commission to local sculptor Thomas Earle by Zachariah in 1860 for his park. She was carved from a 12-ton block of flawless marble from the same Carrara quarries in Italy that Michelangelo had used for his David and the Pietà. Earle carved her in his London workshop, but her installation was delayed because of Zachariah's bankruptcy. Mr Moss stepped forward to complete the payment that Zachariah had started, and she was eventually unveiled in 1863.

Continuing the speculation about reasons for Zachariah's ostracism, arguments in the council about the Park provide a further possible source of disquiet. It may be recollected that Zachariah had commissioned the statue of Queen Victoria, and paid a handsome deposit of £100 for it. But his 'crash' intervened before Earle, the sculptor, had completed it, and with frozen assets Zachariah was then unable to pay the rest of the cost. This was highly embarrassing. Ownership of the statue had been legally transferred to the assignees where it became one of the assets which they should be selling in order to pay the creditors. However, it was impounded in Earle's workshop in London. The Queen had seen the work, and was delighted with it. Indeed, it had been exhibited by Earle to much acclaim in the International Exhibition of 1862 – held on the site now occupied by the London museums of Natural History and Science. But it had not been paid for, and so could not be installed in the Park. The statue was in limbo – and the threat of royal displeasure had to be avoided.

Mayor Moss, after some negotiation with the assignees, with great delicacy and generosity, stepped in to settle the remainder of the bill, and bought the statue on behalf of Hull. A potentially awkward situation had been averted, and everyone was grateful to the Mayor for saving the day – but even this brought division in the council. On 5th June 1863 the local paper reported an argument at a meeting of the Park Committee, emphasising the polarisation of opinion over Zachariah. One of the councillors wanted it placed on record as 'a matter of justice', that 'it was well-known that a great deal of Mr Pearson's money went towards paying for the statue, and therefore it ought not be understood that the Mayor was the sole giver of the statue'. Mr Samuelson objected vehemently to this; speaking as one of the assignees, he said that the statue would have been sold by auction if Moss had not bought it, and that then they would not have had it all, so Moss should certainly get all the credit. Others flatly contradicted him, adamant that there no way that this particular statue could have ever been auctioned. Heated words were exchanged, for and against having Zachariah recognised – but the message was clear: strident and dominant voices in positions of power were determined to deny Zachariah's role in the statue story.

Zachariah had also started a public fund for a statue of Prince Albert for the park, but money was slow to appear once Zachariah's financial troubles stopped him from campaigning. When there were sufficient resources, Earle carved Albert, albeit long after he had died. Queen Victoria vetoed the notion that he should share a pedestal with her, and he stands some distance away from his wife in the park.

Before the Queen's likeness was installed, another curious twist to the story emerged. Zachariah, it may be remembered, had started a subscription list for a nearby statue of Prince Albert, but with the hardship and distress of the mill operatives caused by the American Civil War, and with Zachariah now off the scene and with no-one to drive it, fundraising for Albert had stalled somewhat before it picked up again. In the meantime, a fundamental change was proposed by the council: why not position Victoria (seated) and Albert (standing) both together on the same shared plinth? After the council had agreed to the plans for this grouping, someone thought to check whether the Queen approved – but apparently she did not. For whatever reason, Queen Victoria preferred the statue of her recently dead husband to be located apart from her in the park – and his likeness was eventually positioned some distance away.

Once the Queen had been seated, alone, on her plinth, the statue was unveiled in the park on 29th October 1863 by Earl de Grey of Ripon, at the same time as he was being installed as the Lord High Steward of Hull. Under normal circumstances, Zachariah would have been there, in the midst of the ceremonial, enjoying playing the role of benefactor yet again in the park which he had given. But circumstances were not normal: Zachariah was in London, desperately wrestling with his accounts. And in any case, by now he was so completely ostracised that he was utterly airbrushed out of the entire process, as we can see from the *Hull Packet*'s account of Mayor Moss' carefully worded speech:

It was not necessary for him [Moss] to say how or in what manner that statue was first designed, it was sufficient that it was intended to commemorate Her Majesty's visit to Hull some time ago, and that it had been thought desirable to have recollection of that event by having some beautiful memento in some public place, and the park was considered as suitable as any. The park had been designed for the recreation of the people, and it was therefore most fitted for the reception of this statue, and he [Moss] had much pleasure in presenting the statue as an ornament to the park...

(30th October).

This was an outrageous *post hoc* rationalisation of the facts. By using the passive voice, and avoiding all reference to Zachariah, Moss had succeeded in making it sound as though the whole statue idea had come from the council, and that, having decided they would have it, they then searched around for a convenient spot to locate the statue, finally picking the park as most suitable. To be fair to Moss, having picked up the tab when Zachariah could not pay, he certainly deserved his day of glory – but he deliberately sidestepped Zachariah's role altogether by refusing to say *'how or in what manner that statue was first designed'*.

A conspiracy of silence had clearly been agreed behind the scenes over the central role that Zachariah had played. Perhaps, given the polarisation of views, the whole business, coming as it did whilst the bankruptcy case was still being prepared, was rather a hornet's nest, and best avoided. The use of the passive voice here was neutral. Even the local paper, the *Hull Packet*, colluded with it on this occasion: Zachariah's name was not mentioned once in all the column inches devoted to that day. And needless to say, as can be seen today, the inscription on the plinth of the statue only recognised Moss as the donor.

It was unlikely that Zachariah was omitted in order to spare his feelings while he was in such public trouble, otherwise he would have at least been mentioned tangentially. It was far more likely that sweeping Zachariah and his part in the park and statue under the carpet was due to the simmering – now boiling – resentment. We can trace the build-up through local press reports of the council subcommittee meetings leading to this day when the statue was unveiled. There were arguments on a weekly basis, and bad feeling gathered momentum: there was both personal anger over being owed money, and council anger over the promised income not materialising.

The unwritten rule of being a Victorian philanthropist was that a benefactor would continue to endow his grand gesture, in this case the park, and not leave it for the recipients to pick up ongoing costs. Zachariah had bought the land, gifted it, and stipulated the manner in which the park should be laid out – and he had his plan in place to finance this from the sale of the villa plots. But he had then had the temerity to lose his fortune and, once the assignees had gone into action, Zachariah had been powerless to contribute further monies. The council felt his gift was turning into a liability, and now, compounded by the hawks rubbing salt in Zachariah's wounds at every opportunity, things were turning very sour indeed.

By April in 1863, the members of the Park Committee and Local Board of Health were arguing bitterly regarding ongoing costs of establishing the park, and in the hothouse of council micropolitics some wild rumours and proposals flew about, as reported by the *Hull Packet* on 3rd April 1863. Under the provocative heading 'ATTEMPT TO DEPRIVE THE TOWN OF THE PARK' there was reportage from a comment made in the Park Committee meeting:

> Alderman Bannister intimated that it was not a secret that the assignees of Mr Z. C. Pearson's estate contemplated the step of testing the validity of the gift of the park to the town [...] His informant was one in authority, and the statement might be relied upon.

Bannister, described by Hovell as '*a big rough-speaking coal exporter*', was one of the opposing creditors in the court case, and he seemed to be quite good at fomenting trouble. An anonymous but even more preposterous suggestion was reported: '*a contemporary, seized suddenly with a fit of virtue, last week declared it to be the duty of the town to pay Mr Pearson's creditors the value of the land given by him as a public park!'* The concept of offsetting the people's park against Zachariah's debt now truly set the cat among the pigeons. The outcry and repercussions echoed around town. People were outraged at the prospect of losing their beloved park. There was, as the local press pointed out in their counter-argument, a legal question and a moral one. Had the transfer of the park been legal? And if it was legal, was the corporation morally justified in retaining the park for the people of Hull?

The furore in the newspaper ultimately did the council hawks no good. Ordinary townsfolk wrote indignant letters, incensed about the way the council was behaving towards Zachariah, *'unjustly reflect[ing] on the conduct of an individual who, whatever may be the opinion formed of his mercantile transactions, in the matter of the park, at all events, did good service to Hull.'* And just as today when politicians fear negative public opinion at the hands of the media, there was some inevitable back peddling. The main protagonists were shamed into publicly distancing themselves from the rumours about wanting to take the park back. Councillors saw that they needed to disassociate themselves swiftly. Samuelson, on this occasion opposing Bannister, and no doubt with his electorate in mind, made it clear that Bannister's view was without foundation – he should know, as he was one of the assignees. This was a malicious rumour, he said, and it needed to be nipped in the bud: *'He could positively state that the assignees had never contemplated or discussed the matter, and, to the best of his belief, never would.'* After this, even Bannister was forced to moderate his comments.

The press, of course, came down assertively on the side of common sense: the gift had indeed been legal, Zachariah had indeed donated in good faith while he had plenty of money, and he would indeed have handed over the £1700 profit from the sale of the building plots if the assignees hadn't taken it. All the same, the money for laying out the park was not there, and the arguing on the council was turning increasingly personal, as Alderman Samuelson's outburst shows: *'The town would have been better if we had never seen either Mr Pearson or his Park!'* It was a measure of how desperately let-down the council was feeling. They were lashing out against Zachariah himself, and by association the park bearing his name, which was now costing them money. But this personal attack was a step too far for Alderman Ellison, who took Samuelson to task: *'Only 12 months ago Mr Pearson was lauded with praises, and now all kinds of ill remarks are made upon him. If the park had been called 'Samuelson's Park', these remarks would never have been made!'*

Not to be silenced, Samuelson snapped back: *'When I've swindled as many people as Mr Pearson has, then you may say what you have said. I'm not ashamed of myself, and therefore 'shut up', and when you're on your legs you may reply to my remark.'* Samuelson sounds, from this and other local paper reportage, like a thoroughly unpleasant bully, but he was nevertheless an opinion-former, and it took a brave man to oppose him. Some of these people, of course, had a double agenda: as well as wearing council hats, many were also wearing creditor hats, and finding it difficult to retain the objective perspective expected of public servants.

1863 was possibly the lowest year in Zachariah's life. He was distinctly 'out-crowd' by now, and the opinion-forming cognoscenti of Hull lost no opportunity to kick him while he was down. One of these was a Mr Pease, whose diary refers to Zachariah as a swindler, although, as the Commissioner had pointed out, Pease was not even someone who had lent him money. Samuelson, Bannister, Pease, Brodrick: these were all men who had enjoyed Zachariah's hospitality, most having made generous speeches about him at the grand dinner following the Colossal Fete, and here they were turning on him. As Zachariah had written to Richardson, it was indeed *'in adversity when a man's friends [were] tested.'*

His mood was very low. He had been through 18 months of adjournments and preparations, and the formal Court hearings were about to take place; he was facing an unknown future with a high profile trial, not only of his finances but also of his character. Right now, Zachariah was in London, and voiceless. His main protagonists were in Hull, and certainly not voiceless as they prepared to sink him. He may have derived some comfort from the local press which, while maintaining a discreetly neutral stance on the micropolitics, nevertheless left its readers in no doubt that the outrageous suggestion that the people should be deprived of the park was 'simple robbery':

It is very easy, and perhaps very natural, for living asses to kick at a dead lion. Hence we can understand the fling of Aldermen Samuelson and Bannister at ex-Alderman Pearson yesterday [...] Still, let Mr Pearson's failings be what they may, in giving a park to the town he gave what the town most wanted, and every week thousands of our pent-up poor rejoice at having the chance of inhaling a breath of pure air in Pearson's Park. Whether Mr Pearson was wise and prudent in giving the Park to this town may be a question. But whether the Park, having been given to the public, should be kept up on their behalf, is no question at all. It would be simple robbery to deprive the people of Hull of the full enjoyment of the Park given to them by Mr Pearson.

(*Hull Packet*, 31 July 1863).

With the 'living asses' kicking the 'dead lion' in frustration, it is easy to understand why any overt mention of Zachariah was vetoed at the unveiling of the statue – so deep was the controversy surrounding him.

In the end, perhaps it was just as well that Zachariah was not present to witness the various events of the day on which Queen Victoria's statue was unveiled. Had he been a fly-on-the-wall, he would have winced to see his now-arch-enemy lapping up glory as four new vessels were launched by Earl de Grey from Samuelson's shipyard earlier in the day – while, at that very moment in time, Samuelson was doing his best to ensure that Zachariah would be ripped apart in the Bankruptcy Court. No doubt Zachariah later read accounts of the day in the press: the event was apparently well-attended, and included '*a very good sprinkling of the fair sex*'. The reports would have exacerbated his misery: he should have been in the park for the ceremony. The fact that it was a nasty wet day would have been little comfort to him.

Zachariah did, though, have a narrow escape from yet one further ignominy. It may be recollected that one of the MPs, speaking at the grand banquet at the Station Hotel after the handing over of the deeds, had called (to cheers) for the donor's statue to be placed in the park. History has shown that no such statue was ever installed, but now the enigma of the missing statue that initiated the research for this biography can be understood in context. In 1860 Zachariah was certainly a rather popular chap, and the Colossal Fete was his day of maximum glory, so perhaps this speech was what sowed the seeds of the idea and gave him grand designs to position himself in the park near the Queen. One scrap of evidence supports this hypothesis: a summary of his life, written by a member of the Minerva Lodge after his death, stated that '*in 1860 Thom Earle completed a bust of His Worship the Mayor which the* Hull Advertiser *considered a marvellous likeness, upon which Pearson then [...] commissioned a portrait bust of himself (now lost).*'

Although the statuette that had found its way onto my grandparents' mantelpiece was a full length model rather than what we would describe today as a bust, it is quite feasible that this was the work of Earle. It was symbolic, with Zachariah wearing the Mayoral tricorne hat, and leaning on a ship's rudder at his side. We know from the way that Zachariah secretly organised the Queen's statue, presenting a *fait accompli* to the council, that he was inclined to make grand unilateral gestures without conferring, so it is very plausible that he told no-one about this new statue of his. But the timing was all wrong. Zachariah's financial crash occurred between the maquette being made and the statue itself. He certainly could not now, in the throes of bankruptcy, be seen to flaunt himself so audaciously. Quite apart from the over-zealous campaign against him, his ignominy and social ostracism meant that he was morally obliged to keep a low profile. In any case, he would certainly not have had the money now to pay for the finished product. We cannot be certain whether Earle ever started the large statue or not, but we can confidently guess that at an early stage Zachariah judiciously pulled the plug on the project. What a fortuitous cancellation – and at last a solution to the mystery of the missing statue. It *had* been agreed, the maquette *had* been made – and then the project was aborted prematurely.

Schadenfreude – such a useful German word for which we have no English equivalent. Composed of the words for Harm and Joy, it denotes delight in the misfortunes of others. In Zachariah's story there was indeed a lot of both delight and misfortune, and a good deal of *schadenfreude* as well. The build-up and court case had been very wounding, and Zachariah had felt battered from all sides. Although he must have been delighted that he did not end up in gaol, and relieved at the Commissioner's final verdict and kind words, he was heavily bruised by the whole process and its accompanying poison. Coming from his straightforward Wesleyan background, this took him by surprise. He was a gentle and kind man who had not set out to harm anyone, so the personal attacks came as a shock. He had probably never paused to consider the effect that his meteoric rise up the business and social ladder was having on others at the time. How many of us are that self-aware *at the time?*

It was over – and life from now on would be very different. Despite the misgivings expressed in his letter-from-the-heart to Mr Richardson, he did, in fact, return to his beloved town, where he picked up the threads of his life, and worked hard to repay his creditors. Ugly feelings still existed in some quarters but his friends rallied around to support him. He was never to hold public office again, and he lived a low-key life in a humble corner of the park that he had donated. By now, Zachariah had learnt his lesson: those who keep below the parapet can't get their heads blown off.

13

The quiet life

Keeping below the parapet was a new concept to Zachariah, but his learning curve was steep and he recognised the new order. This was the only way he could pick up the pieces and manage his life. Needless to say, his dramatic and prolonged disaster had been splashed across the local and national newspapers, and his name was well-known at all levels of society. It was a case of 'how the mighty fall'; but for his collapse, it was widely reckoned that he would have gone on to be the richest shipowner in the country.

Living again in Hull, Zachariah still had to tolerate the *froideur* towards him from the opinion-forming businessmen of Hull to whom he still owed money but his real friends were greatly supportive at a personal level, and this enabled him to hold his head up again. He also drew great comfort from the massive amount of sympathy among the working people of Hull; they did not judge him on his 'American adventures'. They had their precious park. Today we take for granted our access to green spaces and clean air so it is hard to understand at this distance in time how extraordinarily grateful the ordinary people were for the park. For the great majority of the town's cramped population the park added real quality to their lives: freedom, fresh air and enjoyment. Zachariah was still 'the people's friend' and 'Hull's greatest benefactor'.

At an immediate, practical level, we can only guess at the devastating impact of the bankruptcy on the family as they picked up the pieces in 1864. Zachariah still had to maintain a wife and seven children, and the oldest, Charles, being only 18 years old, was hardly in a position to support the family effectively. Mary Ann had given birth to their last child, Eveline Rose, a few months before the crash in August 1862. At this stage, Beatrice was almost two years old, Emma, my great-grandmother, was seven, and the older boys, Charles and Alfred, were boarding at naval school in Kent; no doubt they must have had to leave precipitously for lack of fees.

Today bankrupts seem to pick themselves up after only a couple of years and carry on their businesses as they did before, but back then the aftermath of bankruptcy was much more serious. We don't know for certain how destitute Zachariah was, but he could not return to his flamboyant ship-owning business, nor hold public office. Nevertheless, he still needed to 'bring home the bacon' – to earn enough for the family to live on.

Being surrounded by extended family probably helped, although Mary Ann's father, Edward Coleman, working in Bermuda on behalf of Zachariah, had presumably been stranded out there in mid-1862 when the business failed. The name of an accountancy firm used by Zachariah had a Coleman in its title – probably Robert Gordon, one of Mary Ann's brothers. Interestingly, despite Zachariah having so many older siblings of his own, nothing is ever heard of them in this story. One might conjecture that this was the result of losing his mother so young, and being shunted out of the family home to live with relatives but there is no evidence for this. It was almost certainly Mary Ann's family which supported him mentally through his rehabilitation phase.

The disgrace of a bankrupt as high-profile as Zachariah was deep and long-lasting, and it continued well after the time allotted to secure one's discharge. For a man who had been held up as an upright pillar of society, this would have been torture. Zachariah had been legally free of all his debts by October 1864, six months after his formal hearing. To pay off his debts, he had sold everything that he did not directly need for living expenses. All his properties, vessels, land, companies and goods had been sold, and had realised a considerable, though still insufficient, sum.

The earliest known photograph of Zachariah, taken on one of two glass plates discovered in an attic in Melbourne by John Pearson, descended from Charles, Zachariah's oldest son. John's parents had emigrated to Australia in the 1920s, but died when he was young, passing on only vague rumours about his ancestor. Curiosity drove John to the internet to find out more, and we were all delighted when he made contact and the glass plates in his attic were at last identified. This photo is undated, but possibly taken soon after Zachariah's financial crash.

The companion plate was of Mary Ann, Zachariah's wife, and one of their daughters aged about seven, possibly either Emma Jane or Beatrice Maude, since our best guess for the age of the photo is around 1864-66. Victorian photography involved lengthy posing, which is why everyone looks rather strained.

Needless to say, he got very little of what he felt he was owed by the American Prize Courts, the Confederate Government or the Italian Government – although he did think at one stage that the *Indian Empire* insurance company might pay up. In the midst of the torrid time Zachariah was having during the bankruptcy proceedings there had been a small-yet-temporary bright spot to alleviate his misery. In the Court of Common Pleas at Westminster Hall in July 1863, Zachariah won a case against the Commercial Union Insurance Co. for the ship that had burnt in the Thames. He had taken out a three-month policy on her for £10,000 insuring the hull whilst in dock and travelling between docks, and Zachariah claimed that, as her paddles had needed to be removed in order to fit into the narrow dock while she was being worked on, these could only be refitted in the wider space of the open river, the location where the ship caught fire. The insurance company had refused him compensation. When Zachariah challenged their decision in court, though, the jury found in his favour, and awarded him the £10,000. This fell well short of the total loss of the refurbished vessel, but at least it reduced his debt by that much – until the insurance company's lawyers appealed the decision and won. The jury's verdict was overturned on a technicality: the *Indian Empire* was not travelling 'to' or 'from' a dock, but 'detained' in the river for paddle-fitting. Zachariah's minor victory was short-lived – he received nothing.

The immediate question for the large Pearson family must have been housing. In theory, they were still entitled to the property that Zachariah had transferred in 1858 into Mary Ann's name in the post-nuptial settlement when he was rich. However much the assignees had wanted to get their hands on the large house in Grosvenor Terrace, it was protected from being absorbed into Zachariah's pool of assets. Nevertheless, they moved house. Presumably Zachariah and his wife felt that they could not in all conscience live in a grand house under the circumstances, and they relocated into a small terraced house in the north east corner of Pearson Park. Number 2 Elm Villas (now No. 64 Pearson Park) was a far cry from the large Beverley Road house that had been the family home until 1862, though it did have three stories – enough room for the large family and one servant. When they moved there, who owned it or how it was paid for is not apparent.

The house in the NE corner of Pearson Park where Zachariah lived with his family until his death in 1891. No. 2 Elm Villas was far less impressive than his grand house in Grosvenor Terrace, but still roomy enough for the family and a maid. Today it is merely No. 64 Pearson Park.

What is clear, though, is that Zachariah's affairs continued to be publicly trawled through for years. Why else would there be a letter in the local paper in 1867, three years after his discharge, on the housing issue? Signed by *'one of the toiling millions'*, the correspondent urged ordinary folk to come together to present Zachariah with a house in the park: *'the working men of Hull would gladly subscribe to do honour to a gentleman to whose public spirit they are deeply indebted'*. The newspaper editor wisely advised finding out what Mr Pearson thought about it first, though history does not tell us whether Zachariah, having contributed so much of his wealth to charity, now appreciated being a potential recipient.

There are unsubstantiated rumours that Zachariah's friends from the Masonic Lodge and Trinity House were instrumental in helping him rebuild his life, but again there is no proof; supportive gestures would have been made quietly behind the scenes. It is not inconceivable that he did receive some support from this quarter, as the Masons were committed to helping their Brethren in need. Barry Hovell's research into Hull Masons shows that Zachariah paid no membership fees to Minerva Lodge after 1861, most likely leaving because of his ignominious situation. Despite still being ostracised by a number of men in Hull, he did still have some real friends that he had made in the Lodge, one of these writing after his death that, *'despite his ruination, he continued to command regard and assistance from loyal friends'*. And these friends apparently continued through life, because later on, after he had to some extent reinvented himself, he picked up his Masonic links again.

When a box of assorted Pearson family artefacts revealed a piece of soft, white leather identified as Zachariah's by the black ink 'ZCP 1605 Hull', Barry Hovell played detective once again. This had been part of a Masonic apron belonging to lodge number 1605, the De La Pole Lodge, founded in 1876. Zachariah and six other members of the Minerva Lodge to which he had belonged, together with some from other lodges, had apparently made up a group of 20 founding members. He was thus a member for six years of yet another Lodge which was later to meet in the remnants of 'his' chapel in Beverley Road.

This piece of soft white kid leather has been handed down the generations but no-one knew why. It bears the scars of unpicked hems and circular badges. Barry Hovell, Masonic historian in Hull, played detective once more. The number of the De La Pole Lodge is 1605, so Zachariah's mark identifies this artefact as the remnants of his Masonic apron. Additionally, the registration book shows that Zachariah became one of the founder members of this Lodge in 1876.

Hull Trinity House was another probable source of support. This seaman's organisation had always been at the core of Zachariah's being, and its members shared Zachariah's values, standing well apart from the partisan sniping at his character. There were strong affiliations with generations of Pearsons who had given their time voluntarily to ensure safety at sea and to share concern for welfare. Zachariah's father had been one of the Younger Brethren, and his son Arthur Henry was later to become one. Sea was in their blood, and in 1874, ten years after his bankruptcy, Zachariah was re-established enough to be made a Board Member. By 1880 he was one of the twelve Elder Brethren, and he was Warden twice after this. Whether Trinity House helped with Elm Villas is not known, but in any case Zachariah probably benefited in other ways from his Trinity House connections; he was rebuilding his business and needed all the contacts he could get.

Trinity House, Hull, one of Zachariah's most constant haunts all through his life. After his financial crash, Zachariah continued to be heavily involved with all matters marine, and took particular interest in the welfare of seafarers and their families. He became Warden here twice, and was one of the Elder Brethren.

Luckily, being a 'self-made man', a term variously applied with both negative and positive connotations, Zachariah had a formidable array of skills and plenty of business experience to carry him through the last twenty seven years of his life. He used appropriately the links that he still had, though he would not be requesting favours of people, and certainly not asking for credit. Who, after all, would lend to a bankrupt? He needed to rebuild everything step-by-step from first principles, in the same way that he had built up his shipping business in the 1840s: work, earn, invest and grow.

Little by little, then, he did eventually make a success of his post-crash career, operating from Prussian Chambers in Posterngate as a United States Commercial Agent, a shipbroker and a coal exporter. His oldest son, Charles, also in the shipping business, was capitalising on his father's experience: it would have been a shame to waste it. There are references to the two of them working together from time to time, Zachariah staying in the background while Charles headed up transactions. We find Zachariah's name appearing in 1875 as managing director of a new shipping company that Charles was involved with, Hull Steam Shipping, but he was not on the subscribers' list. His other family connections also came in handy and there are references to his association once more with James Coleman. Zachariah, as a bankrupt, had to work through other people. As ever, Zachariah dipped his fingers into several pies to earn enough to keep the family, and in his merchant role we find a notice in the *Yorkshire Gazette* in 1880 dissolving a partnership between him and a Mr Brown.

He would certainly have had more time to focus on earning now that he was not required to play a public role in Hull life. In his first few years after the bankruptcy, Zachariah's name only appeared in the local press associated with small business adverts while he was focussing on rebuilding his life. There were no public appearances reported. He was not in demand to open buildings, make speeches, entertain politicians, or sit on the council. While he was serving time in his disgrace, he was still keeping his head well below that parapet.

One of the things he enjoyed was 'spending more time with the family' – the mantra of all public figures who step out of the spotlight even today. We know that Zachariah sometimes took his family on voyages: his daughter, Emma Jane, described to her grandchild, my mother, how she had visited the Tsar's court in St. Petersburg when a girl. With his business and family maritime connections, we can assume that an occasional sea voyage to somewhere interesting was now possible in Zachariah's less cluttered life.

Even as he focused on rehabilitating himself in Hull's society after his disgrace, Zachariah was still hoping (in vain) that the American Prize Courts would find in his favour and compensate him for at least some of his losses of ships and cargoes. In this picture, four of these ships awaiting adjudication belonged to him: Circassian, Stettin, Patras *and* Ann, *justifying the description of Zachariah as one of the biggest British losers of the American Civil war.*

Alongside rebuilding his businesses, a major preoccupation was actively pursuing compensation from the American government for what he claimed were illegitimate seizures of some of his ships. An engraving published in *Harper's Weekly* (July-December 1862) depicts a collection of assorted captured vessels awaiting judgement by the Prize Court and no fewer than four of these were Zachariah's: *Circassian, Stettin, Patras* and *Ann.* Needless to say, his efforts to reclaim money via this route were largely a waste of time, and Zachariah's sense of justice was disappointed. He was, however, eventually awarded a small amount of compensation for the barque *Empress*. It may be recollected that she had been carrying a legitimate cargo (coffee) to a legitimate port (New York) and she had been captured on circumstantial evidence. The situation was ambiguous, though, and this swung the verdict of the Prize Court in his favour. Ironically, the *Empress* had been the least costly of his ship losses. All the same, this was still a victory, however minor.

This portrait photo of Zachariah was taken when he was about 56-57 years old, and it shows how rapidly the traumatic events of his life had aged him. Calling cards often bore the photograph of the bearer, and Zachariah probably had the picture taken for this purpose.

Once the fog of the ongoing debts started to clear, Zachariah gradually began his reintegration back into the social fabric of Hull life, but 1866 was far too early for him to be considered suitable to be present at the opening of the Town Hall which he himself had instigated. At least on this occasion, two years after his bankruptcy case had ended, he was not air-brushed out of it. On the contrary, in the speeches he was publicly and gratefully acknowledged as the initiator of the project, and the new Town Hall was opened to great acclaim. Zachariah's 'street cred' was slowly being re-established. As time went on, his integration into mainstream life picked up speed, and he resumed some of his previous interests: representing seamen, attending charity functions, supporting candidates for local politics elections and other public duties – but all now in his own right as a private man, not a civic dignitary.

By the mid-1870s, eleven years after his bankruptcy case, Zachariah was reintegrated enough to be invited once more to take part in ceremonial functions. Pearson Park was by now planted and established, and some grand residences had sprung up on the plots around the periphery. It had turned out just as Zachariah had planned all those years ago; the park had not only transformed this area of Hull but was now having a positive effect on the environs. Muckypeg Lane, the thoroughfare to the west of the park, lived up to its name, and in the words of the *Hull and Lincolnshire Times*, was *'made more interesting by a green-covered ditch on either side'*. It was ripe for development, and David Garbutt was the man who turned this into a pleasant road, soon following it by creating the desirable residential area known today as The Avenues.

On the Easter Monday of 1875, at the opening ceremony of the new road which marked the start of the whole development project, Zachariah was an invited guest of honour at the banquet, which was held in a massive marquee in Pearson Park. He must have been quietly delighted when his name was loudly cheered after a speaker referred to him as the originator of the park. As ever on such occasions, many toasts were proposed, and Zachariah responded. Not being a member of the Town Council these days, he had no legitimate channel for his ideas on how to improve the trade of Hull, so he had to seize any opportunity that arose. On this occasion, he used his toast to urge the council to set up a dock-railway trust to break the current monopolies that were binding the town 'hand and foot'. The toast he chose was 'The Town and Trade of Hull'.

At last he was able to speak again in a public position and to be valued for it. And he must have taken pleasure in the fact that his Park had precipitated such an attractive development in this area of Hull. He himself was still living relatively humbly at No. 2 Elm Villas, but – and here is another intrigue – Zachariah's address given in the De La Pole Lodge registration records in 1876 was given as Grosvenor Terrace, their old home. The Pearsons could not live it in under their reduced circumstances but did they perhaps retain it for letting purposes, keeping part of it as an office or a business address?

Zachariah was now returning to the things he valued most in life; as well as Trinity House and all things marine, he was free to pick up his interest in the Volunteers and by 1880 he was being invited to, and was speaking at, their annual inspections. He was also attending charity functions, such as Founders' Day at the orphan's home which he had helped to set up, and he sometimes supported local politicians seeking election. He campaigned personally on behalf of school boards, and attended other functions as a representative of Trinity House, for whom in 1881 he opened a bazaar to raise money for the repair of the Mariners' Church. In April 1881 he introduced HRH the Duke of Edinburgh (Prince Alfred) as a member of the Brethren of Trinity House and in 1885 he was nominated by the Local Marine Board as an assessor for the Court of Survey, in which role he had to make decisions about whether or not ships were seaworthy.

BELLMAN CARTOON.

Z. C. PEARSON, ESQ.

"A man that Fortune's buffets and rewards
Hast ta'en with equal thanks."

A cartoon of Zachariah published in 1878 while he was re-establishing himself in Hull. His features are clearly modelled on the portrait photograph he'd had taken. The cartoon celebrates his civic achievements – he is standing in front of the new Town Hall and clutching the plans for the new waterworks – but at the same time his careworn face betrays his troubled past. The apt caption is stolen from Hamlet: "A man that Fortune's buffets and rewards hast ta'en with equal thanks".

He must have been gratified that, following in the wake of Pearson Park, other Hull parks later appeared, and his name was always linked with them. So at the opening of the West Park in 1885, Alderman Leak said that *'on an occasion like the present they could not forget the name of Z. C. Pearson (applause), for if they had forgotten him that day, the future of Hull would never forget that generous donor (renewed applause)'*. His legacy as elder statesman and benefactor had now largely overtaken his financial disgrace. His name appeared increasingly on the invitation list of important luncheons, and he was present at high-profile funerals, such as that of his long-standing friend, Dr Kelburne King. The families had remained close, as illustrated by a legacy that King made to Beatrice Maude, one of Zachariah's daughters.

One of the unanswered questions of Zachariah's life was his political allegiance. Somewhat mysteriously, after spending a lifetime apparently supporting Liberal candidates at elections, in 1880-2 we find him as an officer for the West Sculcoates Conservative Association (supporting the wonderfully-worded motion that *'"In the opinion of this Association, the deplorable condition in Ireland is due in a great measure to the imbecility of the present Government, combined with the indirect encouragement given by Mr Gladstone in his wild and erratic stump oratory when grasping for the power he has gained, and for which the country pays the penalty of increased taxation at home, dissatisfaction in our colonies, and rebellion in Ireland"* – *passed unanimously'*. Mincing their words was not apparently part of this branch's policy...). History does not tell us what made him switch politics. And then in 1889 we find him supporting the independent local candidate.

A similar mystery surrounds Zachariah's religion. We know that he supported Methodism, had a new Wesleyan chapel built, sat on Methodist committees and fundraising bodies and was publicly described in the local press as a Methodist.

At the same time, he contributed generously to the restoration of Holy Trinity, the main Anglican church in the centre of Hull. But where did he worship? No church records of this can be traced, but all the reports we have of his family marriages show that these took place in his local Anglican parish church of Sculcoates. Perhaps the morals and the belief system of Methodism appealed to him – but were the Church of England services more appealing? As ever, he had kept his options open. He was eventually buried by the incumbent of the Anglican church for seafarers, the Mariners' Church – not in a church at all, but in a graveside ceremony.

In rebuilding his public presence, he maintained a lower profile than his previous flamboyant one, as the celebrations for Queen Victoria's Golden Jubilee demonstrated. The *Hull Daily Mail* in June 1887 reported that the Park Committee had passed a resolution to ask Zachariah to mark the ceremony by planting trees in Pearson Park – but then nothing more was heard of the plan. The day of the Golden Jubilee arrived, and Zachariah attended the Mayor's Breakfast, and then the church service at Holy Trinity Church. Celebrations were extensive, and Pearson Park was filled with joyous townsfolk, but there was no tree-planting. Eventually the tree ceremony *did* take place, albeit a few weeks after the Jubilee celebrations. The *Hull Daily Mail* on 1st August 1887 reported that *'Mr Pearson wished the event to be kept as private as possible'*. This was completely in keeping with Zachariah's wanting a less visible role for himself these days. A further incentive to avoid the actual date may have been the fact that the opening of the East Park was planned to coincide with the Jubilee; Zachariah would not have wished to steal this park's limelight.

The event took place in the evening, and despite Zachariah's wish to keep it low-key, the council invited the Mayor, the Police Band and representatives of trade associations, justifying this ceremonial by including it as part of the Jubilee events. Zachariah diluted his role by making it a family affair, and the prime tree-planter was the third Pearson daughter, Beatrice Maude, still unmarried and living at home at the age of 26. She 'gracefully' planted the first tree 'amid ringing cheers', with a specially-made oak spade, inscribed in silver, one of the very few family heirlooms to survive. Zachariah briefly thanked everyone for their kindness towards his daughter and himself, and followed by planting the second tree, the Mayor planting a third. Zachariah, now aged 68, had carried out his civic duty but had also avoided the spotlight glare of the Jubilee.

The spade with which Beatrice Maude planted a tree in Pearson Park to mark the occasion of the Queen's Golden Jubilee in 1887. It is silver-plated with an inscribed shaft, and the blade depicts the three crowns of Hull. Zachariah at this stage in his life wished to keep a low profile, and when asked to carry out a ceremonial planting he shared the honours with the family.

Coming to the end of his life now, Zachariah was not only reintegrated into society, but playing a full role in it as well – at the level where he was most comfortable. He attended a Remembrance Day service 1887 at Holy Trinity Church with the Mayor and Corporation and was a guest at a ball in March 1889 in honour of HRH Prince Albert Victor coming to Hull. He was fully engaged with the workings of the Hull Conservancy Commissioners and the Hull Pilotage Commissioners, who also honoured him by changing the name of their new acquisition, the racing yacht *Camilla*, purchased for pilotage duties, to the *Z. C. Pearson*.

Even in his old age Zachariah could not relinquish the things that mattered to him; he remained alert and vigilant in safe-guarding 'The Park'. When in January 1890 he noticed in the newspaper a request to the council by some local residents for a path across the middle of the park for their own convenience, Zachariah was on the case at once, tackling the proposal head-on and stifling the idea at birth. He wrote to the Parks Committee that '*it was never intended that [the Park] should be cut up into roads for a thoroughfare for the inhabitants of a district*', especially that section of the park: '*why destroy the best piece of grass where children can play?*'. Knowing how much the general public would agree with him, he copied his letter to the local paper, putting the issue in the public gaze. The letter warned the council about the consequences of breaking the covenant under which the Park had been donated and helpfully offered to lend them a copy. He felt very strongly about protecting the park, as his unambiguous post script made clear: '*I should not like to have to apply for an injunction to restrain the council from destroying the Park and alienating it from the purpose for which it was devised. You may make what use of this note you think proper*'.

Nothing more was heard of the proposal.

As he grew older, Zachariah and Mary Ann had their fair share of family joys and tragedies. While Zachariah was getting re-engaged with his old life in Hull, the children were growing up and there was a steady stream of marriage celebrations. The older children were married in the 1870s: Charles Edward to Louisa Brown in 1872, Alfred Coleman to Matilda (known as Mabel) Fisher, in 1874, both producing a healthy crop of grandchildren. In 1877 Mary married Joseph William Smith, a solicitor, and in 1881 Arthur married Edith Searby, but no evidence of children from either has come to light.

There were worries, too, when his offspring had their own business crises: just 18 months after getting married, Alfred Coleman Pearson became the third generation of Pearsons to face bankruptcy. His new bride must have wondered what sort of family she had married into. The *London Gazette* of 24th September 1875 announced that Alfred, of 'Pearson and Co., coal merchant', was summoned to the Town Hall to a meeting of his creditors. His grandfather had been 39 when summoned to the Dog and Duck, his father had been 41 in the London Bankruptcy Court, and Alfred was aged only 24. Was bankruptcy in the Pearson blood?

Another worry for Zachariah and Mary Ann was Emma Jane, their second daughter. In August 1882 she married a University student, Bruno Adolph von Hohnfeldt. He had arrived in England with his mother, Ottilie, just at the time when the Jews were fleeing from the Prussian pogroms in the 1870s, although the Jewish Immigrants list did not include Bruno's father, an army officer. Emma and Bruno had not been married many years before it became clear that Bruno was a cruel and heartless man with few morals. Emma bore him three sons in the first five years of their marriage, but the man was impossible. Apparently, as related by Emma's grandchildren, he would not tolerate washing in the house, he disapproved of toys around the place, and could also be extremely violent towards Emma, as the grisly details in the divorce papers were to spell out many years later.

Zachariah and Mary Ann must have been distraught to see Emma Jane treated like this, but she escaped from Bruno when her youngest was still a baby. She was well out of it; Bruno turned out to be a confidence trickster, as witnessed by his Old Bailey records. She later used to tell her grandchildren: *"they said he was a wrong'n, and I wouldn't believe them"*. Life for a single mother was difficult enough, but being separated from one's husband added extra stigma. Emma achieved security by moving in with her parents at Elm Villas, where the three little boys had plenty of green space to run around in the park. No doubt the grandchildren brought Zachariah and Mary Ann a great deal of pleasure in their old age, and Zachariah was now the closest male role-model the boys would have had.

The last two girls were married in 1883 and 1889. Eveline Rose, the youngest, was first, marrying George William Webster. Beatrice Maude, at the age of 28, was the last of the brood to marry, and Zachariah's restored standing in the community earned her a comment in the local press. She was described as the *'daughter of our most respected fellow-townsman, whose memory will always be cherished for his noble and princely gift to the town of Pearson Park'.* She married a physician, Dr Henry Fairbank, at the parish church in Sculcoates, where the bride *'entered the sacred edifice, leaning on the arm of her venerable father'.* As the wedding breakfast was held at Elm Villas, it could hardly have been over-lavish, but would have been well in keeping with the Pearsons' lower profile.

Zachariah must have been pleased to see his son Arthur Henry following in his marine footsteps. As reported in the *Hull Packet*, Arthur *'passed the necessary examination and was sworn in as a Younger Brother of the Corporation of the Trinity House Dec 1885'.* His career, though, was later to be his undoing; the vessel he was commanding, the *Volo*, ran aground and was holed on a rock in fog at Gothenburg just after Christmas 1896. Although no-one was lost, and the vessel was eventually refloated, it seriously affected Arthur, for he died in that town a few weeks later; the official cause was 'dropsy' (probably congenital heart failure), but it was considered to have been precipitated by the accident. Luckily, having predeceased his son, Zachariah did not have to suffer the tragedy of his son's death.

In the whole of this story we hear very little about Mrs Mary Ann Pearson; society was run by men, and wives were generally invisible. We can assume she was some sort of stoic to bear eight children, raise seven, and cope with Zachariah's very public life and disgrace while still producing children.

We know that in April 1862, just having given birth to her eighth child, as Mayoress she was the treasurer of a charity raising funds for the new Orphan School for the Port of Hull Society and Sailors' Orphan Institution, an indication that she shared the social conscience of her husband. We do not know how she managed both the family and Zachariah across the difficult times, but she clearly stood by him as his main support throughout his turbulent years. When their whole world crashed and Zachariah was in despair, she would have had to reassure, to exercise patience, and to maintain the family while Zachariah was fighting with his collapsed reputation, his public ignominy and his predatory creditors. How demanding this must have been – and all at the same time as housing and feeding the seven children.

At this stage in their lives, untroubled by ill-health, and having clawed back their respect and social standing after their stormy years, we can imagine that Zachariah and Mary Ann were enjoying their family to the full. They were living in their beloved Hull in the park he had created. With Emma Jane and her three little boys living under the same roof, they were surrounded by family, and they also had the help of one general servant. Given that No. 2 Elm Villas had been big enough to host a wedding reception earlier in the year, we can guess that Christmas 1889 saw another large family party there – although it is not clear how many of their other 13 grandchildren (whose ages ranged from a few months to 16 years) were living in Hull at the time, or visiting from London, where Charles and his brood of five boys were now living.

Hopefully, this last Christmas all together was a happy one, as a month later Mary Ann tragically suffered a cerebral haemorrhage – a stroke caused by a bleed in the brain. She was attended at their home by physicians, including her son-in-law, Dr Henry Fairbank, but there was little anyone could do, and she died 17 days later on 12th February at the age of 67. Strokes are by their very nature unexpected, and his wife's sudden death affected Zachariah deeply. She had been his soulmate, and after losing her he grew frail.

He continued to live in Elm Villas with his daughter Emma Jane and his three grandsons, and carried on taking an interest in Hull life, especially those aspects connected with Trinity House. But eighteen months after his wife's death, he took a turn for the worse, and the *Hull Daily Mail* of 19th October 1891 announced: *'we regret to hear that our respected townsman, Mr Z. C. Pearson, is lying dangerously ill at his residence, the Pearson's Park, Hull. Prayers were offered at church last evening for his recovery'*.

On 29th October, in his home at Elm Villas, *'despite every care and skill which his medical men, Dr Fairbank (son-in-law) and Dr Wilson, could bestow, he quietly passed away in the presence of various members of the family'*. One of the newspapers reported: *'Mr Pearson, though in delicate health for some time, was only taken seriously ill a few days ago, and his decease has therefore been somewhat sudden'*. He was 70, and the certificate gave the cause of his death as *'inflammation of stomach 3 weeks exhaustion'*, which might have implied one of several conditions, including possible stomach cancer. His family was around him, and the certifying medic was Dr H. S. Fairbank, Beatrice's husband; also in attendance was George Webster, Eveline's husband.

The funeral took place a few days later, and the *Hull Daily Mail* of 3rd November 1891 described the event. Messrs Bladon and Son hired out the 'mourning habiliments' for the family, and Mr Wilson was the undertaker, providing a coffin of oak with brass mountings, bearing *'a suitable inscription and [...] covered with beautiful wreaths which had been sent by relatives and friends of the deceased'*. The cortège of four carriages drawn by black-plumed horses came from the extensive funeral stables of Mr Hudson, and Zachariah left his home in Pearson Park for the last time for his final resting place in what is today the Spring Bank Cemetery. Zachariah's sons, Arthur and Alfred, together with Mary and Emma, his two older daughters, led the mourners in the first carriage. The second carriage conveyed his daughter Eveline and her husband, George Webster, together with Arthur's wife and Beatrice's husband. James Coleman, his ex-business partner and brother-in-law was in the third carriage, while the fourth carriage was reserved for grandchildren and servants.

Assuming the account was accurate, the list of mourners is just as interesting for its information as for its omissions: where was Charles, the oldest son? Now living in London, he was still working as a shipping merchant, and maybe he was also sea-faring, so perhaps he was at sea at the time? And what about Beatrice? Her husband, Dr Henry Fairbank, who had been present at Zachariah's death, apparently attended the funeral without her. Was she ill? She was destined to remain childless, so whether now, at the age 30, she was suffering from the consequences of a failed or precarious pregnancy, we can only conjecture.

The Revd. Hay Rea, incumbent at the Mariners' Church, conducted the funeral service. Although this church was physically situated down near Queen's Dock it was the only church in Hull without a defined catchment area or specific membership – any seaman could belong to it. It is impossible to know whether Zachariah planned his own funeral or not but it seems that this would certainly have been how he would wish to be buried – by the sea-farers' minister and without too much high-profile ceremony. The service was conducted around the graveside rather than in a church, and *'at the conclusion of the beautiful ritual of the Church of England, the mourners departed after taking one last look into the grave which contained the remains of the one who had rendered such valuable services to the town at large'*.

Regardless of what Zachariah may have intended, there was a good civic presence, including several prominent names, such as two well-known surgeons: Dr Lowson and Mr T. E. Evans. Together with other personages in Hull, this was an indication of how well-respected Zachariah was in the town generally by the time he died. Naturally, a great many members of Trinity House and associated maritime contacts attended. They gathered around his graveside to honour a man who had done so much to better the lives of seaman and their families. In the words of one obituary: '*no man was held in higher esteem by his brethren of the Trinity Board, and no member of that board has ever been more solicitous for the welfare of poor seamen than has Captain PEARSON, whose memory will long be cherished*'.

Zachariah's grave stone in the Spring Bank Cemetery. As well as his name and that of Mary Ann, the stone also commemorates their infant son, James Harker, who died of slow fever, and Mary Ann's brother, Robert Gordon Coleman.

In addition to the great and the good of maritime Hull, many working folk came to pay their respects to a man they recognised as 'on their side'. As one 'ordinary' mourner at his funeral remarked: '*the vote of the poor is the best*', and the *Hull Times* commented that '*the deceased gentleman was more than respected by those in the humbler stations of life. The many of this class who were in attendance testified to the late Mr Pearson's generosity and kindness, and many were the incidents related of his courteous consideration to all who had sought his advice or assistance. Surely no higher tribute could be paid to the memory of any man.'*

He was interred with his wife, and their infant son James, and either in the same grave or alongside it, was buried Mary Ann's brother as well. The inscription on his gravestone reads:

SACRED TO THE MEMORY OF
Z.C.PEARSON
DIED 20TH OCT 1891,
AGED 70 YEARS.
LEAD KINDLY LIGHT.
MARY ANN,
46 YEARS THE MUCH-LOVED WIFE OF
Z.C.PEARSON
WHO DIED 12TH FEB. 1890,
AGED 67 YEARS
"AT HOME WITH THE LORD"
ALSO
JAMES HARKER PEARSON
SON OF THE ABOVE,
DIED SEPT. 28TH 1851
AGED 2 YEARS
ALSO
ROBERT GORDON COLEMAN
UNCLE OF THE ABOVE
DIED 28TH SEPT 1881
AGED 43 YEARS

The obituaries which followed extolled Zachariah's skills and humane character: *'success never made him so proud that he had not a kindly word in his most prosperous days for the humblest seaman, and adversity could never quench his even flow of spirits, or destroy the kindliness of his disposition. Of him it may be more truly said than of most men, that to know him was to love him.'* Another praised his leadership at sea:

No more careful navigator ever had command of a vessel, or one that was more attentive, or took greater heed to the changes of weather. He had a stout heart, but he was also possessed of correct judgement, and was known to "crack on" only so long as it was prudent. His command was during the balmy days of British seamanship, before the men had been spoiled by having all their work at sea done for them by steam appliances and the men who sailed with him were always proud to call him captain. It is a common thing, even in these days, for sailors to refer to the captain of a ship, no matter what may be his years, as "the old man," and when Captain PEARSON was in command his crew always entertained for their master that love and respect that sons are at least supposed to have for their fathers.

Zachariah was held up as a good example of a man to be emulated; later on the day of the funeral, a Mr Hamilton, delivering a talk to the Missions to Seamen about the Holy Land, urged his audience to *'live godly lives, as had Mr Pearson, at whose funeral he was present during the day, and having known him personally thought his Christian character worthy of imitation'.*

Although Emma Jane, having left her beastly husband, was living at Elm Villas with her boys at the time of her father's death, the house had been rented in Zachariah's name, and everything was now sold by auction before the house was put up for letting again. The list of Zachariah's personal effects throws a final light on his life: the rosewood piano and the 'music Canterbury' (music storage unit) give the first, and only, indication of any music in the Pearson household. Other effects paint a picture of a genteel middle class Victorian family at the end of the nineteenth century, with mahogany dining tables, red velvet chairs, and gas fittings. It is sad to see a great life reduced to a list of effects for sale, but here it is, as advertised in the local paper:

At the residence of the late Z. C. Pearson Esq., 2 Elm Villas, Pearson Park, Hull, on Thursday 12th November, 1891, at 11 o'clock without reserve Mr Charlesworth will sell by auction the genteel household furniture and effects, comprising costly cottage pianoforte, in rosewood case, by Collard and Collard; music stool, six-feet mahogany sideboard, with plate-glass back; mahogany centre table, mahogany dining room suite, 10 pieces, in maroon velvet; music Canterbury, large gilt chimney glass, pictures, marble clock with bronze mount; bronze statuettes, silver tea and coffee service, lady's easy chair, velvet pile carpet and hearth rug, mahogany 8 foot dining table, six mahogany hair-seated chairs, easy chairs and couch, mahogany 4 ft sideboard, with plate-glass back; drumhead marble clock, ornaments, gilt chimney glass, stand table, two mahogany hall chairs, bronze umbrella stand, six iron bedsteads, feather beds, mattresses, Spanish mahogany 4ft 6" wardrobe, mahogany, birch, and painted chests of drawers, dressing tables, wash stands, dressing chests, toilet glasses, cane chairs, towel rails, chamber services, toilet sets, curtains, cornices, Venetian blinds, gas fittings, kitchen furniture and utensils etc.

Thus the last tangible possessions of Zachariah were disposed of, though one item that was not for sale here was his illuminated copy of the 'Deed to Pearsons Park'. Shortly after his father's death, Charles Edward, the oldest son, came back from London to present this Deed to the reference department of the Hull Free Library.

The portrait of Zachariah that today hangs in the Guildhall. Painted by T. Tindall Wildridge, it was acquired by Mayor Robson after Zachariah's death through public subscription. Zachariah appears here to be middle-aged, after his bankruptcy, so with no money of his own it is not clear how, when or why it was painted – unless the public subscription was actually to paint it.

The man had died, but his memory in Hull lived on in diverse gestures of recognition. The following year, Mayor Robson wrote a letter to the *Hull Daily Mail*, saying: *'I have for some time thought that there should be placed in the Town Hall a memorial of the late Z. C. Pearson, who during his career gave many instances of his great regard for the welfare of this town'* (21st September 1892). He went on to describe Zachariah as *'a man with many qualities endearing him to those with whom he came into contact'*, and that he had *'accordingly seen fit, in conjunction with others, to secure the portrait now painted of Mr Pearson, by Mr T. Tindall Wildridge'* and wished to present it to the town.

It is not clear when this portrait was executed, how Robson came to acquire it, or even why it was painted. Zachariah is portrayed as slightly grizzled, but not old. It looks as though he had sat for it when he was middle-aged, and well after his financial embarrassment. Who would have commissioned it at that stage in his life? And why? Whatever its origin, Mayor Robson was inviting people via the local paper to contribute towards its purchase price of £100. It seems from the council meeting minutes the following year that raising the cash had been no problem, as the portrait had by then been bought and *'its disposal was referred to the Hanging Committee'* [sic]. This portrait today hangs in a council chamber in the Guildhall.

Another tribute to Zachariah was a road name; the short street leading from Beverley Road westwards into the park through the ceremonial gateway was named Pearson Avenue. And now, with some predictability, the idea of the statue was resurrected. Never far beneath the surface, it only needed his death to trigger letters in the local papers calling for him to be memorialised in marble. But this rekindled the old polarised positions. Memories were long, and the acrimony over the financing of the park was still firmly in the council's mind. Even in death Zachariah was unwittingly at the centre of controversy. The old animosities had been suppressed during his later years as he became ever more re-established in Hull society, but now that he was dead the old battle lines were redrawn. The pro-statue lobby argued their case publicly via the local newspapers, but the council's opposition was of a more subtle behind-the-scenes nature. This made little difference. The anti-statue movement's position was common knowledge. There was no way the powerful of Hull society could stomach a marble statue raised to the man who had left the council to pick up the bill when the assignees swallowed the income from the building plots.

But the growing groundswell of opinion from ordinary citizens could not be ignored, which forced the council to justify their negative stance by repeating the argument that the park had been given illegally. This, of course, was fought ferociously in the press. Typical correspondence focused on the key issue of the park donation, and dismissed the spurious anti-Zachariah arguments: *'It is nothing to the point to say that Mr Pearson was influenced in his gift by business motives and objects. The real and only question is – Did he in conveying the land to the town confer upon the inhabitants a benefit for all time?'*

A subscription list was proposed, calling upon the rich to top up the working man's pennies, but this was clearly to no avail. A letter in the *Hull Daily Mail* of April 1895 was pointedly addressed to the powerful foot-dragging lobby: *'there is a growing feeling in favour of the movement, and it only needs the countenance and support of our leading representative men to ensure success'*. Another fund-raiser for a statue bemoaned that *'various causes operated against its success, and though a considerable amount of money subscribed lies at the bank, the proposal has not been brought to fruition'*. The background resistance to the idea was well-understood, but by these letters the correspondents hoped to shame the 'leading representative men' publicly into raising the funds for a proper memorial.

It was not to be. Eventually, in the face of all this psychological posturing, a strategic compromise was reached. In August 1896, the *Hull Daily Mail* recorded that The Pearson Memorial Fund was now seeking permission from the Parks Committee for a bas-relief in marble to be carved by the local gifted sculptor William Day Keyworth (Jr), this *'to be placed in a prominent position in the Pearson's Park'*.

This white marble bas relief was the compromise reached after the stand-off between those who demanded a statue to memorialise Zachariah and those who adamantly opposed one. It was carved by William Day Keyworth (Jr).

Celebrating Queen Victoria's Diamond Jubilee in Pearson Park in June 1897.
The park was packed for the joyous occasion, but as can be seen from the
photo, his memorial plaque has not yet been mounted on the ironstone pillar.

Almost seven years after Zachariah's death, then, the oval marble bas-relief that we see in the park today near the lake was attached to the huge reddish pillar of oolitic limestone, or ironstone, that had been presented to the park initially when Zachariah had invited people to endow the park in whichever way they wanted. Its installation took place in July 1897, just after the Queen's Diamond Jubilee celebrations in the park – presumably delayed out of tact with the intention of avoiding any further controversy.

Under the oval of Zachariah is the simple inscription:

ZACHARIAH CHARLES PEARSON
MAYOR OF HULL, 1860
HE PRESENTED TO HIS TOWNSMEN
THE LAND FOR THIS PARK

From this vantage spot, and high on his fossil-laden pillar, Zachariah watches over ensuing generations of children, bowlers, picnickers and dog-walkers in the park which he had presented to 'his' town in his heyday.

But did this relatively low-key memorial put pay to the *sotto voce* mutterings? Well, not quite, although it did help to lay a ghost. As one correspondent to the local paper wrote: '*private individuals have even disputed the rightful donor as being the late Z. C. Pearson. I however think such opinion cannot now live*'. But he was not alone in feeling that a bas-relief was an inadequate memorial, and the call for a full statue continued to limp on for a little while longer before fading. Then in May 1898, when a statue to the late Mr Gladstone was mooted for Hull, 'One who appreciates the Park' did not mince his words to the *Hull Daily Mail* in suggesting a more appropriate local subject for a statue than Mr Gladstone:

> Take a stranger for a stroll through Pearson's Park, and inform him gently that this beautiful park was the gift of a fellow townsman, who in his day was as popular to us, locally, as Mr Gladstone is to all. Now take your friend and show him (if you dare) that mean miserable apology for a memorial that is fixed to that ugly piece of iron stone near the main road. I think that before we attempt to erect any further memorial, let an attempt be made to place in Pearson's Park something worthy of Mr Z. C. Pearson and his magnificent gift.

Needless to say, a statue never materialised. And if we are permitted to second-guess his wishes, by the end of his life Zachariah himself would probably have approved of the more modest memorial. The working-class swell of good-will, stifled by those in positions of power, had kept the controversial nature of Zachariah's legacy alive to the last. And we must assume that throughout this unedifying public wrangle no-one knew about Zachariah's secret: the plans which had been aborted some 35 years earlier for his statue – the maquette for which led to this book.

Epilogue

Zachariah Charles Pearson had led, albeit inadvertently, a colourful life, and even today opinion in Hull is divided about him – mainly from reputation and rumour handed down in folk law. Reputations, though, are created as stories are told and re-told, and generations come to believe the spin of the tellers. But how should *history* remember him? Many epithets have been applied to Zachariah over the years, and rumour has swirled around him like a complex eddy. Was he a philanthropist, a victim, or a swindler? Was he even, as some modern-day name-callers have suggested, a supporter of slavery?

History tends to be told by the winning side and it is easy to look back at events through the lens of the victors. Now, a century and a half after the American Civil War, it is tempting to suggest that anyone who sold goods to the Confederates must have supported slavery and all that it stood for. But before the war started, despite Wilberforce's Slavery Abolition Act having been passed by Parliament in 1833, the British Government had apparently no qualms in trading with America for the cotton they desperately needed to keep the economy going. The moral situation did not change with the Confederate secession in 1861. The same slaves were being used on the same plantations to produce the valuable cotton crop – and yet no-one accused Britain of being pro-slavery.

Because he traded with the Confederate Government, Zachariah's 'American adventures' are some sometimes superficially interpreted today as being pro-slavery although there is not a scrap of evidence to indicate that Zachariah was in any way sympathetic to slavery. Even Zachariah's worst enemies after his crash did not try to pin that on him. Indeed, it would have been anathema to his Methodist principles. However, coming from the same town as William Wilberforce, some have even contrasted the moral stance of these two men – ironically, since they both stood up for the disenfranchised.

Attributing motives and moralities when looking back after the event is a mistake. As Hilary Mantel, Thomas Cromwell's biographer, has remarked, people tend not to know they are in history at the time they decide to do something; they make decisions on the basis of what is known to them at the time, and it is wrong of historians to interpret their motives in the light of our *post hoc* knowledge. Imagine if, in 100 years from now, people accuse the CIA operatives in 2001 of being active supporters of jihadism because they failed to recognise the significance of the prior intelligence they had on the men who flew planes into the twin towers. This is clearly nonsense, and known as 'hindsight bias'. But who knows what twists and turns events will take in the future and how people will interpret actions looking back through history? Zachariah's motives were good, clean and moral when he tried to trade with the Confederates. We can safely conclude he was certainly not a 'slavery supporter'.

To his angry creditors at the time of the bankruptcy, he must have fitted into the 'swindler' bracket, as their humiliating comments make clear. The massive financial disaster impacted on many men's lives, and certainly created an immense amount of fury and upset at the time. But to deserve the title 'swindler' Zachariah needed to have deliberately set out to cheat people, which he clearly did not. The Bankruptcy Commissioner was clear in his summing up that Zachariah was not dishonest. He may have lost his usually sound business judgement, and compounded his situation by borrowing more and more in an attempt to cover his losses till the cargoes were sold, but this did not add up to deliberate dishonesty. And he did, reputedly, repay his debts. In the face of the light 'sentence' dispensed by the Bankruptcy Court, though, one can understand that people might wish to lash out with verbal abuse. These were people with whom Zachariah had been most closely associating, which all added to his humiliation and shame – they knew how to kick a man when he was down. But as the Commissioner remarked, he had taken quite enough punishment by the end of the court case. He was not a swindler.

The 'victim' label has considerable credibility. Zachariah was too naïve to handle the dog-eat-dog etiquette of the London discount market and he had no adviser on the inside to help him avoid being ensnared. He was personally targeted as a successful and unimpeachable shipowner, and he fell directly into the cynical machinations of the bankers Overend and Gurney. Then with impeccable timing the American Civil War started and, in an effort to deploy his newly-acquired-but-unnecessary vessels to bring back cotton and re-open Hull's cotton mills, Zachariah became the victim of bad luck – albeit probably enhanced by bad judgement. He was entering a whole new line of business which he did not understand. Enthusiasm triumphed over common sense. His skills and experience lay in understanding how to run ships, find crew, and buy the right cargoes to sell to the Confederates. Knowing how to dodge Abraham Lincoln's defensive fleet to get in and out of the Southern ports was quite another matter – one that was completely alien to him. He described it as an adventure, and he knew he was taking a risk, but did not realise at the time how big a risk it was. He was inspired by the vessels he saw getting through the blockade – but Zachariah was not to be one of these winning shipowners. Losing all ten of his vessels with their cargoes certainly placed him in the 'victim to bad luck' category, and the tragic burning of his newly-restored *Indian Empire*, compounded by his successful compensation claim being overturned on appeal, reinforces his 'victim' status.

The term 'philanthropist' appears to be the most persuasive. All the evidence indicates a socially-minded man, driven by an innate Methodist sense of fairness and honour. Zachariah always had the well-being of Hull at heart, and though we only have a rare glimpse from his own lips about his personal ideology, he did articulate on a number of occasions how his aims in life were to *'benefit this Town of Hull'*. In the words of the newspaper columnist Whiting, Zachariah was one of nature's 'nice fellows'. Plenty of evidence backs up this view: the Commissioner's praise for Zachariah's character, the regained respect of his townsmen after his disgrace, and the obituaries which were lavish with their adulation.

But history must judge him by his deeds rather than his ideals. Having built up wealth though his own hard work, he went on to spend some of it for the good of others, mainly the poor and voiceless, even whilst living relatively modestly. Instead of leaving Hull once he'd made his pile, and living out his life with his family in the clean air of the Yorkshire countryside, like so many of his contemporaries had done, he stayed to defend and improve it, jealously guarding its reputation against the fierce competition from nearby docks. In a world with neither national health system nor social services, the poor, the working class, the orphans and the disenfranchised relied on those who, like Zachariah, had the social conscience to create charities and share their wealth philanthropically. Such deeds are more persuasive than philosophy: Zachariah was undoubtedly a philanthropist.

Today, the only lasting legacy to Zachariah's philanthropy is Pearson Park, which nestles on its original site, between the main road north out of the city, and 'The Avenues', the residential area designed for the emerging middle classes of the nineteenth century. The twentieth people's park in England to be opened, it remains today very much as Niven planned it. Nevertheless, in keeping with its original principles, it continues to evolve. Under the enthusiastic management of a Charitable Trust of the City Council, a Heritage Lottery Fund is hopefully, at the time of going to press, about to be awarded and some of the original features of the park are to be restored.

That Pearson Park is there at all is due to an adventurous Victorian philanthropist who wished to improve conditions for the workers and advance the development of Hull. Behind this peaceful oasis in a bustling city, then, is a fascinating slice of history – and if you look again you may notice that Queen Victoria's expression is a little more enigmatically 'Mona Lisa' than it seemed before.

Bibliography and References

Bankruptcy Report, 1864, in *The Hull Advertiser*, April 27th

Bennett, J., 2008, *The London Confederates*, McFarland and Co., Jefferson, N.C. and London

Bourne, John. T. (Letters from), in Vandiver, F., 1947, q.v.

Bradlee, F. B. C., 1974, *Blockade Running during the Civil War*, Porcupine Press: Philadelphia

Brander, M., 1975, *The Victorian Gentleman,* London: Gordon Cremonesi

Carr, D., 1998, *Grey Phantoms of the Cape Fear,* John F. Blair: Winston-Salem, NC

Correspondence respecting the Seizure of the British Steamer "Orwell" in 1860 by the Followers of General Garibaldi. Harrison and Sons: London

Crawford, P., *The Impact of the American Civil War on Hull, 1861-1865,* in 'The Journal of Regional and Local Studies,' 1984, vol. 4, no. 1

Crossfire, 2008, *The Lasting Legacy of the Blockade Runner 'Modern Greece'* Magazine of American Civil War

Davis L. and Engerman, S., 2006, *Naval Blockades in Peace and War,* Cambridge University Press

Elliott, G., 2006, *The Mystery of Overend and Gurney*, Methuen: London

Fort Fisher Museum: www.nchistoricsites.org.org/fisher

Gibson, Paul, 2008 & 2010, *Hull Then and Now, Parts 1 & 2,* Paul-Gibson publishing

Horner, Dave, 1968, *The Blockade Runners,* New York: Dodd, Mead and Co.

House of Commons Hansard: www.hansard.millbanksystems.com/commons

House of Lords Hansard: www.hansard.millbanksystems.com/lords

Hovell, B, 2009, *The Minerva Lodge,* Yorkshire History

Hovell, B., 2011, *Kingston upon Hull: The Masonic Heritage,* Barry Hovell

Ketchell, C. (Ed.), 1989, *An Illustrated History of The Avenues and Pearson Park Hull,* Avenues and Pearson Park Residents Association

King, W.T.C., 1936, *History of the London Discount Market,* Routledge: London

Lincoln, A., 1861, *Proclamation of Blockade against Southern Ports,* http://www.historyplace.com/lincoln/proc-2.htm

Livingstone, Rebecca, 1999, *Civil War Cat-and-Mouse Game: Researching Blockade-Runners at the National Archives* in Fall, vol. 31, no. 3

Markham, J. 1992, *John Markham's Colourful Characters,* Beverley

Mayfield, J.W., 1909, *History of Springhead Waterworks and How the Pearson Park was obtained for the People,* A. Brown and Sons, Hull

Mercantile Navy List, 1861, Bradbury and Evans, London

Minutes of Hull Town Council: various

National Centre for Preservation Technology: www.ncptt.nps.gov/rising-from-the-depths/

Neave, D, 1991, *Lost Churches and Chapels of Hull,* Hutton Press

Nepveux, E. T. S., 1999, *George A. Trenholm, Financial Genius of the Confederacy,* The Electric City Printing Co.: Anderson SC

Niven, J., letter dated 17th Feb. 1860 recorded in Minutes of Local Board of Health Kingston upon Hull Park Committee, BHH/1/38 HCA

Official Records of the Union and Confederate Navies in the War of the Rebellion 1861-1865, published 1894-1922, digitised at http://cdl.library.cornell.edu

Particulars and Conditions of Sale, 1860. Auctioneer's Publicity, Hull Archives

Pearson, Z. C., 18.10.1862, Private Letter, Hull Archives

Pearson, Z. C., in Smith, J., 1860, *Proceedings Relative to Pearson's Park,* , private publication, Hull

Riall, Lucy, 2007, *Garibaldi, Invention of a Hero,* http://www.sc.edu/library/spcoll/hist/garib/garib.html

Shaw, M. L., 2008, *Pearson and his Park,* in Historic Gardens Review, issue 19

Shaw, M. L., 2008, *Zachariah Pearson: philanthropist, victim or swindler?* In East Yorkshire Historian, Vol. 9

Sheahan, J. J., 1866, *History of the Town and Port of Kingston upon Hull*, John Green: Beverley

Shipping Register, Hull City Archives

Smith, J., 1860, *Proceedings Relative to Pearson's Park*, private publication, Hull

Sprunt, J., 1916, *Chronicles of the Cape Fear River*, Edwards & Broughton Printing Co: Raleigh

Tar Heels Wheels, October 1962, volume X1X, number 10

The Westminster Review, 1840, vol. 35

Vandiver, F., 1947, *Confederate Blockade Running through Bermuda*, University of Texas

Victoria County History: www.victoriacountyhistory.ac.uk

Victoria County History of the County of York, 1961, University of London Institute of Historical Research, Oxford University Press

Whiting, C. S., 1858, *Mr Councillor Pearson,* in *Portraits of Public Men,* Hull; pp 152-157

Wise, S. R., 1988, *Lifeline of the Confederacy: Blockade Running during the Civil War*, University of South Carolina Press

Wrigglesworth, E., 1991, *Browns' Illustrated Guide to Hull,* Hull

Xenos, S., *Depredations, or Overend, Gurney, & Co., and the Greek and Oriental Steam Navigation Company.* Private publication: London, 1869.

Newspapers / Journals

Economist, The

House of Commons Select Committee reports

Hull Advertiser

Hull Daily Mail

Hull News

Hull Packet and East Riding Times

Hull Trade Directory

Illustrated London News

London Gazette, The

New Zealand Railways Magazine

Runner, The : Newsletter of the Cape Fear Civil War Round Table

Times, The [London]

Westminster Review

York Gazette

Illustration Credits

I am grateful to the following for permission to use these images.

Barry Hovell
    Illustrations on pp. 68, 78
Brian Rylance
    Illustrations on pp. 103, 110, 280
Guildhall: Hull Museums:
    Illustrations (Accn No. 2005.142) on cover and p. 269
Guildhall, Hull
    Illustration on p. 64
Harpers Weekly
    Illustrations on pp. 123, 251
Hull History Centre
    Illustrations on pp. 3, 5, 23, 62, 90, 93, 96, 109, 112, 220,
        225, 225, 273
Maritime Museums: Hull Museums:
    Illustration (Accn No. 1993.156.1206) on p. 71
NC Historic Sites: Fort Fisher
    Illustrations on pp. 170, 171, 172, 176
Wilberforce House Museums: Hull Museums:
    Illustration (Accn No. 2005.4557) on p. 148
Wrigglesworth, Edmund: *Browns' Illustrated Guide to Hull*
    Illustration on p. 66

Index

Lightning Source UK Ltd.
Milton Keynes UK
UKOW02f1330121216
289791UK00002B/258/P

9 781845 301569